JESUS for
the NON-RELIGIOUS

Books by John Shelby Spong

Honest Prayer

Dialogue in Search of Jewish-Christian Understanding
  (with Rabbi Jack Daniel Spiro)

Christpower (compiled and edited by Lucy Newton Boswell)

Life Approaches Death: A Dialogue in Medical Ethics (with Dr. Daniel Gregory)

The Living Commandments

The Easter Moment

Into the Whirlwind: The Future of the Church

Beyond Moralism (with the Venerable Denise Haines)

*Survival and Consciousness: An Interdisciplinary Inquiry into the Possibility
  of Life Beyond Biological Death* (editor)

Living in Sin? A Bishop Rethinks Human Sexuality

*Rescuing the Bible from Fundamentalism: A Bishop Rethinks the Meaning
  of Scripture*

*Born of a Woman: A Bishop Rethinks the Virgin Birth and the Role
  of Women in a Male-Dominated Church*

This Hebrew Lord: A Bishop's Search for the Authentic Jesus

Resurrection: Myth or Reality? A Bishop Rethinks the Meaning of Easter

Liberating the Gospels: Reading the Bible with Jewish Eyes

Why Christianity Must Change or Die: A Bishop Speaks to Believers in Exile

The Bishop's Voice: Selected Essays (1979–1999)
  (compiled and edited by Christine Mary Spong) (Crossroad)

Here I Stand: My Struggle for a Christianity of Integrity, Love, and Equality

*A New Christianity for a New World: Why Traditional Faith Is Dying
  and How a New Faith Is Being Born*

The Sins of Scripture: Exposing the Bible's Texts of Hate to Reveal the God of Love

JESUS for
the NON-RELIGIOUS

Recovering the Divine at the Heart of the Human

John Shelby Spong

HarperSanFrancisco
A Division of HarperCollins*Publishers*

JESUS FOR THE NON-RELIGIOUS. Copyright © 2007 by John Shelby Spong. All rights reserved. Printed in the United States of America. No part of this book may be used or reproduced in any manner whatsoever without written permission except in the case of brief quotations embodied in critical articles and reviews. For information address HarperCollins Publishers, 10 East 53rd Street, New York, NY 10022.

HarperCollins books may be purchased for educational, business, or sales promotional use. For information please write: Special Markets Department, HarperCollins Publishers, 10 East 53rd Street, New York, NY 10022.

HarperCollins Web site: http://www.harpercollins.com
HarperCollins®, ♨®, and HarperSanFrancisco™
are trademarks of HarperCollins Publishers

FIRST EDITION
Designed by Joseph Rutt

Library of Congress Cataloging-in-Publication Data available.
ISBN: 978–0–06–076207–0
ISBN-10: 0–06–076207–1

07 08 09 10 11 RRD (H) 10 9 8 7 6 5 4 3 2

Dedicated to:

Katharine Shelby Catlett
John Baldwin Catlett III
John Lanier Hylton
Lydia Ann Hylton
Katherine Elaine Barney
Colin David Barney

Grandchildren of great promise and integrity in whose hands the world seems full of hope.

John Shelby Spong
Christine Mary Spong

CONTENTS

Part 2
The Original Images of Jesus

Part 3
Jesus for the Non-Religious

PREFACE

Dietrich Bonhoeffer once called on the Christian world to
separate Christianity from religion and he spoke of something
he called "Religionless Christianity." . . . I hope to build on
Bonhoeffer's idea and to find a way through the human Jesus
but beyond the confines of religion that will lead me into all that
I now believe the word "God" means.[1]

There is a sense in which I have been writing this book for
my entire lifetime. Finally, in what is likely to be the last
decade of my life, I have been able to bring together two powerful
streams of thought that have been flowing separately inside me for
almost as long as I can remember. The first stream has been formed by
my deep commitment to Jesus of Nazareth, who has always stood at
the center of my faith tradition; the second has been created by my
deep alienation from the traditional symbols and forms through which
the meaning of this Jesus has been communicated through the ages.
Together these two streams have produced a profound tension that has
shaped both my personal and my professional life.

The Jesus who attracted me was always the Jewish Jesus—deeply
real, intensely human, yet in touch with something that was both eternal and transcendent. For some decades I have been convinced that
the secret to understanding this Jesus has to be found in the Jewish
context that produced him, nurtured him and shaped him. Yet when I
listened to the Jesus who was worshipped inside the Christian church,
both his Jewishness and his humanity seemed to me to be either ignored or vigorously repudiated.

This profoundly Jewish Jesus first appeared in my writing in 1974, in a book entitled *This Hebrew Lord*. That book touched something deep and significant in me, and obviously it did in my audience as well: it has gone through three revisions, four new covers and countless reprintings, yet thirty-three years later, copies of it are still rolling off the presses every year. HarperCollins now calls it "a classic," which probably means they do not quite know what to do with it: it is too old to promote and it still sells too well to cancel!

One year after the publication of *This Hebrew Lord*, that book became the catalyst for a dialogue in which I engaged Rabbi Jack Daniel Spiro, then the spiritual leader of Temple Beth Ahabah in Richmond, Virginia, but now the head of the Department of Judaic Studies at Virginia Commonwealth University. These discussions would later be published under the title *Dialogue in Search of Jewish-Christian Understanding*. In that encounter my attraction to the Jewish Jesus was expanded to new levels of intensity.

Still later, under the influence of a great New Testament professor, Michael Donald Goulder, of the University of Birmingham in the United Kingdom, I moved dramatically deeper into the Jewish roots of Christianity. Out of that study, I published a book entitled *Liberating the Gospels: Reading the Bible with Jewish Eyes*, in which I sought to demonstrate that when the Christian church was formed it was a movement within the life of the synagogue, where it lived for the first fifty to sixty years of its life. Christianity separated itself from Judaism somewhere around the year 88 CE. This means that of the four canonical gospels in the New Testament, two, Mark and Matthew, were written before that fracture occurred; Luke, which was probably penned after 88, was nonetheless so influenced by Mark that Mark's pre-split framework is still operative in that third gospel. John was thus the only one clearly on the other side of that split, and so John reflects, quite obviously, both the separation and indeed some of its bitterness.

Given this close connection between Christianity and the synagogue, it was inevitable that when Jesus' earliest followers tried to talk about their experience with him, they did so using the God language of their familiar Jewish background. In investigating this process we discover that it was Jesus' humanity that inspired the talk of his divinity.

The second stream flowing through both my professional life and my writing career was the recognition that the expanding knowledge of my secular world had increasingly rendered the traditional theological formulations expressed in such core Christian doctrines as the incarnation, the atonement and even the trinity inoperative at worst, and incapable of making much sense to the ears of twenty-first-century people at best. Time after time I watched the church fight and lose rearguard defensive battles as it was forced to adjust its thinking to the waves of new discoveries that compromised what the church once called "revealed and unchanging truth." That "truth" proved to be not only not revealed, but also not eternal!

To compound the problem, I discovered that this expanded secular and scientific knowledge, which I saw eroding the formulas of my faith tradition, was actually aided by a second knowledge revolution arising from within Christianity itself. Over the last two hundred years, the Bible has become the subject of new and critical scholarship that has quite literally torn away the biblical support for most traditional Christian thinking. It has been Christian scholars whose study has led them to challenge creeds, relativize doctrines and dismiss dogmas. At first this critical thinking was confined to the Christian academy, but it finally broke into public awareness in 1834 with the publication of a monumental book by David Friedrich Strauss entitled *Leben Jesu*, or in English *The Life of Jesus, Critically Examined*.[2] This book raised publicly questions about the accuracy, the authenticity and the reliability of the crucial details in the gospel accounts of the life of Jesus. That was the opening shot in a battle that would ultimately infuriate the fundamentalists, in both their Catholic and Protestant forms, driving them to more and more hysterical claims for the infallibility of their teaching authority or the inerrancy of their sacred texts. At the same time this knowledge would totally demoralize the mainline traditions that no longer knew how to talk about either their God or their Jesus.

No one today can realistically pretend that this biblical revolution is not real. Critical biblical scholarship, having now passed through several generations, forms the frame of reference in which the Christian academy works, dramatically separating the Bible from the assumptions held by the average pew-sitters in our various churches. Yet clergy, trained for the most part in the academy, seem to join a con-spiracy of silence to suppress this knowledge when they become pas-tors, fearful that if that average pew-sitter learned the content of the real debate, his or her faith would be destroyed—and with it, more importantly, his or her support for institutional Christianity.

I have always felt, in the words of Clifford Stanley, my first theol-ogy professor, that "any God who can be killed ought to be killed." We also need to face the fact that any deity who must be protected from truth, arising from any source, has died already. God and truth cannot be incompatible. As I wrestled with this new biblical scholar-ship, I began to process publicly the issues it raised for me in such books as *Rescuing the Bible from Fundamentalism, Why Christianity Must Change or Die, A New Christianity for a New World* and even *The Sins of Scripture.*

My devotion to Jesus, whom I increasingly viewed through a Jewish lens, and my need to reformulate all of the traditional Christian sym-bols under the impact of new learning were the sources of a profound restlessness within me. No matter how deeply I loved the church, both its creeds and liturgies made assumptions I could no longer make. In-creasingly, Jesus was real to me, but the theological language that I used to talk about him was not.

It was only when this tension began to be resolved that this book, *Jesus for the Non-Religious*, became a possibility. I began to see that it was the Jewish portrait of Jesus of Nazareth, as a first-century fully human man, that opened my eyes to what the church meant when it proclaimed in Paul's words that "God was in Christ." It was the full humanity of Jesus that enabled his followers to perceive divinity in him. Humanity and divinity were not two different things that needed to be reconciled, as the church had struggled so valiantly to do in the first five hundred years of Christian history. The whole premise on which that reconciliation was postulated was simply wrong. "Or-thodoxy," which by definition means "right thinking," has always as-sumed a dualistic world divided between nature and supernature, body and soul, humanity and divinity. That worldview no longer exists and so the attempt to reconcile the human with the divine has become inoperative. It was this "orthodoxy" that brought about the loss of Jesus' humanity; then the divine Christ, which was all that remained when the human Jesus was "divinized," was destroyed by the combination of the explosion in secular knowledge and the insights that came out of the new field of biblical studies. I now began to sense that the new starting place, which Christianity so obviously needed, had to be one that did not force believers into this divine-human debate about Jesus.

In this book, I seek to locate that new starting place. I will not shrink from allowing the scholarship of the Christian academy to dismantle piece by piece either the literalized stories of the Bible or the theological constructs that were placed on Jesus of Nazareth. I will follow where truth leads. Once these constructs have been shattered, as surely they have been and will be, then I will take what remains, the Jewish Jesus, and begin to look anew at that life to determine just what it was about his humanity that caused first-century Jewish people to assert that in this life the holy God was somehow met and engaged. I will work from the known to the unknown, from the human to the divine, from earth to heaven, not the other way around. I will seek to separate the Jesus of history from the layers of interpretive material, from mythology and from the miraculous claims that derived from a supernaturally oriented world. I think I can demonstrate that most of these aspects of the Jesus story were not part of his original meaning, but were later interpretive additions. The question I will seek to address is: Can a full understanding of Jesus be developed by looking at him as a fully human one through whom what God means can be experienced? If the answer to that question is yes, as I believe it is, then the two parallel streams that flow inside me can come together and flow as one. If that can be the result of this study, then I believe I will have set the stage for the emergence of a new burst of Christian energy and power that has not been seen for hundreds of years.

The choices before the Christian world are clear to me. We can pretend that there is no problem with the continued use of the literalized, dated and inoperative language of our faith, changing nothing, and the result will be that Christianity will die. The other choice is that we can develop a whole new way of seeing Jesus and conceptualizing God that will lay the groundwork for a radical reformulation of what we call Christianity. In this book I will make it quite clear which choice I have made.

Traditional Christians dedicated to the dying patterns of the past will, I am sure, find this book to be difficult and, from their perspective, negative. New truth always offends the security systems that have operated in the world of yesterday. If it is truth, however, it is ultimately freeing and it must never be compromised by fear. All of my professional life I have kept before me the motto of my theological seminary: "Seek the truth; come whence it may, cost what it will."[3] My only request of my traditional readers is that they do not stop their journey through this book until they reach the end. This study is too important to be aborted before new conclusions are reached, even when the pain is intense.

People who are no longer committed to traditional Christian patterns, but who, nonetheless, still seek the "transcendent" and the "holy," and who just might be willing to look anew at a reformulated Christianity, will, I hope, find this book both refreshing and hopeful. They are the ones who know themselves to be living with the emptiness of what someone has called a "God-shaped hole" that nothing else quite fills. I call them "believers in exile." My hope is that here they will find a path they can walk that will lead them into a vibrant Christianity for tomorrow.

For me the process of thinking through and then writing this book has been deeply integrating. For that reason I have a lively hope that a new Christianity can grow out of what I perceive to be the death of the old supernatural forms of yesterday's Christianity. As we move beyond that definition of religion, the Jesus who might be able to move with us is the one I call "Jesus for the Non-Religious." Dietrich Bonhoeffer once called on the Christian world to separate Christianity from religion and he spoke of something he called "religionless Christianity."[4] His execution at the hands of the Nazis, in a prison camp in Flossenburg in 1945, never allowed him to develop this concept beyond that tantalizing hint. I hope to build on Bonhoeffer's idea and to find a way through the human Jesus, but beyond the confines of religion, that will lead me into all that I now believe the word "God" means.

I have one further literary task that I hope to complete in my already more than the "three score and ten years" presumably allotted to us by the biblical text. I want to take the idea of a nontheistic but eminently real God met in the human Jesus and from that vantage point address the subject of death and dying, as well as what the church has tried to say through the ages about eternal life. I want to test these insights against what human beings still identify as the ultimate threat of nonbeing. Death terrifies the self-conscious human being perhaps more than anything else. Beyond what most of us have yet embraced, it was the fear of death that first created the theistic deity, which in turn was the concept that captured the Jesus experience. How will a nontheistic God, a human Jesus and the new Christianity that I see emerging all around us today speak to us when we come face to face with death, the ultimate barrier to meaning? It is a book I could not write until I came to the place where I began to live it existentially. If my idea of God and my vision of a redefined Jesus cannot speak to the human anxiety of death, then I do not believe that I have found either the new beginning for the Jesus story that I seek or one that will survive. I hope I live long enough to write this final book and to make this case publicly. This proposed book is scheduled for publication in 2009, by which time I will be seventy-eight! It will be a good race. Time alone will tell whether I will succeed in accomplishing this ambitious goal.

Allow me now to extend my gratitude to a number of people who have helped to make this book a reality. My thanks go first to people in those places where the ideas found in this book were initially broached as lectures and from whom I received both the encouragement that enabled me to continue walking this path and the refinement that comes with interacting with others over new ideas.

At the top of that list is the warden of St. Deiniol's Library in Hawarden, Wales, Peter Francis, with his wife, Helen, and their wonderful redheaded daughter, Lucy. St. Deiniol's Library originally housed the private book collection of Prime Minister William Gladstone, but its shelves have received thousands upon thousands of additional volumes over the years. It is today also a conference center at which I have been a leader on many occasions, usually offering the content that would constitute my "next" book. The encouragement and friendship I have received from Peter Francis and his family, together with that of the people who attended my conferences, have made this library a very special place for both my wife, Christine, and me. I was deeply honored several years ago when the Board of St. Deiniol's Center elected me a "Fellow" of that institution, over the objection of the frightened Archbishop of Canterbury, Rowan Williams. This book was really born in that place.

Later, I delivered lectures on parts of the content of this book at various congregations of the United Church of Canada, in places like Edmonton, Peterborough, Toronto, Markham and Guelph. My ideas were further developed at an Episcopal Church in Dayton, Ohio, at Congregational, Presbyterian, Unitarian, Unity and Religious Science churches in such places as Silver Bay, New York; San Diego, California; Colorado Springs, Colorado, and Naples, Florida. Next lectures on the content of this book were given in Highland/Cashiers, North Carolina. My chapter on anger was first delivered at the Scargill Center in Kettlewell in Yorkshire, England. In each place the interaction of the various audiences not only forced me to clarify these ideas again and again, but they also made me confident that a book designed to present Jesus to a non-religious, non-church-oriented world not only is needed, but also is a worthy undertaking.

My special thanks go to my former publisher at HarperCollins, Steve Hanselman; my present publisher, Mark Tauber; my editor, Michael Maudlin; my publicist, Julie Rae Mitchell, and all the staff at the San Francisco office, including in particular Cindy DiTiberio, Claudia Boutote, Laina Adler, Kris Ashley, Jan Weed and Lisa Zuniga. I also want to thank Kelly Hughes of the DeChant-Hughes public relations firm in Chicago, which has launched my last six books.

I am grateful to my online publisher, WaterFrontMedia, especially its owners, Ben Wolin and Mike Keriakos, as well as my liaisons and editors Mekado Murphy, Tony Brancato and Mark Roberts, who have helped me turn my weekly column into a major communication piece that is now opened about a hundred thousand times a week.

I salute friends around the world who are working in their countries to do the same thing that I am trying to do: to transform Christianity into a twenty-first-century force. People are generally unaware that this groundswell of reforming energy is operative in so many places.

In Canada, I think of the Reverend Gretta Vosper, who heads Canada's Center for Progressive Christianity; the Reverend Mary Joseph in Markham, Ontario; the Reverend Randy MacKenzie in Brantford, Ontario; the Very Reverend Peter Eliot in Vancouver, British Columbia; the Right Reverend Michael Ingham, the Bishop of New Westminster in British Columbia, and the retired Anglican Archbishop of British Columbia, David Somerville, the spiritual godfather of so much of the energy for change in western Canada.

In New Zealand there are close friends and exiled Christians Liz and Geoff Robinson, as well as the Reverend Dr. Lloyd G. Geering, New Zealand's courageous voice for a new Christianity.

In Australia, there are the Reverend Dr. Greg Jenks, who heads an organization called Faith Futures Forward; Uniting Church of Australia pastors the Reverends David Carter, Rosemary Carter, Sean Gilbert and the late Nairn Kerr, who together established the Progressive Christian Network in that land. Other Australian archbishops, bishops, and ordained clergy who have been particularly supportive are Peter Carnley, Philip Aspinall, Ian George, Ian Brown, Roger Herft, Nigel Leaves, Ian Pearson, Carolyn Pearce and Dorothy McMahon.

In the United Kingdom I salute the Reverend Hugh Dawes and his wife, Jill Sandham, who together head up the Progressive Christian Network in Great Britain, as well as such outspoken and heroic lay and ordained Christians as Richard Kirker, Don Cupitt, Keith and Marian Ward, Michael Goulder,[5] Fred and Anthea Kaan, Hylton and Joan Boothroyd, Adrian and Christine Alker, John and Judith Sadler and Richard and Helen Truss. I also acknowledge my three ordained soul mates in the United Kingdom, Richard Holloway in Scotland, Andrew Furlong in Ireland and Susan O'Hare in Wales.

In Scandinavia, I acknowledge my deep appreciation to people like the Archbishop of the Swedish Lutheran Church K. G. Hammer, Bishop Claes-Bertil Ytterberg and ordained pastors Christer Beijer, Pelle Soderback, Marianne Blom, Hans Ulfvebrand, Nils Aberg and Johan Linman. The Church of Sweden is, I believe, the most vibrant expression of Christianity in all of Europe. In Finland, I stand in awe of the single bishop there who seems, almost alone among the bishops of that country, to understand the issues facing the church, Wille Riekkinen. Thankfully he is supported by such able clergy as Hannu Saloranta, Jarmo Tarkki and Sakari Hakkinen. In Denmark it is both a publisher named Henrik Brandt Pedersen and two pastors, Eric Fonsbol and Thorkild Groesboll, who keep expanding the boundaries of Christianity. In Norway it is again two remarkable pastors, Grete Hauge and Helge Hognestad, and two energized lay people, Jane Robertson and Else Margrethe Stromay.

On the continent of Africa I am grateful to three great Anglican bishops, Desmond Tutu, Njongonkulu Ndungane and Khotsu Mkullu, who have consistently stood against the mindless homophobia that seems to grip so much of the organized Christian church on that continent.

I also want to pay tribute to two people who have headed two organizations that have helped to change the religious debate in this country. They are the Reverend James Adams, who founded and directed for over a decade The Center for Progressive Christianity in Cambridge, Massachusetts, and the late Dr. Robert Funk, the founder and president of the Westar Institute, which has given the world the "Jesus Seminar." Both organizations have provided my work with tremendous encouragement and both should occupy an important place when the history of twentieth-century Christianity in the United States is written.

This book could not have come into being without the work of Gail Deckenbach, who translated my scratchy handwritten legal pads into Microsoft Word. Gail has worked with me professionally for over twenty years and in retirement came back to assist once more. She is one of the finest people I have ever known.

Finally, I wish to acknowledge the members of my family: My fantastic and beautiful wife, my life partner, my primary editor and the organizer of my new career are all the same person, Christine Mary Spong. I love her with what some people think is an unseemly passion for someone my age, and I also respect her incredible competence and the totality of her personal integrity. I cannot imagine life without her and consider myself the luckiest person in the world to be her husband. Next are our children: Ellen Elizabeth Spong and her husband, Gus Epps; Mary Katharine Spong and her husband,

Jack Catlett; Jaquelin Ketner Spong and her partner, Virgil Speriosu; Brian Yancy Barney and his wife, Julieann; and Rachel Elizabeth Barney. Finally, there are our six grandchildren, Shelby, Jay, John, Lydia, Katherine and Colin, to whom this book is dedicated. Each of them has brought something very special to our lives, as have the assortment of granddogs and grandcats, which thankfully live at their homes not ours!

Life has been an exquisite pleasure, and these are the people who have made it so.

Shalom!

John Shelby Spong
Morris Plains, New Jersey
February 27, 2007

THE LAMENT OF A BELIEVER IN EXILE

Ah, Jesus!
  Where have you gone?
    When did we lose you?
Was it when we became so certain that we possessed you
  That we persecuted Jews,
    Excommunicated doubters,
      Burned heretics,
        And used violence and war to achieve conversion?
Was it when our first-century images
  Collided with expanding knowledge?
Or when biblical scholars informed us that the Bible does
  Not really support what we once believed?
Was it when we watched your followers distorting people
  With guilt,
    Fear,
      Bigotry,
        Intolerance,
          And anger?
Was it when we noticed that many who called you Lord
  And who read their Bibles regularly
    Also practiced slavery,
      Defended segregation,

Approved lynching,
Abused children,
Diminished women,
And hated homosexuals?
Was it when we finally realized
That the Jesus who promised abundant life
Could not be the source of self-hatred,
Or one who encourages us to grovel
In life-destroying penitence?
Was it when it dawned on us that serving you would require
The surrender of those security-building prejudices
That masquerade as our sweet sicknesses?

We still yearn for you, Jesus, but we no longer know where
To seek your presence.
Do we look for you in those churches that practice certainty?
Or are you hiding in those churches
That so fear controversy that they make "unity" a god,
And stand for so little that they die of boredom?
Can you ever be found in those churches that have
Rejected the powerless and the marginalized,
The lepers and the Samaritans of our day,
Those you called our brothers and sisters?
Or must we now look for you outside ecclesiastical settings,
Where love and kindness expect no reward,
Where questions are viewed as the deepest
Expressions of trust?

Is it even possible, Jesus, that we Christians are the villains
Who killed you?
Smothering you underneath literal Bibles,
Dated creeds,
Irrelevant doctrines,
And dying structures?
If these things are the source of your disappearance, Jesus,
Will you then reemerge if these things are removed?
Will that bring resurrection?

Or were you, as some now suggest, never more
   Than an illusion?
By burying and distorting you were we
    Simply protecting ourselves
      From having to face that realization?

I still seek to possess what I believe you are, Jesus:
   Access to and embodiment of
     The Source of Life,
       The Source of Love,
         The Ground of Being,
           A doorway into the mystery of holiness.

It is through that doorway that I desire to walk.
   Will you meet me there?
    Will you challenge me,
      Guide me,
        Confront me,
           Reveal your truth to me and in me?

Finally, at the end of this journey, Jesus,
   Will you embrace me
    Inside the ultimate reality
      That I call God
       In whom I live
        And move
          And have my being?
For that, Jesus, is my goal in this book.

Part 1

SEPARATING THE HUMAN JESUS FROM THE MYTH

1

INTRODUCTION: OPENING THE DOOR ON A NEW QUEST

Whatever it was that people experienced in Jesus has today come to be identified with medieval doctrines based on premodern assumptions that are no longer believable.

What is it that drives me to pry loose from Jesus of Nazareth the layers of supernatural miracles, creedal formulations and ancient mythology? The answer is quite simple: I am a Christian. As a Christian, I live inside a faith system which, at its core, asserts that in the life of this Jesus, that which we call God has been met, encountered and engaged. My deepest sense of self-identity is found in this conviction. That, however, is only half of what compels my search.

The other half driving me into this study is my conviction that I am living at the end of the Christian era. I believe that I am witnessing the death of Christianity, as it has been historically understood. The Christianity that is now emerging in America and in the Third World is something with which I do not choose to be identified. I do not want to be filled with competing claims or disturbing anger. I do not want to worship a God that I cannot challenge, or be loyal to a tradition that requires me to shut down my mind. Many of the things historically said about Jesus I, as one who yearns to be a believer, can no longer hold with credibility. I need to be publicly honest about this.

Some voices inside the official church delight in telling me that my inability to assert my allegiance to these ancient formulas means that I have walked away from my ancestral faith and can no longer claim the title "Christian," or at the very least can no longer refer to myself as an "orthodox Christian." These critics seem not to recognize how badly compromised that entity called Christian orthodoxy has become. No thinking person can today assert, for example, that the earth is at the center of the universe. Yet that assertion remains a far greater component of orthodox Christianity, including orthodox Christology, than these defenders of the faith seem willing to admit. Despite the enormous revolution in our understanding of the immensity of space, God is still defined by these people as a supernatural being, external to the life of the world, who lives somewhere above the sky and who continues to intervene periodically in human history. The primary way that the Jesus story is still told is that he was the critical example in history of that divine intervention. Traditional Christian doctrine continues to portray Jesus as a heavenly visitor who came from the God above the sky in a miraculous birth and who, when his work was complete, returned to that God by way of a cosmic flight. That completed work, says this orthodoxy, was to bring salvation to a fallen world, and this was accomplished by Jesus' death on the cross. On every level each of these assertions has become for me not only literal nonsense but also little more than theological gobbledygook. Yet they are repeated in some form in the liturgies of most Christian churches every Sunday morning. I have no wish to pretend that such concepts still mean anything to me or that they are worthy of being preserved.

Sometimes when I have to respond to the constant harassment of those who live within the narrow bounds of yesterday's Christianity, I feel as if I am being gummed to death by a herd of clacking geese. Most of these traditional believers are so busy defending the answers of yesterday that they no longer know what the questions were to which these answers were originally directed. They do not understand that they have actually entombed Jesus in the caskets of another world, another time and another place. Out of their fear and defensiveness, they regularly accuse me of abandoning Jesus, not recognizing how absolutely impossible that would be for me. My commitment to Jesus is deep and steadfast. He stands not only at the center of my faith, but also at the center of all that I am. My commitment, however, is to the reality of Jesus as a God experience; it is not a commitment to the reality of the traditional explanations of that God experience in Jesus. There is a vast difference.

For the life of me I cannot understand why it is not today universally recognized that propositional statements can never capture eternal truth. Whenever a powerful, timeless experience is explained, the truth of that experience is captured inside the language, the level of knowledge and the worldview of the explainer. Explanation always places perceived truth inside time-bound words and time-warped concepts. To identify the ultimate truth of God with the explanation of that truth is to confuse the ultimate with the transitory. It is to proclaim that something which is clearly less than real is to be equated with that which is ultimately real. That is the mistake that religious systems always make, and that is why those religious systems always and inevitably die. Christianity, it is now obvious, will prove to be no exception.

Whatever it was that people experienced in Jesus has today come to be identified with medieval doctrines based on premodern assumptions that are no longer believable. That identification means that serious theological discussion seems to accomplish little more than to erect a division between the shouters and the disinterested. Jesus becomes the captive of the hysterically religious, the chronically fearful, the insecure and even the neurotic among us, or he becomes little more than a fading memory, the symbol of an age that is no more and a nostalgic reminder of our believing past. To me neither option is worth pursuing. Yet even understanding these things, I am still attracted to this Jesus and I will pursue him both relentlessly and passionately. I will not surrender the truth I believe I find in him either to those who seek to defend the indefensible or to those who want to be freed finally from premodern ideas that no longer make any sense.

It was my church, not some alien agency, which taught me in one of its own accredited theological seminaries to approach the Bible critically. Why should I now be fearful of my own church's approach to scripture? I intend, therefore, to employ that scholarship in everything I do to reveal to my readers how little we know historically about many of the assumptions we have made when telling the Jesus story.

Some people will be shocked by my ensuing analysis, not knowing that these conclusions have been commonplace in academic circles for centuries. I do not stop there, however. I take the story of the Bible so seriously that I am compelled to probe its pages for revelatory but still largely hidden clues. I intend to use these clues that permeate the gospel tradition to probe the meaning of that original Jesus experience. It was the experience people had with Jesus that created the supernatural language of explanation. It was not the other way around. These clues become visible, I hope to demonstrate, only when we put on Jewish lenses to read these essentially Jewish documents that we Christians call Mark, Matthew, Luke and John. I list them in that order, because that is the order in which they were written historically, which I hope to show is itself a valuable tool for interpretation. By laying out these clues in clear relief, I will seek to lead my readers into the meaning of the Jesus experience, the power of which caused the story of Jesus to be written in the first place.

This driving inner need to probe the Jesus behind the gospels has been part of who I am since I, as a young boy, first encountered the power present in his person. I discovered in him a firm rock in the storm of my insecure life. He provided the security that was promised to me in my evangelical fundamentalist church. His appeal is obvious to me in retrospect. I grew up with an alcoholic father who died when I was twelve, and a mother who was forced by those circumstances to live in the poverty that comes to those who try to survive in this world with less than a ninth grade education. I desperately needed the certainty which my church assured me that Jesus offered. All I had to do was "trust and obey"! The Bible, literally understood, would be my guide.

By the time I was an adolescent, I had made a slight transition from that early biblical rigidity to a somewhat more sophisticated ecclesiastical rigidity. However, the quest for personal security still drove me. My expanding world of knowledge had challenged successfully my literal understanding of the Bible. I could never return to that, but I was also unwilling to let go of this Jesus. That was when I sought and found a momentary repose in what I contended was the accuracy of the Catholic claim that in the church's teaching authority, the ultimate truth of God had been received. Here the "unchanging faith" resided. In time that too turned out to be little more than another illusion destined to be cast aside as my world continued to expand when I was at the university.

The next phase in my developing life came when I began to perceive that Jesus had become for me primarily the familiar, but nonetheless the human face of the ultimate mystery I called God. My spiritual life, I now came to recognize, was destined to be an endless journey into that mystery. One of my shaping theological teachers, Paul Tillich, referred to this God as "Being Itself," which meant to me that my search for God would be identical with my search for my own identity. I am today still on that journey. I do not expect to arrive at any final destination so long as I am living "on this side of the Jordan." Nonetheless, I do not think that I am pursuing something of my own creation. God for me is a reality that can be experienced, but when I try to speak of this experience, I discover that God always transcends the grasp of my explanations. That fact alone drives me beyond any religious system that claims to possess the truth of God in any ultimate sense. Religion from that day to this has had to be open-ended for me and its forms can never be allowed to be final.

I relate these things because I want my readers to know that I understand better than most the appeal that comes from religious systems that offer security, that claim the unchallenged authority of an inerrant Bible or an infallible pope, but I now regard those claims as nothing more than the traditional conclusions of religious hysteria. These things satisfy me no longer. I join my secular friends in renouncing them as little more than delusional ideas, in which I no longer am willing to participate. I do not, however, reject the search for what Jesus represented or the journey into that ultimate mystery that I call God. That journey, I believe, is undertaken by every human life in some form, for to search for God is part of what it means to be human.

I still read regularly the biblical stories about Jesus, but I am repelled again and again by the imposed assumptions that we seem to think undergird those narratives, none of which I, as a twenty-first-century person, could ever make. I do not believe that food can be expanded by anyone from five literal loaves to a volume sufficient to feed a multitude. If that were possible world hunger would clearly never be a problem. Since people starve in this world every day, the obvious conclusion of those who cling to such an understanding of God must be that in our day this God has chosen to let the hungry die. They never face the fact that this would be a demonic deity.

I do not believe that anyone can, with supernatural power, cause the blind to see, the deaf to hear, the mute to sing and the lame to walk in any literal way. If that were possible, the development of medical science would have been quite unnecessary. That development, however, was necessary, because the discovery of both the causes and the cures of illness or the lack of wholeness is now and has always been a human, not a divine, responsibility.

People say somewhat defensively that the age of miracles is now over. That allows them to accept a supernatural worldview while explaining why supernaturalism does not operate in the modern world. It serves to counter the dawning realization that there never was an age of miracles and that the things our ancestors once called miracles were in fact either tales of fantasy that grew over the passing years or misunderstandings of reality based on a lack of knowledge about how the world operated so many hundreds of years ago. The ability of anyone to walk on water exists in our world not in reality, but only in very bad golf jokes. Storms are understood today to be the result of moving, impersonal weather fronts. They serve no ulterior or divine motive. They can, therefore, not be stilled by any person's command.

Dead people, whether they be Jairus' daughter, the widow's son at Nain or the man called Lazarus, do not in our time rise from their graves to take their places in the life of society for a second time. We know death to be a permanent state, and to be so total a shutdown of bodily functions that the brain is irreversibly destroyed if it is without oxygen for a very few minutes. We now recognize death as a natural part of life, not punishment inflicted on us by an angry deity for our sins. Certainly a crucified man, executed and buried on Friday, cannot walk out of his tomb resuscitated and alive on Sunday, nor can a body defy gravity in order to ascend into the sky as the way to return to the God who was once believed to dwell above the clouds.

These are but a few examples of why the story of Jesus sounds to me more like the world of make-believe than it does like the "word of God"! I must reject all of these things as not possible and therefore as not true in any literal sense. Yet the rejection of these tangential things does not prevent me from still believing that Jesus offers me a doorway into the realm of transcendent otherness and I continue to pursue that meaning through him.

I find myself unable to believe literally the supernatural things said about Jesus in the Bible and reiterated in Christian history, yet I am still drawn deeply and expectantly into the Jesus experience. If this tension is one that any of my readers have felt or engaged, then perhaps I can be an asset, or a companion with you on your own journey. That at least is my hope.

I speak first to the tyranny of religious fear. Is faith so weak and life so afraid that those who dare to pose questions must expect to be attacked for faithlessness by the religiously insecure? I am not some enemy of the Christian faith who has, by raising these issues, forced this debate upon others. The religious debate in our time results rather from the exploding new horizons of learning that have reshaped our perceptions of reality, coupled with a new biblical scholarship that previously had not been allowed to escape the academy for fear that it might erode the confidence of the people who sit in the pews. Why should new truth be so totally resisted by both the Christian church's evangelical and catholic wings? It was New York's late Senator Daniel Moynihan who said, "Everyone is entitled to his or her own opinions, but no one is entitled to his or her own facts." Religion cannot hide from truth by seeking to accumulate its own facts. How, we need to ask, can the heart be warmed if the mind is violated? Will the heart worship what the mind rejects? Hardly, unless the fear of nothingness creates hysteria that in turn replaces all rationality. The other side of this equation, however, is that the heart will not tolerate emptiness forever. It is, therefore, that human sense of emptiness that forces the mind to break new ground, to open new possibilities and to develop new alternatives. The spiritual reality we seek in this postmodern world cannot be achieved without enlightened minds, but it will also never be discovered without warm hearts. That is what drives us, I believe, to learn new ways in which to worship God with both heart and mind. Before we can do that, however, we must first be willing to allow our minds to destroy any formulation from the past that no longer works. There is something secure about the fantasy of unexamined truth, or a life that is so closed that it will not step beyond yesterday's human explanations, yet no God is well served who is not seriously questioned. We must face that fact openly and directly.

I intend to start this quest with a radical probe of the details found in the traditional Jesus narratives as they are written in the gospels. Most of those details will not stand up to scrutiny. People will be surprised, perhaps threatened, maybe even angered, to discover step by step that so much of what has been said and written about Jesus is not history at all. It never has been. I will analyze it thoroughly and carefully. If the data then requires it, I will set that narrative aside or expose it for what it is. I plan to do that boldly and overtly. Some will worry that when this process is complete the traditional faith story will be in shreds. That is not my concern. Destroying Jesus is not my goal; destroying the layers of ever-hardening concrete that have encased him is. Once that task has been completed, we will be ready to move toward seeing Jesus in a new way—a Jesus for the non-religious.

I hope this goal intrigues you. The journey now begins.

2

THERE WAS NO STAR OVER BETHLEHEM

Birth stories are always fanciful. They are never historical.
No one waits outside a maternity ward for a great person to
be born.

W e start our probe into the Jesus story at the beginning of
the Bible's description of his life. Was Jesus born in
Bethlehem, the city of David? The answer is a very simple no. There is
almost no possibility that this claim is a fact of history.

Jesus' place of birth was quite probably in Nazareth. He was, in all
likelihood, born in exactly the same way that every other person is
born. He had a human mother and a human father. Both the Bethlehem birthplace and the virgin birth tradition are aspects of a developing interpretive process that did not begin to manifest itself inside the
Christian written tradition until well into the ninth decade, or some
fifty to sixty years after the earthly life of Jesus had come to an end.
Traditional believers, most of whom have learned what they know
about Jesus' birth from Christmas pageants in which they were actors
and actresses and not from the Bible itself, will find this first probe into
the birth myth to be immediately disturbing. Romantic, nostalgic, unchallenged tales die hard.

Birth stories are always fanciful. They are never historical. After all, no
one waits outside a maternity ward for a great person to be born. An individual has first to become great; then tales presaging that future greatness begin to circulate around his or her origins. Tales are developed that

hint of the presence of peculiar gifts of strength, character or intelligence in the heroic person at a very young age. In time the moment of that person's birth might well begin to be marked with magical signs and portents of things to come. It is, therefore, essential to begin this search for the reality of the man Jesus by looking at the biblical narratives that purport to tell of his birth, which for far too long have been mistakenly read as history.[1] These stories are filled with unusual details. They tell us of singing angels, stars that announce earthly happenings and even a fetus leaping to proclaim the anticipated power of another fetus. These details should quickly be recognized for what they are: interpretive symbols, not literal history. Listen first to some pertinent facts that do come from the realm of history:

According to secular records, King Herod the Great appears to have died in the year 4 BCE, after which the land of the Jews was divided into three procuratorships. In time Pontius Pilate became the Roman Empire's procurator for Judea, one of those three areas. Pilate, according to secular records, held that position between the years 26 CE and 36 CE. If the tradition is accurate that Jesus was born when Herod was king, a detail attested in two gospel narratives (Matt. 2:1, 22, Luke 1:5), and if his crucifixion took place during the reign of Pontius Pilate, as all of the gospels assert (Mark 15:1, Matt. 27:2, Luke 3:1, 23:1, John 18:29ff.), then we can get a fairly accurate fix on the actual time dimensions of his life. By squeezing those numbers with the use of other known data, a consensus among scholars has emerged suggesting that the life span of Jesus of Nazareth began around the year 4 BCE and ended in the crucifixion somewhere around the year 30 CE. With those dates fairly firmly set, we are ready to focus on the specifics of his life.

Where was Jesus born? Since he was widely known as Jesus of Nazareth (Mark 1:24, 6:1–6, 16:6, Matt. 21:11, 26:71, Luke 4:16, 18:37, 24:19, John 1:45, 18:5), the probability is that Nazareth was his place of origin. That is certainly the assumption made by the author of the book we call Mark, the earliest gospel to be written. In Mark's narrative there is not only no reference to Bethlehem, but also no hint of a miraculous birth. This means that the account of a Bethlehem birthplace for Jesus did not enter the Christian tradition until Matthew wrote his gospel sometime in the eighties of this Common Era. When the Bethlehem tradition does appear, it seems to have been driven not by some firsthand memory, but solely by the use of a messianic text found in the book of the prophet Micah (Mic. 5:2), a late-eighth-century-BCE work. Matthew, in his story of Herod responding to a query from the magi, says that the king directed his scribes to determine where the "promised one" would be born. Those scribes searched the scriptures and interpreted the words of Micah as a hidden messianic clue (Matt. 2:5–6). Why would Micah write that the messiah would be born in the village of Bethlehem, just a few miles from Jerusalem? Because this city was the birthplace of the great King David and Jewish expectations had long ago added the restoration of the throne of David to their developing messianic tradition.

Matthew and Luke, the only gospel writers to give us a birth tradition or indeed any information about Jesus' family of origin, lend support to the shakiness of Bethlehem being the birthplace by disagreeing on how it was that Jesus happened to be born there. Indeed, the two accounts vary in many places. In the common mind, however, they are blended: most people cannot separate Matthew's details from Luke's. It is essential for our purposes to make the two stories distinct.

Matthew assumes that Mary and Joseph live in Bethlehem. That, of course, makes it easy to say that Jesus' birth occurred there. Mary and Joseph, according to Matthew, lived in a quite specific and identifiable house in Bethlehem over which, he would say, a star could pause and on which it could pour its steady and illuminating light. Yet Matthew also clearly knows the historical fact that Jesus was a Galilean, and he shares the general assumption of those who knew Jesus as an adult that he hailed from the village of Nazareth. In that day there was virtually no migration from Jerusalem and Judea toward Galilee. No one desired to move out into the country or even the suburbs. All the factors present in the life of the Jews, whether they were social, political or economic, favored migration, if at all, *toward* Jerusalem, not *away from* it. Jerusalem represented opportunity, while Galilee represented poverty. Even Roman oppression was tempered by the political weight of the city. Yet that is the direction Matthew has the family of Jesus move so that he can account for Jesus' Galilean background. To explain this counterintuitive behavior, he had to develop in his infancy narrative a rather forced drama to explain what it was that motivated the family of

Jesus to leave his noble Judean place of birth in Bethlehem in order to grow up in rural and rustic Galilee. That contrived explanation involved a number of supernatural messages received through dreams and even included a little royal intrigue, pitting the household of the monarch, King Herod, against this humble child who was supposed to be a threat to the king's power (Matt. 2:7–23). To make the story even more obviously a mythical creation, Matthew will tell us later that this Jesus was a carpenter's son (Matt. 13:55). Very few kings in real life will notice the birth of a commoner, much less become involved in a defensive plot of protecting the throne from the threat such a child would bring. These motifs in Matthew's original birth story of Jesus are clearly not history, but rather reflect the growing power of claims made well after Jesus' death that he was somehow the heir to the throne of King David, a popular prerequisite for the Jewish messiah.

The literal accuracy of the Bethlehem birthplace for Jesus also depends heavily on the story of the wise men being true. Yet no reputable biblical scholar today would seriously defend the historicity of these magi. This story, which is told only in Matthew, has about it all the marks of an interpretive sermon, developed rather dramatically from a passage in Isaiah 60. In Isaiah's account kings are said to have come to "the brightness of [God's] rising" (60:3). These kings come on camels, they come from Sheba, and they bring with them gold and frankincense (60:6). That is the core of the story of the magi.

How then did the myrrh get into the story of the wise men? Myrrh clearly does not appear in Isaiah 60. The answer is simple, but it requires an understanding of Jewish history. One of the things that does appear in Isaiah, as noted above, is that these kings came from Sheba. The word "Sheba" would remind Jewish interpreters of another story in their history in which another royal visitor came to pay homage to another king of the Jews, and back into their sacred scriptures they would plunge. In 1 Kings the story is told of the visit of the Queen of Sheba to King Solomon (10:1–13). She was also said to have come on camels and to have brought truckloads of spices. Myrrh, in all probability, entered the story of the wise men through this doorway.

In Matthew's rendition these kings or magi are led by a magical star that from its heavenly perch in the east announces the birth of a king of the Jews (Matt. 2:2). That star then floats across the sky so slowly that these Middle Eastern stargazers can follow it to their destination (Matt. 2:9). Stars that appear in the sky to announce earthly events are conceivable only in a world that viewed the sky as the roof of the earth and the floor of heaven. Stars in that worldview were a kind of heavenly lantern that God could hang out to be seen on earth to announce important births and were often so used in Jewish folklore. In one interpretive tradition of the rabbis, a star was said to have announced the birth of Abraham, the father of the nation; another announced the birth of Isaac, the child of promise; and still another, the birth of Moses, the one who most dramatically shaped Jewish consciousness. If God lived beyond the sky, as people in that day generally assumed, with the earth as the object of constant divine attention, perhaps such a thing might be imaginable. It is not imaginable, however, in our space age. We live with a consciousness of the dimensions of space that first-century people could not have conceived. In our world, first airplanes linked us to destinations on the other side of our globe and then spaceships carried us to the far reaches of the moon. Unmanned spacecraft later carried us to other planets in our solar system. With help from the Hubble telescope we have learned that our galaxy, known as the Milky Way, has over 200 billion stars in it, most of them larger than the star that we call the sun. Our single galaxy measures over 100,000 light years in size; in other words, it would take light 100,000 years (traveling at its approximate speed of 186,000 miles per second) to go from one end of our galaxy to the other. To find the distance roughly in miles, multiply 186,000 by 60 seconds and then by 60 minutes and then by 24 hours and then by 365.25 days and you will have the distance traversed in a single light year; then multiply that total by 100,000 for the total mileage. The result is beyond our ability to count. Our modern consciousness has also had to embrace the fact that the whole visible universe, of which our enormous galaxy is but a tiny part, contains hundreds of billions of other galaxies, with more being discovered almost routinely as space continues to expand outward up to and including this very moment. Stars are impersonal physical objects that do not announce earthly events. There are no wandering stars in our galaxy. Each star travels in a fixed trajectory that can be charted by computers, and its exact location in the sky on any date in the past or in the future can be calculated precisely. So in the real world there can be no such thing as a star able to lead the magi first to the palace of King Herod, where they learn from the king's scribes that Bethlehem is to be the birthplace of the Jewish messiah, and then to their final destination — Bethlehem. Those ideas, so essential to the biblical story, are simply not credible except when we travel into the world of make-believe. They are premodern fantasies.

Bethlehem was the city of David. The throne of David had been vacant or filled with pretenders since the early sixth century BCE, when the Babylonians put an end to the Jewish royal line by killing all the children and heirs of King Zedekiah, after which they put out Zedekiah's eyes and marched him into Babylonian captivity, where he died (2 Kings 25:7). Well after Jesus' death, when messianic thinking began to swirl around him, his memory was wrapped in these traditions. Jesus' birthplace in Bethlehem is not history. The prophet Micah did not predict it. A star did not announce it. Wise men did not follow that star. It did not lead them to the king's palace or to the house in Bethlehem where tradition says the Christ child was born. These magi did not present their gifts of gold, frankincense and myrrh. All of these details are part of a developing mythology that must be separated from Jesus if we are ever going to see him as he really was.

Almost as if to signal that he was spinning a mythological interpretive web, Matthew takes a Moses story out of the Jewish past and weaves it around Jesus' birth as a secondary theme. A wicked pharaoh (or Egyptian ruler) had once struck a blow against Moses, God's appointed deliverer, by killing all the Jewish male babies born in Egypt. His aim, according to that Hebrew story, was to destroy the child Moses before he could grow up to be the one who freed the Jews from Egyptian bondage. In that story Moses was spared because his mother hid him in the bulrushes of the Nile River, where he was found by the pharaoh's daughter, taken to the pharaoh's palace and raised as her son (Exod. 1:15–2:10). Moses' sister, Miriam, popped up in this ancient narrative at just the proper time and offered to get a Hebrew wet nurse for the baby to assist in his royal upbringing. Miriam's candidate for this job was her mother, who was, of course, also Moses' mother. All the circles are closed. That happens in developing mythology. It does not happen in history.[2]

Matthew integrates this Moses theme into his story of the wise men by having them go to Bethlehem with the king's blessing. King Herod, says Matthew, only requires them to return to him when they have found the "royal child" so that "I too may come and worship him" (Matt. 2:8). Journeying down the six-mile wagon track of a road from Jerusalem to Bethlehem, the wise men are led again by the magical star they had seen in the east (Matt. 2:9). It now stops over the house where Jesus is living so that the magi can present their gifts of gold, frankincense and myrrh (Matt. 2:9–11). These Middle Eastern astrologers, however, are warned by God in a dream not to return to Herod, so they go home by a different route (Matt. 2:12). Herod, soon realizing that these perfect strangers have declined to do his intelligence work against this pretender to his throne, becomes angry and resorts to plan B (Matt. 2:16–18): Herod gathers his army and goes to Bethlehem with orders to kill all the Jewish boy babies in a vain attempt to destroy God's promised deliverer. That is, of course, exactly what the pharaoh did when Moses was born. Matthew further links the two stories by saying that Herod's actions necessitated an escape to Egypt. All of these interpretive clues are, in this masterful narrative, linked quite beautifully to the supposed Bethlehem birthplace of the messiah. They are romantic and fanciful, but there is not one shred of history in them. The Bethlehem birthplace is just another part of a developing messianic interpretive tradition. If history is our primary agenda, we ought to sing at Christmas "O Little Town of Nazareth," for that is overwhelmingly the probable place in which the one known as Jesus of Nazareth was born.

Turning next to Luke, who wrote about a decade later, we discover an entirely different spin on the story of Jesus' origin. Luke also suggests that the birth of Jesus occurred in Bethlehem. However, that is about all that his birth story has in common with Matthew's account.

Luke was not only aware of the developing birth tradition, but he also had Mark in front of him as he wrote. Because he wanted to introduce the themes he would develop in his gospel, it was important to him to assert the developing conclusion that Jesus was heir to David's throne, so he too had him born in Bethlehem. Unlike Matthew, however, Luke agreed with Mark that the family of Jesus lived in Nazareth. His problem, therefore, became how to figure out a way that the Nazareth-based couple could have had this special baby in the town of Bethlehem in order to fulfill the Davidic expectation. He chose a rather fascinating, but, as we shall see, historically suspect literary device. Before Jesus was born, Luke wrote, a census or an enrollment was ordered by Caesar Augustus, requiring people to return to their ancestral home for registration (Luke 2:1–5). Joseph, Luke asserts, was of the "house" of David, so he was required to return to Bethlehem. Joseph took with him his wife, described in King James English as being "great with child" (2:5, KJV). That was the reason, Luke then argues, that this Nazareth couple just happened to be in Bethlehem when the child was born. It was an ingenious solution to a mythological problem.

Filmmakers Cecil B. DeMille and Mel Gibson might both be proud of Luke's rich imagination. His narrative is not, however, anything close to history, and unless all rational faculties are suspended, there is no way to pretend that it is. Many issues in this story reveal again and again that these rich, interpretive, even inaccurate data were designed primarily to make a point about who the writer believed Jesus was. They were not employed in the service of presenting actual historical data.

First, Luke says that this registration or enrollment, ordered by Caesar Augustus, occurred when Quirinius was governor of Syria. Secular records, however, reveal that Quirinius became governor of Syria in the winter when the year 6 CE turned into 7 CE. If Jesus was born when Herod was still king (4 BCE), as Luke states (1:5), he would have been ten or eleven years old before Quirinius assumed power in Syria. The story's historicity begins to wobble on this fact alone.

Second, there is no record anywhere in ancient history of any authority ordering people to return to their ancestral home for enrollment or taxation. Such a requirement assumes a level of governmental efficiency and record keeping that does not exist today and would have been unimaginable in an ancient world that did not issue birth certificates, marriage certificates or death certificates. There is one other fact that makes this an absurd proposition. In Luke's genealogy (3:23–38) there are forty-one generations between David and Joseph. Try to imagine how many direct heirs of a person are produced in forty-one generations. It would be approaching a number in the millions. King

David had multiple wives—perhaps not a thousand like his son Solomon, but probably hundreds. Within a very few generations almost everyone could accurately claim the distinction of being the heir of David. The idea, then, that any government would know who those heirs were and could thus order them to return to the city of David for an "enrollment" is inconceivable, if not preposterous. If such a tactic were literally employed, it would be no wonder there was no room at the inn! There would have been no city or nation in the Middle East or indeed in the modern world that could have handled the influx of such a crowd. History this is not!

Other details in Luke's birth narrative are equally untrustworthy if one tries to read them literally. Most people do not know that it is approximately ninety-four miles from Nazareth to Jerusalem and perhaps one hundred miles from Nazareth to Bethlehem, making such a journey one of at least seven to ten days. The modes of transportation available in that era were either walking or riding a donkey. There were no restaurants or motels on the way. Travelers had to sleep in the fields and eat whatever food could be purchased to supplement what they might have taken with them. The heat in the middle of the day would have driven travelers off the road in search of shade; the darkness of the midnight sky would have been so profound one could not safely walk after the last traces of twilight disappeared. When these facts are assembled in our consciousness, the question arises as to what husband in his right mind would take his eight- to nine-months pregnant wife on such a journey? Why would he even think about taking her? After all, women were not enrolled for tax or voting purposes in that day. Women did not participate in the decision-making processes of the civic society. Clearly the literary device that Luke used to try to get Jesus into Bethlehem for his birth in order to keep the mythology growing was full of holes.

Next Luke has Jesus and his parents, not fleeing to Egypt as Matthew had suggested, but rather remaining in the Jerusalem area for his circumcision on the eighth day of his life and his presentation and the rite of purification on the fortieth day. Only then does the family return in a leisurely fashion to their home in Nazareth, where the tradition makes it quite clear that Jesus grew up. He was undoubtedly born there too.

The Bethlehem birthplace for Jesus is an image-building bit of mythology. He is a child of Nazareth, an uninspiring town out of which people would later say "nothing good could come" (John 1:46). Yet it was out of Nazareth that Jesus surely came, and this is very clear in the biblical story once we get beyond the interpretive myths that were being laid upon him in the gospels of Matthew and Luke.

This analysis forces a number of questions upon us: What was there about this Jesus that made it necessary for people to surround his birth with a Bethlehem origin and with cosmic signs and wonders? Around how many lives does this kind of mythology gather? Why was it attached to him? What operated in history that caused people to think it appropriate to pull Jesus out of a humble origin and relocate him to a place of royal beginnings?

The interpretive myth of Jesus unravels as soon as it is literalized. The meaning of his life, however, still cries out for an explanation. When our analysis is complete, perhaps that explanation can be formed. For now, however, it is sufficient to say he was born in Nazareth of Galilee. There were no stars, no angels, no wise men, no shepherds and no manger. This is our first conclusion. We move on from there.

3

THE PARENTS OF JESUS: FICTIONALIZED COMPOSITES

Is not this the carpenter, the son of Mary?

Mark 6:3

Is not this the carpenter's son? Is not his mother called Mary?

Matt. 13:55

Once the birth stories are dismissed as history, the question arises as to who the parents of Jesus were. What if anything can we know historically about these two people?

There will be some who are startled even to have this question asked, for we have treated mythology as history for far too long. Everyone knows, we say, that Jesus' earthly father was named Joseph. After all, we have seen him thousands of times in art, in crèche scenes and on Christmas cards. He is so familiar that we recognize him immediately when we see him portrayed. He is either walking beside a donkey on which the pregnant Mary rides sidesaddle on the journey to Bethlehem, or he is standing resolutely behind the manger with his staff in hand as if to protect his recently delivered wife and the infant child who is lying in the manger. Most of us have never questioned the accuracy of these portraits, or even the assumption that the man's name was Joseph.

If that is true for Joseph, it is hundreds of times more true for Mary. Her portrait has dominated the art of the Western world for centuries. She is either depicted in stained glass or remembered in some other way in almost every Christian church throughout the world. We are so sure of what she looks like that throughout history people have claimed to see her in visions. Shrines at Fatima and other places owe their existence to such appearances. Recently she was said to have appeared under a bridge in Chicago, the report of which tied up traffic for miles. Television documentaries have been made about her various sightings. Vatican investigations are carried out to distinguish between those appearances that are deemed to be "real" and those that appear to "lack proper documentation." Throughout history Mary has been a far more important figure than Joseph. We will be surprised to learn that this is not necessarily the way it was in the earliest books of the New Testament. Nothing reveals more clearly the power of the mythology that developed around Jesus between the time of his death and the writing of the gospels than the study of the biblical details of his parents. Yet those details do not uphold the myths about his origin that entered the developing history of Christianity, to say nothing of our emotions. That is why once we have dismissed the birth stories as history, we have to focus on the historicity of those two people whom, along with Jesus, we have called the holy family.

The first note to inform our study is the fact that neither parent receives any mention in any written material available to us prior to the eighth decade of the Christian era, nor is there any hint present that anyone regarded either parent as particularly significant in the tradition until the ninth decade. In the entire Pauline corpus, written no earlier than 50 and no later than 64 CE, there is not a single reference to the parents of Jesus. When Paul talks about Jesus' origins, the only thing he says is that Jesus was "born of a woman, born under the law" (Gal. 4:4). The word translated "woman" in this text has in it absolutely no connotation whatsoever of the word "virgin." Indeed, in Jewish circles, just as in ours today, a virgin mother would be a contradiction in terms. A child simply could not be born of a virgin. What Paul is saying in this earliest text on the origins of Jesus is that Jesus had a perfectly normal birth. He was born of a woman, like everyone else, and he was born under the law, like every Jew. The book of Galatians was written in the early fifties. Paul appears never to have heard of Jesus' miraculous birth, probably because this tradition had not yet developed. In that same epistle to the Galatians Paul refers to James, whom he identifies as "the Lord's brother," so a permanent virgin status for Mary would also have been inconceivable to him (1:19). A few years later, in the mid to late fifties, Paul wrote the epistle to the Romans, in which he became the first person to make the claim of a Davidic connection for Jesus. This is the place where the Bethlehem birth tradition was born. For Paul, however, this claim was not one of divine paternity. He simply wrote that "according to the flesh" Jesus was descended from David (Rom. 1:3), only to become one who was "designated Son of God in power according to the spirit of holiness by his resurrection from the dead" (Rom. 1:4). Paul seemed neither to know nor to care about further details of Jesus' parentage.

One might reasonably ask whether there are any other documents that might be earlier than Paul's writings to which we could turn for additional information. The answer is that there are two possibilities, but their dating is still a matter of some debate in New Testament circles, and how much weight they can bear is questionable. Nonetheless, they deserve mention. One is the material that scholars refer to as the Q document, a hypothetical text that has never been seen. Its presumed existence results from an inference born out of the study of both Matthew and Luke. Scholars universally assert that Mark was the primary source underlying both those gospels. Matthew used about 90 percent of Mark in his work; Luke, a bit less, perhaps 50 percent. This means that scholars can delete from both Matthew and Luke all their Marcan material—that is, everything that the gospels share with Mark—and can study the ways each used Mark and what each added to or deleted from Mark. Once the content of Mark is removed from both gospels, however, it then becomes obvious that in addition to their dependence on Mark, Matthew and Luke have a second source in common, for there are non-Marcan passages in the two gospels that are identical (or nearly so) in content. The assumption of the majority of scholars is that this second source, now presumably lost, was a written source. It was named Q, short for the German word *Quelle*, which simply means "source." The Q hypothesis was the gift of nineteenth-century German scholarship. When this Q material is isolated, it turns out to be primarily a collection of the sayings of Jesus. Even if this theory is accurate, however, we still have a dating problem. We know only that the Q material had to be earlier than Matthew and Luke, since both used it. Mark clearly did not use this source, so one might argue that it was later than Mark, but it could have been earlier than Mark and simply unknown to him. The Q material has in it no narrative material at all. There is not even a mention in Q of so vital a moment in the Jesus story as the crucifixion or the resurrection. There has been a strong push in some circles, like the Jesus Seminar (a group of scholars dedicated to finding the historical Jesus), for an earlier date, even as early as the fifties. It is not essential that we enter that debate in this book. It is essential, however, that we note that regardless of its date, the Q material includes nothing at all about Jesus' parents, not even their names.[1]

The only other Christian source that some scholars argue was written earlier than the canonical gospels is called the Gospel of Thomas. Discovered in the twentieth century in a cave at a place called Nag Hammadi, the Gospel of Thomas, only one chapter long, is also a collection of the sayings of Jesus, again with no narrative material, no birth story, no crucifixion story, no resurrection story and no miracle stories. Regardless of when Thomas is dated, it provides us with no data at all about Jesus' family of origin.[2] The content found in the later gospels about the presumed parents of Jesus is therefore built on very flimsy historical data.

In Mark, the only other New Testament source written before the birth narratives entered the tradition, we note that nothing is recorded about Jesus' birth. It is hard to imagine this story being left out if it had been known by Mark. What Mark does say about the family of Jesus, however, makes it obvious that he had never heard about any developing birth legends. In two places Mark gives us references to the family of Jesus, both of which are quite pejorative (3:31–35, 6:1–4). Mark suggests that the family of Jesus consisted of a mother, four brothers (who are named James, Joses, Judas and Simon) and at least two sisters (who are unnamed, but the plural for "sister" is used). No father is mentioned. These family members come into Mark's story expressing concern about Jesus' mental health and about the effect his strange behavior is having on their social standing. "When his family heard it [referring to Jesus' teaching and public activity], they went out to restrain him, for people were saying, 'He has gone out of his mind'" (3:21, NRSV). The scribes then called him demon-possessed (v. 22). Jesus, according to Mark, rejects this intrusion of his family members into his life and in effect publicly disowns both his mother and his brothers, claiming that the only mother and brothers he recognizes are those who do the will of God. To think Jesus is out of his mind would hardly be an appropriate response of a mother to whom an angel had appeared to tell her that she was to bear a divine child. These passages simply cannot be harmonized with angelic annunciations and the promised expectation of a life described as being the Son of God or the son of "the Highest."

The actual naming of Jesus' mother as Mary is uttered only once in Mark's entire gospel. Indeed, this is the only mention of her name in Christian written records until the ninth decade. On this single occasion her name is placed on the lips of an anonymous member of a hostile crowd that, Mark tells us, is both astonished and angry about what Jesus has said in the local synagogue. The question the crowd is raising in this episode is: How is it possible that this local boy has acquired such knowledge? A voice from the crowd calls out, "Is not this the carpenter, the son of Mary?" (6:3). Mark understands this remark as clearly meant to be rude and offensive. A grown Jewish man would never be called the son of a particular woman unless the person meant to imply that Jesus' paternity was either questionable or unknown. These words carry with them something of the connotation of our word "bastard"! Mark had to be aware of that when he wrote this passage.

When we become clear about what the factual baseline appears to be in the Jesus story, then we can watch the tradition developing without any threat that, by exposing these developing details, we are actually calling some established truth into question. There was no established truth about Jesus' family of origin. We are rather identifying the accretions to his life story at the moment they enter the developing tradition.

Joseph, the name of Jesus' earthly father, is introduced into the tradition for the first time by Matthew near the midpoint of the ninth decade. Once the idea of a virgin birth had become part of the tradition, there was a need for a male figure to provide the protective cover for the pregnant Mary in that cruel and patriarchal society.

In Matthew's birth story Joseph is actually the primary character, with Mary only a bit player in his drama. She is introduced simply as a virgin betrothed to Joseph. Before they came together, says Matthew, Mary was found to be "with child" (1:18). Matthew adds the words "of the Holy Spirit" to that verse.[3] It is, however, clear from the rest of his story that the earlier presumption was that something scandalous had happened. Matthew describes Joseph as "a just man" (1:19) who is unwilling to put his presumably unfaithful fiancée to shame by making a public issue of her illicit pregnancy, so he plans to divorce her quietly. That is when Joseph is said to have had the first of a series of dreams that will form part of the interpretive drama that Matthew is creating. An unnamed angel informs Joseph in this dream first that the child was conceived not by another man but by the Holy Spirit, second that the child's name is to be Jesus, and third that his birth is the fulfillment of the words of the prophet Isaiah (Matt. 1:20–23). Only then does Joseph, obedient to this revelation, take Mary as his wife and give his male protection to her infant. This protection is symbolized by the fact that Joseph names the child with the name revealed to him by the angel.

This is the place where the legend of the virgin birth entered the Christian story. It appears to be a Matthean creation. It is a beautiful but obviously contrived tale. Matthew even seeks to ground this story in the Hebrew scriptures, which was his signature mark. This pregnancy, he says, fulfilled the scriptures, and he offers a Greek translation of Isaiah to provide the biblical basis for this miracle. There were and still are many problems with this effort. First, the word "virgin" is not in the original Hebrew text of Isaiah 7:14. Second, the Isaiah text in Hebrew implies not that a woman will "conceive," as Matthew quotes it, but that a woman *"is with* child." Where I come from, that means that she is not a virgin! Third, the young woman with child about whom Isaiah speaks is to be a sign of the continuity of the nation of Judah, which at that moment was under siege from an alliance of the kings of the Northern Kingdom and Syria as they tried to force the kingdom of Judah into taking up arms with them against the might of Assyria. Isaiah offers this sign to the king of Judah to stop his fear that

Judah will fall to these kings. A sign from God that would in fact not transpire for eight hundred years would hardly have had any real value in the midst of that crisis.

It is amazing to me how these inconsistent, almost incoherent explanations first got literalized and then managed to exert such influence on Christian thought. The use of this text from Isaiah was, first of all, a real stretch, and Matthew must have known this. Even second-century Jewish writers pointed out this fact to Christian leaders, but to no avail.[4] Their minds were made up and facts would not be allowed to interfere with the developing institutional power of Christianity. For us to unravel them now, as I think we must, and as Christian scholarship has done now for almost two hundred years, is to recognize that even originally they had no literal substance. The story of Jesus' miraculous birth clearly must have served some other agenda. Perhaps it was designed to cover some unprotected flank of the Christian story. Maybe there were rumors about Jesus' paternity in addition to the previously mentioned rude comment in Mark. The suggestion that a scandal needed to be covered up is apparent in a number of places in the New Testament. Luke has Mary say in the passage known as the Magnificat that God "has regarded the low estate of his handmaiden" (Luke 1:48). Is that a hint of scandal? There was no lower estate in that era than being a pregnant out-of-wedlock woman. When John has the crowd say to Jesus, "We were not born of fornication" (John 8:41), is that another hint? The implication of that comment surely is that Jesus *was* born of fornication. Those passages certainly cause scholars to wonder, but whether or not we can today discern the reason that the virgin birth story first developed, we do need to note, at the very least, that it is not an original part of the Jesus story. Rather, it is a late-developing, interpretive tradition that obviously incorporates symbols that were never meant to be literalized. Virgin births were a familiar tool in the ancient world to explain the extraordinary qualities of a leader.

Once the virgin tradition has been introduced, however, an earthly father has to be provided for the drama; a patriarchal society requires that. Thus the virgin birth and the earthly father appear in the tradition simultaneously. If there had been no virgin tradition, the character of Joseph would never have been created. I use the word "created" quite deliberately, because that is surely how Joseph came into being. Joseph never makes an appearance in the gospel tradition anywhere outside the birth narratives.[5] There is an interesting and I believe revealing redaction by Matthew on Mark's story about Jesus' family being embarrassed by him and coming to take him away. While Mark has a person from the crowd shout, "Is not this the carpenter, the son of Mary?" Matthew, with Mark clearly in front of him as he writes, has a problem, for he has already created the birth story with Joseph as part of it. So Matthew rewrites this brief bit of dialogue. He changes these fourteen words so substantially that he removes the scandal and provides a reference to Joseph. Matthew's rewrite reads, "Is not this the carpenter's son? Is not his mother called Mary?" (Matt. 13:55). From this Matthean rewrite of Mark alone comes the tradition of Joseph being a carpenter. Matthew smooths Mark's text so that it will harmonize with his newly introduced account of a miraculous birth.

I do not believe that a person named Joseph who was the protective earthly father of Jesus ever existed. The texts we have examined above support that assertion. Joseph is from start to finish a mythological character created out of whole cloth, by the author of the gospel we call Matthew.

Supporting this assertion even more powerfully is the way Matthew draws the character of Joseph.[6] The only biographical details on Joseph in the entire Bible come in this gospel's birth narrative. There we are told three primary things: First, this Joseph has a father named Jacob. Second, God appears to communicate with Joseph only through dreams. (Four separate dream encounters are related: 1:20, 2:13, 2:19, 2:22.) Third, Joseph's role in the drama of salvation is to save the child of promise from death by taking him down to Egypt (2:13–15). Each of these details would certainly be familiar to Matthew's Jewish audience, who knew quite well the story of the patriarch Joseph in the book of Genesis (37–50). That Joseph also had a father named Jacob (Gen. 35:24). That Joseph was also deeply associated with dreams (Gen. 37:5, 9, 19; 40:5ff., 16ff.; 41:1–36); in fact, he rode into power in Egypt as the interpreter of dreams (Gen. 41:38). That Joseph's role in the drama of salvation was to save the people of the promise from death by taking them down to Egypt (Gen. 45:1–15). These biographical connections can hardly be coincidental. They are too obvious and too fanciful to be remembered history. This was just another part of the process of grafting Jesus into the Jewish epic, which was the mythological self-understanding of the people called the Jews.

There is one final reason that the name of Joseph was essential in the Jesus story. The Jewish people were, after the reign of Solomon, divided into the Northern Kingdom, called Israel at the time of the political separation but known as Galilee in the New Testament, and the Southern Kingdom, called Judah at the time of the separation and Judea in the New Testament. So deep was this division in the history of the Jews and so abiding was the hostility that flowed from this division that the Jewish storytellers located its source in their prehistory by portraying their founding patriarch Jacob as having had two principal wives: Leah, the mother of Judah whose tribe dominated the Southern Kingdom, and Rachel, the mother of Joseph whose tribes (Ephraim and Manasseh) dominated the Northern Kingdom. If Jesus were in the first century to have a valid claim to being messiah, he would be required to bring these two factions together. Matthew accomplishes this by a genealogy (1:1–17) that first grounds Jesus' life, indeed his DNA, clearly on the line of King David, which would relate him to the tribe of Judah genetically and by bloodlines. Then Matthew gives Jesus an earthly father whose name is Joseph (Matt. 1:16), and by patterning Joseph's life after the patriarch Joseph in the book of Genesis, he brings the other strand of the Jewish story, the Joseph tribes, into his interpretation of Jesus. It is a clever twist, but it is not history. I do not think anyone knows who the father of Jesus was, including the writers of the New Testament. Mark never says. Matthew and Luke say that the Holy Spirit was his actual father. John, frequently called the Fourth Gospel, omits the miraculous birth story, but refers to Jesus as the son of Joseph on two occasions (John 1:45, 6:42).

The reason Joseph has remained a shadowy figure throughout Christian history is that he was a literary character from the very beginning, created out of the stuff of a growing interpretive mythology. So the inquiry deepens and the plot thickens. First we jettison Bethlehem as the birthplace of Jesus. Next we dismiss the virgin birth as pure fantasy. Then we show that the character we have called the earthly father of Jesus is a recognizable literary device, not a person of history.

With Joseph now seen as a Matthean creation, our attention next turns to Mary. As already noted, her name is introduced in a single verse in Mark. Her behavior in Mark is portrayed as being negative to Jesus. So we raise an even more disturbing question: Was Mary, the mother of Jesus, a person of history? Clearly, the person Jesus had to have had a mother that at least he, to say nothing of the other members of his family, would have known, but whether she was actually named Mary is open to question, and her identity as a virgin is obviously nothing but a later developing tradition. When Mark, at least a decade earlier, had introduced without name the mother of Jesus, he said, as noted earlier, that she was the mother of four other sons besides Jesus and at least two unnamed daughters (6:3). A mother of seven was certainly not a virgin in the mind of Mark! Matthew thus appears to be the creator of the legend of the virgin.

Near the end of that ninth decade, or perhaps even as late as the beginning of the tenth decade, Luke writes his gospel, in which he reinforces the virgin story with more details. He also begins to develop Mary's character much more fully than Matthew had done in his one-dimensional presentation. In Luke the mother of Jesus is overcome with fear at the role thrust upon her (Luke 1:29). She is, says Luke, related to Elizabeth the mother of John the Baptist (Luke 1:36). She sings the song called the Magnificat (Luke 1:46–55). She ponders the various signs in her heart (Luke 2:19). She goes with Jesus at age twelve to Jerusalem for the Passover (Luke 2:41). (One wonders if that was intended to be something like the later-developing bar mitzvah celebration.) In that story she rebukes Jesus when he remains in the temple after her departure (Luke 2:48). Then her name disappears from Luke's narrative.[7] She is mentioned by name only one other time in the entire Lucan corpus, and that comes in the book of Acts (1:14), where she is said to be in the company of the disciples in the upper room at the time of Pentecost. She is not mentioned in the crucifixion story in any of the first three gospels.

One of the above-mentioned Lucan references raises, at least for me, the question of the historicity of the name Mary. Luke refers to Elizabeth, the mother of John the Baptist, as Mary's "kinswoman." The King James Version translates that word "cousin," but the specificity of the relationship is not spelled out (1:36). The suggestion that

Jesus and John the Baptist are cousins, however, derives from this text in Luke alone. What makes me suspicious is that Elizabeth, in Hebrew, would be Elisheba, a name that appears only once in the entire Bible. She is the wife of Aaron, the brother of Moses. Now bear in mind that Luke introduces Elizabeth as the daughter of Aaron (1:5). Clearly Luke had Aaron and Moses in mind when he wrote his gospel. Recall that Moses also had a sister named Miriam, who plays a very important role in the Moses story, from guarding him at his birth (Exod. 2:4) to rejoicing at his crossing of the Red Sea (Exod. 15:2ff.). When the Hebrew name Miriam is written in English, the result is Mary. Did Luke use the family of Moses as his model in the creation of the family of Jesus? It is a question worth at least raising, since we know that he used the story of Abraham and Sarah to form the content of the story of the parents of John the Baptist (Zechariah and Elizabeth). Also, echoes about Mary, drawn from characters in the Hebrew scriptures, but primarily from the book of Genesis, can be found in the birth story of Luke.[8]

It is in the Fourth Gospel only that the mother of Jesus is said to be present at the cross. John's purpose in putting her there is to allow her to be commended by Jesus into the care of "the disciple whom he loved," who is to be her "son" (John 19:25–26). This gospel always portrays the beloved disciple as heroic. No biblical scholar believes that episode is remembered history. Certainly the Catholic piety that has the mother of Jesus mourning at the cross, cradling the deceased body of her son, is sheer devotional fantasy. It might make a good movie theme, but it is not history.

The only other time that Mary is mentioned in John's gospel is anything but flattering. It occurs in the story of the wedding feast in Cana of Galilee (2:1–11). Here the Johannine text provides an embarrassing jolt to the pious tradition that surrounded the virgin in history. In this story Jesus rebukes his mother for trying to force his hand. Jesus addresses her: "O woman, what have you to do with me? My hour has not yet come."

People are surprised when they realize that this is the total extent of the material about the mother of Jesus in the entire New Testament. It is scanty, sometimes even hostile and rejecting. Almost the entirety of the positive biblical content about Mary in the Christian tradition comes out of the birth stories, which are all but universally dismissed as history. The embarrassing stories about the mother of Jesus have either been ignored by the church fathers or been "creatively" reinterpreted. Mary's journey continues through the centuries, however, with ever-expanding and highly miraculous mythology. She becomes both a perpetual virgin and a postpartum virgin. Then she is removed from a real human identity by stories of her having been immaculately conceived at her birth and bodily assumed into heaven at her death. None of these Mary narratives, however, makes any pretense at historical grounding.[9]

The tree of our literalized faith story shakes when historical data are sought to affirm these claims. Once the birth stories are dismissed as history, both of the supposed parents of Jesus fade substantially. These stories have had enormous emotional power in the developing tradition, but they have almost no factual basis. To pretend that they are factual is to be delusional and to ignore everything we now know about biblical scholarship. So we dismiss them as nothing more than mythology. The Jesus of history now begins to come into view so that his humanity can be properly seen.

Our traditional religious games of pretending are over. We can close our minds to reality no longer. In the debris of this process, however, we are enabled to find the clues through which we can begin to understand the one upon whom this heavy tradition has been laid and we are driven to wonder what there was about him that made this mythological development seem appropriate. That is the question that emerges over and over, demanding an answer.

THE HISTORICITY OF THE TWELVE DISCIPLES

You are those who have continued with me in my trials; as my Father appointed a kingdom for me, so do I appoint for you that you may eat and drink at my table in my kingdom, and sit on thrones judging the twelve tribes of Israel.

Luke 22:28–29

Have you ever wondered about the makeup of that group of people who were said to rotate around the Jesus of history as his disciples? The tradition is fairly consistent that they were twelve in number. The designated twelve also appear to be all males, a tradition that no less a person than John Paul II argued supports the Roman Catholic Church's requirement of an all-male priesthood. The names of the disciples are given in a number of places in the New Testament, although these texts do not agree on what the names were of those who constituted the twelve. The first three gospels also tell a rather stylized story about the moment when the twelve were chosen. The Fourth Gospel does not.

If this group represented the people who founded the Christian church, as so many ecclesiastical leaders have argued over the centuries, then it is strange that Christians do not know much about them. Indeed, the very people who are so certain that there were twelve disciples and who treat that number as both real and sacrosanct generally could not name the twelve even if their lives depended on it. The ability in our society to name Santa Claus' reindeer is quite frankly more common. Have you ever wondered why it is that we claim something to be of great significance, but do not act in such a way as to affirm that importance? Many politicians say the Ten Commandments are important, but they cannot recite them. Evangelicals claim the Bible is the word of God, but their speech indicates that very few of them know much about it. The church says it follows the faith and witness of Jesus' apostles, but we cannot tell anyone who those apostles were. The fact is that what we say we believe and what we really believe are two different things, and our religion so often acts to hide that fact even from ourselves.

So let me bring the twelve disciples into focus by tracing the makeup of this group through all four gospels. It may prove to be more than the average reader wants to know about them, but it is vital to my developing thesis. Even naming the disciples proves to be impossible, since as noted earlier the gospels simply do not agree on their identities. We need to be prepared to discover that even the twelve are more symbolically real than they are actually real.

The association of Jesus with a band of twelve enters the tradition fairly early. By the midfifties, Paul, writing to the Corinthians, lists two things that have been handed down to him as of prime importance. First were the details of the Last Supper (1 Cor. 11:23–26); second was the chronicle of the last events in Jesus' life (1 Cor. 15:3–8). It is in his recounting of Jesus' final events that Paul introduces the concept of the "twelve" into the Christian story. The resurrected Jesus, said Paul, manifested himself to certain witnesses. The first was Cephas (or Peter) and the second was the "twelve." It was as if "Peter and the twelve" was a common phrase. Certainly the gospels are clear that Peter was one of the twelve; in fact, he was presumed by Paul to be their leader. The name Cephas is an Aramaic word that means "rock." It was translated "petros" in Greek and becomes the name Peter in English. Cephas was actually a nickname, probably similar to the way we use the nickname Rocky today. It became attached to one whose real name was Simon, causing this figure to be popularly referred to as Simon Peter—that is, Simon the Rock. There is in the gospels some sense that Peter was the rock on which the Christian church was built.

Interestingly enough, even though Paul gives us the earliest reference to the number twelve, as a synonym for the disciple band, he never mentions their names. In the epistle to the Galatians Paul tells us of his visit with Peter, a few years after Paul's conversion. Paul states that prior to this meeting he made no attempt to be in touch with those who were "apostles before me." Here, however, we run into another problem. Are the "twelve" and the "apostles" the same group? Paul does not seem to think so. He refers to James, the brother of the Lord, as an apostle. No biblical record suggests that this James was one of the "twelve." Paul does not hesitate to assert constantly his own right to be called an apostle. In 1 Corinthians 15:5 Paul refers to the "twelve" as a single group with a corporate identity, but two verses later, in 15:7, he refers separately to the "apostles," suggesting that he sees them as a different group. While tradition has tended to blend the two, that is not an accurate reading of Paul.

Much later, in the book of Acts (written about 95–100 CE), Luke says that when Paul came to Jerusalem, "he attempted to join the disciples; and they were all afraid of him, for they did not believe that he was a disciple" (Acts 9:26). When Luke writes this, the term "disciple" appears to mean simply a follower of Jesus, because the context makes it clear that the group is much expanded from what Luke had earlier called the "twelve." Later, when Luke relates another gathering of the leaders of the Christian movement with Paul in Jerusalem (Acts 15:1–35), he uses the words "apostles and elders" to refer to the leadership. By this time the twelve no longer seemed to be a significant body at all.

The point of this analysis is to show that the concept of the twelve may have been an early one, but the exact makeup of the twelve does not appear to have been either significant or clear from these references.

When we turn to the gospels, the confusion grows thicker. The first gospel, Mark, gives us for the first time the names of the twelve, relating a rather dramatic story to describe the process by which they were chosen (3:13–19). Mark's list includes some intriguing data. Simon is not only placed first, but Mark also tells us that Jesus surnamed him Peter. Simon is followed by James, who is identified as the son of Zebedee, and by John, James' brother. About the Zebedee boys Mark tells us that Jesus named them Boanerges, which (Mark says) means "sons of thunder."[1] Then, without supplying us with any further biographical details whatsoever, Mark lists the others. The next four are Andrew, Philip, Bartholomew and Matthew. (Earlier Mark identified Andrew as Simon's brother and suggested that those brothers, along with the two sons of Zebedee, were fishermen who were together when they answered Jesus' call to follow him. Jesus, the text says, promised to make them "fishers of men" [Mark 1:16–20].) Mark's list then continues with Thomas and James, who is identified as the son of Alphaeus, presumably to distinguish him from James the son of Zebedee. Then Thaddaeus is named, followed by Simon, who is called the "Cananaean."

Some commentators, including Jerome, seem to think this label meant that Simon was from the village of Cana, that place in Galilee where the Fourth Gospel suggests a wedding took place early in Jesus' career (John 2).[2] That identification is now, however, believed to be unlikely. Others have tried to identify "Cananaean" with the people who inhabited the nation of Canaan—that is, the inhabitants of the land that the Israelites believed had been promised to them, who thus were the enemies who bore the brunt of Joshua's invasion (Josh. 5). If that were correct, Simon would have been a Gentile. That definition, however, is now also considered unlikely to contain truth. The best guess today is that this word "Cananaean" comes from the word *qan'a na*, which was the name of a onetime adherent of an early revolutionary movement that later would be known as "the zealots." Luke clearly accepts this definition, for on his list he drops Mark's word "Cananaean" and replaces it with the word "zealot." This could be a hint that the band of Galileans around Jesus had some linkage with or connection to the revolutionary movement that would ultimately ignite the Galilean war in 66, which resulted in the destruction of Jerusalem in 70 CE and ended, according to Josephus,[3] in the suicide of the remaining members of the Jewish resistance movement at Masada in 73 CE. We need only to note that the gospel of Mark was written in all probability shortly after Jerusalem's destruction and he may have wanted to blunt this connection with the zealots. In any event this Simon, the "Cananaean," is the eleventh member on Mark's list.

The twelfth disciple is identified as Judas Iscariot, "who betrayed him." Please note that this is the first place where the idea appears in the Christian tradition that one of the twelve is the traitor. Paul, writing much earlier as we have noted, does not appear to know anything about a disciple being the traitor, for while it is Paul who introduces the note of a betrayal in 1 Corinthians as a dating mechanism, he never associates that act with one of the twelve (11:23–26). When Mark tells the story of the betrayal in the Garden of Gethsemane, he says that Judas, "one of the twelve," appeared at midnight, leading "a crowd with swords and clubs, from the chief priests and the scribes and the elders" (Mark 14:43–50). By the prearranged sign of a kiss, Judas was to identify Jesus so that he could be seized and led away. That act was done, says Mark, with the word "master." Mark next tells us that one standing by, who is not specifically identified as a disciple, drew a sword and struck the slave of the high priest, cutting off his ear. It was, Mark suggests, a violent scene in which Jesus was led off to the high priest. After Mark the tradition of the "twelve" seems to grow.

Since we know that Matthew based his gospel on Mark, the places where Matthew altered Mark give us great insight. When we raise the question of why these particular changes, omissions, and additions seem necessary, we open a fascinating doorway into Matthew's mind. Narrowing our focus, however, just to the consideration of how Matthew understood the meaning of the twelve and who was meant to be included on that list, we turn now to his account of Jesus selecting those who would constitute his disciple band.

Mark had said Jesus chose the twelve "to be with him and to be sent out to preach and have authority to cast out demons" (Mark 3:14–15). Matthew modifies their commission to read, "He ... gave them authority over unclean spirits, to cast them out, and to heal every disease and every infirmity" (Matt. 10:1). Then he lists the members of the twelve. "Simon, who is called Peter," is first. Matthew has removed from Jesus the credit for giving Simon his new nickname. Andrew, Simon's brother, is listed next, ahead of the sons of Zebedee. James and John are not described as "Boanerges," thus again altering Mark's text. Thomas and Matthew are reversed in this gospel's order. Matthew is referred to as "the tax collector," which opens the door for him to be identified with Levi, whose story is first told in Mark but whose name is changed in Matthew's gospel (Mark 2:13–14 vs. Matt. 9:9). To confuse matters even more, Mark calls Levi the son of Alphaeus, while

Matthew gives that designation to James. Perhaps that makes Levi James' brother. Perhaps Levi was another name for James. Perhaps there were several Alphaeuses. The interpretive options are plentiful. Matthew concludes his list with no other changes.

Moving into Luke, the plot thickens. A study of Luke reveals that while Luke is dependent on Mark, he does not follow Mark nearly as rigorously as did Matthew. Comparing Luke's treatment of the call of the twelve, we find these variations: Luke adds to Mark's narrative the fact that Jesus went up into the hills not to call into discipleship those whom he desired, but rather to pray (compare Mark 3:13 with Luke 6:12). Only after spending all night in prayer does he choose the twelve, and Luke adds "whom he named apostles" (Luke 6:13). The designation of the twelve as "apostles" is now firm, but remember that Luke is writing some thirty-five to forty-five years after Paul suggested that "disciples" and "apostles" were two separate groups (1 Cor. 15). Then Luke gives us the list. He follows Matthew's order by coupling Peter with Andrew and placing both men ahead of James and John, who are not identified in Luke as either "Boanerges" or "sons of Zebedee." He then goes back to Mark's order, which placed Matthew ahead of Thomas and copies into his text Mark's story of Levi where Matthew had changed his name (Luke 5:27–32). He omits Thaddaeus altogether and goes immediately to Simon, who is identified clearly as "the zealot." Then Luke adds a disciple named Judas, not to be confused with Iscariot, to replace Thaddaeus and finally completes his list with Judas Iscariot, who, he says, "became a traitor" (Luke 6:16).

This means that in Luke's list there is no Thaddaeus and there are two Judases, one of whom wears the title Iscariot. That title appears to be a description of the second Judas' character, since our best guess is that it comes from the word *sicarios*, which means "political assassin." It also may point to the fact that *sicari* was the name given to the zealots in the war against Rome. Luke gives us a list of the disciples once more in the second volume of his work, which we call the Acts of the Apostles, or simply Acts. Here he varies the order very slightly. Andrew has been dropped to fourth and his identity as Peter's brother has been dropped. Thomas has been moved to sixth place from eighth in the gospel. Otherwise the list is the same.

When we come to the Fourth Gospel we discover that there are only three references to the twelve. Two are in chapter 6 (vv. 67 and 71) and the other is in chapter 20 (v. 24). There is, however, no Johannine list in which the twelve are ever identified. To confuse things even more, John tells us about a person named Nathanael (1:43–51), who is clearly part of the innermost circle of Jesus' associates but whose name appears on no previous gospel list. The closest that John comes to naming the group of disciples comes in chapter 21 (v. 2), but those names only add up to seven, including Nathanael. John also has a reference to a disciple named Judas, but not Iscariot (14:22), which seems to validate Luke's list. Finally, John says that Andrew and another unnamed disciple of John the Baptist were the first disciples that Jesus chose. Andrew then went and got Peter; in other words, it was Andrew who brought Peter into the band of disciples. John also gives us the only details we have about either Philip or Thomas. Philip, Andrew and Peter all hail from the city of Bethsaida, John tells us. He then adds that it was Philip who brought Nathanael into the fold. In John's gospel it was Philip to whom Jesus asked, "How are we to buy bread, so that these people may eat?" which set the stage for his story of the feeding of the multitude (John 6:5ff.). Philip responded pedantically, "Two hundred denarii would not buy enough bread for each of them to get a little." In a similar fashion it is also John alone who lifts Thomas out of the clouds of anonymity and names him "doubting Thomas," a label which has become a part of our secular vocabulary (20:24–29). Thomas also appears briefly in the Johannine text on three other occasions (11:16, 14:5, 21:2). The final episode is in what we might call the Johannine appendix, chapter 21, which describes a Galilean appearance of Jesus to the disciples following his crucifixion. Here John lists only Peter, Thomas (whom he now identifies as the "twin"), Nathanael, the sons of Zebedee and two others who are unnamed. It no longer appears that the number twelve is important and Andrew is specifically left out.

Of course the "big four"—Peter, Andrew, James and John—show up again and again in gospel texts. Three of them—Peter, James and John—share with Jesus in the transfiguration and Gethsemane experiences, for example, and Andrew has a number of appearances with these disciples in which he seems not to do the spectacular action, but the ordinary thing, that becomes a means of grace. When the four are reduced to a threesome, Andrew is always the one omitted.

The fact remains that when this analysis is complete, we are left with not one single detail about the lives of almost half of the people who were said to be the closest associates of Jesus of Nazareth. Among these are Bartholomew, Matthew (unless the identification of Matthew with the tax collector found only in Matthew's gospel is accurate), James the son of Alphaeus, Simon (other than his descriptive word "Cananaean," or "zealot"), Thaddaeus and the Judas who is not Iscariot.

The greatest number of details we have about any of the twelve in the gospels are not about Peter, but about the disciple who is portrayed as the antihero of the passion story. Although I have written about Judas Iscariot extensively in other books, I must bring him into focus here to make the story complete.[4]

The more we learn about Judas Iscariot in the gospels, the less he looks like a person of history, and I now believe that he in fact never existed. My study has led me to the conclusion that Judas, like Joseph, is a manufactured literary character who, as the traitor, was not part of the original story but was first introduced by Mark in the eighth decade of the Common Era. Because this will be an idea that confounds many, let me, ever so briefly, list my reasons for what some might find a startling conclusion.

My first inkling that Judas might be a literary rather than a real figure of history came when I noted that Paul does not seem to be aware that a member of the twelve was the one who "handed him over." Paul introduces the idea that Jesus was handed over with these words: "The Lord Jesus on the night when he was betrayed, took a loaf of bread" (1 Cor. 11:24, NRSV). The traitor story, I believe, started with that verse. Four chapters later, when Paul describes the final events in Jesus' life, he does not mention a traitorous act; and he says that when Jesus was raised, he appeared, as we noted earlier, first to Cephas and then to the twelve. The idea that the traitor could be present with the twelve for Easter's resurrection is simply not believable. According to Matthew, by the time of Easter, Judas had already hanged himself. It would seem that Paul had never heard the story of Jesus being handed over by one of the twelve.

Once that seed of doubt about the historicity of Judas is planted, a study of the Judas material in the gospels becomes quite revealing. Judas clearly grows more evil with the appearance of each gospel as they develop chronologically. In a contrary way, Pontius Pilate seems to grow less and less sinister. Both shifts need to be examined to determine what it means that Judas and Pilate are shown to be on opposite journeys.

A study of other stories of betrayal in the Hebrew scriptures is also revealing. Every detail in the Judas story can be found in a previous biblical narrative. In the Genesis account of the twelve sons of Jacob, who handed over their brother Joseph to be sold into slavery, the brother who sought to receive money for this act was Judah (Gen. 37:26–27), the fourth son of Leah. Judas and Judah are essentially the same name. Judah received twenty pieces of silver for his deed. In the story of Ahithophel's betrayal of King David (told in 2 Sam. 15:12–17:23 and referred to in Psalm 41), the text says the traitor ate at the table of the "Lord's anointed." That kingly title, the "Lord's anointed," was derived from the Hebrew word *maschiach*, which was later translated as "messiah," or "Christ." This Ahithophel episode surely lies behind the mealtime detail included in all four gospels, a statement along the lines of "One of you who breaks bread with me will betray me" (Mark 14:20, Matt. 26:23, Luke 22:21, John 13:18). When Ahithophel's act of betrayal is discovered, he goes out and hangs himself just as Judas is said to have done. The story of betraying a friend with a kiss comes out of the story of Joab kissing Amasa as he disembowels him with a dagger in his right hand (2 Sam. 20:9). In the book of Zechariah we find that the shepherd king of Israel was said to have been betrayed for thirty pieces of silver (Zech. 11:14). He later hurled the silver back into the temple just as Judas is said to have done.

When we add to this composite of betrayal details from Jewish scriptures the fact that the antihero of the Jesus story turns out to bear the same name as the Jewish nation itself—that entity which was considered the primary enemy of the Christian movement by the time the gospels were written—suspicion grows. When finally we discover that in both Luke and John there is a not fully repressed memory of a good Judas who was one of the twelve and that the church put into its sacred scriptures an epistle called Jude which also affirms the memory of a good Judas, suspicion turns into raging doubt.

The context of history in which Mark's gospel, which set the tone for at least Matthew and Luke, was written throws additional light on Judas. It is, however, so deeply a part of the crucifixion story that I have chosen to treat it in that later context. Suffice it now to say that the story of Judas, called Iscariot, is a far more complicated and interpreted story than Christians have imagined. My bottom line is that I have come to believe that there was no Judas Iscariot and no act of betrayal.

When we begin to draw conclusions from all these data about the disciples, the first one we reach is that the identity of the twelve in the memory of the earliest Christians did not seem to be as important as the fact that there were twelve. The gospel writers did not agree on who the twelve were, making it quite possible that there never was a particular group of twelve disciples at all, so that when the concept of "twelve" did emerge, the gospel writers had to scramble to give names to them.

Second, if order is a sign of importance, as it seems to have been, the importance of the individual disciples varies from list to list, a fact that could reflect something as simple as the identities of the various competing groups within early Christianity. Thomas appears to be the most volatile name on the list, which, as Princeton professor Elaine Pagels suggests, may reflect a tension between those who produced the Gospel of Thomas and those who produced the Fourth Gospel. Professor Pagels develops the point that a close reading of the Gospel of Thomas makes one aware that the Fourth Gospel was written at least in part to respond to the way Thomas appears to understand Jesus in the gospel that now bears his name.[5]

The third conclusion that needs to be registered is that Jesus also had female disciples who were always with him and who are not counted on any list. Yet Mark tells us that these women, with Mary Magdalene almost always mentioned first, followed him in Galilee and ministered to him (Mark 15:40–41). Matthew refers to these women and repeats the idea that they "had followed Jesus from Galilee, ministering to him" (Matt. 27:55). Luke also mentions these women who "had followed him from Galilee" (Luke 23:49). Perhaps the whole idea that Jesus had twelve male disciples is a claim initiated by Paul and imposed on the Jesus story in the service of another, peculiarly Jewish agenda.

If Jesus was to be the founder of the New Israel, which was one of the claims made for him, then the New Israel must have twelve tribes just as did the Old Israel. In Matthew, prior to Jesus' entry into Jerusalem, Jesus says to the disciples, "Truly, I say to you, in the new world, when the Son of man shall sit on his glorious throne, you who have followed me will also sit on twelve thrones, judging the twelve tribes of Israel" (19:28). Luke quotes Jesus at the Last Supper as saying to the disciples, "As my Father appointed a kingdom for me, so do I appoint for you that you may eat and drink at my table in my kingdom and sit on thrones judging the twelve tribes of Israel" (Luke 22:30). Advocates of the Q hypothesis argue that these ideas, not present in Mark, but close enough in Matthew and Luke to represent a common source, are from that now lost document and may represent a source earlier than Mark. If that is so, then we need also to note that these words are spoken with Judas still part of the twelve. This might indicate that when the Q document was written, the story of one of the twelve being the traitor had not yet developed, which as we saw also appears to be the case with the writings of Paul.

Finally, it is apparent from the story Luke tells in the book of Acts (1:15–26) that it was the number twelve that was important, and not the identity of the twelve. For after the story of Judas' defection was told, there was great pressure to restore to the disciples the number twelve, resulting in the choice of Matthias.

So scrape away another layer from the overlaid tradition. The Bible, closely studied, does not say what most of us were taught to believe. There probably were not twelve disciples. Those who have literalized the gospel stories might well be beginning to feel that everything in which they once trusted is crumbling. Crumble it must, for it hides from us the power of the Jesus experience that brought these explanations into being in the first place. The essence of the gospel story is not, however, in these details, which is why they can be surrendered without compromising the core of the Christian faith. We have not yet completed this phase of the book. More must yet be scraped away. Even at this point, however, some will inevitably begin to wonder what, if anything, will be left by the time this phase is over. Have courage. I am not aware of any other way to get to my goal than this one. I urge you to continue your walk with me even when it begins to feel as if we are walking into an ever-deepening pit.

5

MIRACLE STORIES IN THE GOSPELS: ARE THEY NECESSARY?

I am convinced that a God the mind rejects will never be a god
the heart will adore. I do not wish to be told that faith means
that I have to remain a child or at least childlike before a
parental, supernatural deity.

Did Jesus really perform miracles? Do miracles, defined as
the supernatural setting aside of natural causes, ever
happen? Can someone born blind ever be enabled to see by having
spittle placed on his or her eyes? Can a storm be stilled by a person's
command? For most of Christian history the church's teaching about
miracles has been straightforward and clear. Miracles were assumed to
have occurred for two reasons: First, the Bible says so and the Bible is
the "revealed word of God." Second, since Jesus was assumed to be
God in human form, it followed quite logically that the whole created
world had to be responsive to his divine command. Today both of
these assertions have been challenged quite specifically by the scientific community and also by the world of Christian scholarship, even if
not everyone is yet aware of that fact.

The idea that miracles occur has been claimed in some form in
almost every age. Shrines have been built on the sites where healing
miracles are said to have taken place. Supernatural visions are described frequently enough that numerous studies on these phenomena

have been launched to validate their truth. Newspapers still write accounts of these claims as if they possessed some validity and crowds still gather at the places where the supernatural sightings are said to have occurred. Evangelists who claim the power to perform healing miracles, even in our modern age, continue to attract vast audiences both to their live tent or amphitheater gatherings and via the medium of television. Does this attention or do these claims mean that there is something real going on that we do not understand, or do they point only to a widespread human gullibility and a deep human fear? To ask the question bluntly, Do miracles really occur, or are tales of miraculous power the fictional but inevitable result of humankind's deep-seated need to believe that there is a supernatural being who will intervene on our behalf?

When we examine these miraculous claims, the first thing that is obvious is that there are high levels of acculturated content present in what people assert they have experienced. No one has any idea what either Jesus or the Virgin Mary actually looked like, since we have no photographs or portraits from the first century. However, we could surmise that the Jesus of Nazareth who lived in the first century was in all probability a brown-skinned Middle Easterner with cropped black hair, standing no more than 5 feet 4 inches to 5 feet 7 inches tall and weighing no more than 120 to 140 pounds. That, at least, describes the norm for males who inhabited that region of the world at Jesus' time in history. Yet if a figure looking like the real Jesus of history appeared to any Westerner in a vision, no one would have the slightest idea of who he was, since he would not fit into our culturally created images. The same would be true of the mother of Jesus. Yet in all visions reported by Westerners Jesus and Mary are always seen as if they had just stepped out of a medieval portrait with the features and coloring of northern Europeans. Does that fact not suggest that we are the authors of our own visions and that these supernatural phenomena are not objectively real? It is also a fact that Jesus and his mother seldom if ever appear to people in Hindu or Islamic cultures. High levels of subjectivity, of seeing both what we want to see and what we are programmed to see, color our talk about religiously oriented visions. Stories of miraculous healings also appear to have a wish-fulfillment quality, as well as a self-centered quality, about them. They are focused in the belief that one's own sickness or that of a loved one clearly merits divine attention.

Yet having said all that, we must face the fact that the gospels present a picture of a Jesus who is quite capable of doing supernatural acts with such regularity that when we read the various gospel texts, we expect a miraculous occurrence on nearly every page. Since so many people in the Christian world still assume almost automatically that if something is in the Bible it has to be true, breaking this mind-set open to get to the truth about miracles is quite difficult. Mark, Matthew, Luke and John all portray Jesus as having power over nature, as being able to heal various infirmities and even, on three separate occasions, as being able to actually restore to life one who had died. The questions these stories raise are clear: Are they true? Is this history? Saying yes is not a problem if one is a fundamentalist and admits no evidence beyond the fact that "the Bible tells me so." Saying no is also not a problem if the responder no longer resides inside a Christian faith community, since that person has probably already said no to both questions. Are those, however, our only choices, or is it possible for us to dismiss these tales as not being literally true events in history, but still recognize that they represent something that is not only important but is integrally connected to Christianity? It is to engage this latter question and possibility that I now turn the spotlight of this study on the miracles said to have been performed by Jesus in the gospels.

To begin this discussion let me first isolate and clarify the actual content of the gospel miracles. How are the supernatural episodes associated with Jesus counted in the New Testament? Some evangelical Christians have tried to number them exactly, but the final tally is open to challenge on many levels. Many of the supposed miraculous happenings connected with either the birth of Jesus or his death, resurrection and ascension are generally not included, yet those narratives are filled with supernatural details. We have already noted the ones at his birth and will shortly deal with those around his death and resurrection. That is, however, not the only problem we face when trying to count the miracles in the gospel.

Consider the fact that the story of Jesus feeding the multitude with a small and finite number of loaves, after which large amounts of bread are gathered into numerous baskets, is actually told six times in the gospels. Is that a single miracle, or six miracles? Before one responds too quickly that their similarity in content suggests a single event, one needs to know that Mark and Matthew say this miraculous feeding episode actually happened twice in two different locations with a different number of people, a different number of loaves and a different amount of leftovers (Mark 6:30–44, 8:1–10, Matt. 14:13–21, 15:32–39). Does that make two miracles? Luke and John, however, disagree with Mark and Matthew and say that a miraculous feeding of the multitude happened only once (Luke 9:10–17, John 6:1–14). Even then there is still confusion, since John places the event early in the ministry of Jesus in Jerusalem and at the Passover (6:4). John, who includes no account of the Last Supper, puts all of his eucharistic teaching, which in the other gospels is attached to the Last Supper, into this episode. Mark, Matthew and Luke, on the other hand, locate all of these feeding episodes in Galilee. The study of the gospels is never quite as simple as either the "true believers" or the Bible's critics would have us believe.

This confusion about the number of miraculous events in the New Testament continues when we recognize that both Luke and John record an episode in which the disciples, following Jesus' instructions, throw their nets to the other side of the boat, to haul in a miraculous catch of fish. Each of these episodes features a dramatic change in the life of Simon Peter, and in that sense they are quite similar. Luke, however, says that this miracle took place at the beginning of Jesus' ministry in Galilee (Luke 5:1–11), while John agrees that this miracle occurred in Galilee, but dates it in the post-resurrection period of Jesus' ministry (21:1–19). Are these episodes to be counted as one or two?

If we limit our count of the miracles in the gospels to things Jesus himself did, there are in fact twenty-three different miracle episodes in Mark. There is further an allusion in Mark to numerous healings which are not told individually (Mark 1:34). Matthew copies most of Mark's distinct episodes and adds no new ones, but he regularly heightens the miraculous content in his versions of these stories. Luke, however, adds some miracle stories to the list he has copied from Mark, who presumably was not aware of the additional episodes. Two of these are portrayed as specific events: the raising of the dead son of a widow in the village of Nain (Luke 7:11–17) and the healing of ten lepers (Luke 17:11–19). Luke then adds his own generic verse stating, without giving us any details, that "in that hour he [Jesus] cured many of diseases and plagues and evil spirits and on many that were blind he bestowed sight" (7:21). John adds to this growing list of miracles with four accounts mentioned nowhere else: the story of Jesus changing water into wine at a wedding at Cana in Galilee (2:1–11); the healing of a man who had been in some way infirm, perhaps crippled, for thirty-eight years, which takes place in a pool by the Sheep Gate in Jerusalem (5:1–18); the giving of sight to a man born blind (9:1–41), and finally, the raising of Lazarus from the dead (11:1–44). Each of these Johannine episodes is told in enormous detail, including a narrative about the effects (sometimes negative) these miracles had on others. When all of these separate stories are put together, we have a total of about thirty miraculous accounts about which there are some details, together with the generic lists about which there are no details given.

Beyond the gospels, there are other miracles recorded in the New Testament in the book of Acts. Here it is the disciples of Jesus, rather than Jesus, who are deemed to be the agents of supernatural power. This additional source in the book of Acts forces us to note that in the Christian tradition Jesus is not the only life through which miracles are said to occur. Peter and John heal a cripple in Jerusalem (Acts 3:1–10). Angels are portrayed as miraculously opening the doors of the prison to free the disciples (5:19). Angels also give specific divine instructions to the Christians (8:26) as a sign of God's miraculous care. Paul not only has a supernatural vision on the road to Damascus, but he is also blinded and subsequently healed by the intercession of Ananias (9:17–18). Peter raises a dead woman back to life in Joppa (9:36–43) and has, like Paul, a miraculous and life-changing heavenly vision (10:9–23). Paul heals a cripple in Lystra (14:8–18), casts out a demon from a slave girl (16:16–18) and, like Peter, is also freed from prison by a supernatural event (16:25–34). Supernatural visions direct the course of Paul's ministry (16:9, 18:9, 27:23) and he also raises the dead, restoring to life a young man named Eutychus (20:7–12). Finally, Paul, after being shipwrecked on his journey to Rome, survives snakebite in a manner that was regarded as an act of God, to which the people responded that Paul himself must have been a god (28:1–6).

The fact is that miracles, attributed to the presence of the supernatural, are deeply embedded in the New Testament story of Christianity's foundations. Are miracles then an essential part of that story? Does Christianity fall if these miracles are withdrawn, redefined or even denied? Must Christians today be committed to the historicity of these first-century miracle stories? Or is there another way that these dramatic acts can be understood in our day? Was there perhaps another way to understand them even when they were originally written? Does being a Christian in a postmodern world require that we believe the unbelievable just because it is in the Bible? Those are the issues we face as we seek to enter now the dramatic and powerful Jesus experience that has been transmitted to us through the ancient texts of the Bible, where miracles are assumed.

Let me begin by stating my conclusion both up front and clearly. I do not believe that miracles, understood as I defined them at the beginning of this chapter, ever happen. I also do not believe that the miracles described in the New Testament literally occurred in the life of Jesus of Nazareth or that of his disciples. How can I assert, my religious critics ask, that God was in this Jesus, as indeed I do, and not allow for miraculous action to mark his life? This chapter and the several that follow address that question, tackling the struggle that I, as a Christian, and many others like me who live in the twenty-first century, have to engage, because the only choice we have is to give up Christianity completely or to suspend our thinking processes, deny the insights of our postmodern scientific world, ignore much of contemporary theological thinking and twist our brains into first-century pretzels in order to be or to remain Christians. That is a price I am no longer willing to pay. I insist that there must be a way to be both a believer and a citizen of the twenty-first century. I am convinced that a God the mind rejects will never be a God the heart can adore. I do not wish to be told that faith means that I have to remain a child or at least child-like before a parental supernatural deity.

Nonetheless, I still experience life as something holy. I still believe that there is a reality called God that permeates all that is. I do not, however, believe in a deity who does miracles—nor do I even want such a God. I do not wish to live in a world in which an intervening deity acts capriciously to accomplish the divine will by overriding the laws of nature established in creation. The problems posed by the miracle stories historically associated with the life of Jesus are thus for me something that I must be able to view differently than traditional Christians do. In searching for a new way to read and to understand these parts of the biblical tradition, I do not start by asking whether or not these miracles happened as reported, since I do not believe they did. I ask, rather: What was the experience that my ancestors in faith had with Jesus of Nazareth that made it seem appropriate for them to talk about him by emphasizing supernatural categories? My journey forces me to get beyond the literalism of a premodern world if I am to discover the reality of this Christ who continually transforms my life.

Before addressing the specific miracles found in the Jesus story, I must make my readers aware of the supernatural understanding that was all but universally believed in that period of history and that permeates much of the Bible. Miracles do not begin with the Jesus story; they are present in the Bible beginning with the book of Genesis.

The presupposition of those who wrote the Bible was an almost universal belief in a three-tiered universe. God was thought to live just above the sky and thus to be in touch with and be responsible for whatever happened on earth. This mentality is still present in some believers and is symbolized by athletes pointing to the sky after accomplishing an athletic victory. It also feeds the image of God as the keeper of record books that track everyone's behavior. That is surely being intimately involved! It is depicted in the biblical narrative by the creation story in which God took a daily stroll with Adam and Eve in the Garden of Eden (Gen. 3:8). In that ancient myth when these first people disobeyed God by eating the forbidden fruit, God meted out appropriate punishments directly to the offending man and woman (3:16–17).

By the time the story of Noah and the flood is told, the biblical understanding reveals a displeased deity, fully aware of and angry at the evil that human beings do, deciding to manipulate the weather patterns in order to punish them all in an act of divine vengeance. Only Noah and his family were deemed worthy of being spared this genocidal act, which God was said to have planned and carried out single-handedly. In this account the natural laws of the universe were assumed to be in the service of God (Gen. 7:1ff.). That is clearly the majority view of God on all the pages of scripture, as illustrated in such stories as the exodus, the feeding of the Hebrews with heavenly food called manna in the wilderness, the dictating of the law at Mount Sinai, the raising up of prophets to speak the words of God's judgment to the people and many other narratives.

This external, miracle-working God is by every measure the dominant and the popular biblical image of the deity, created as a direct response to that basic human yearning to be watched over and protected by a supernatural parent figure in the sky, one who can make insecure human beings feel cared for by divine power and thus secure. Miraculous acts were constantly attributed by the writers of scripture to this supernatural God alone, or to one assumed to be God's agent. Miracles, in fact, seem to require this understanding and definition of God. Most people, however, fail to embrace the fact that the miracle-producing majority view of the God of the Bible is a mixed blessing. A deity capable of acting in miraculous ways frequently elicits the child-like responses of guilt and dependency. If God is the source of supernatural power, then it is clearly in our best interests to please this deity, or at the very least not to incur the divine wrath. So fear drives us to please this capricious deity with proper living and proper worship. When we worship such a deity, we are either seeking divine favor or fearing divine retribution. As a result, this God becomes, above all else, a behavior-controlling deity.

This sort of supernaturalism does not encourage maturity or independence. We never grow up if we always have to please a supernatural parent figure; we never take responsibility for ourselves so long as we are not to some degree in charge of our own destiny. Churches want their people to be "born again"—that is, returned to the status of a helpless newborn baby—when what people really need is to be helped to grow up and to recognize that they are significantly responsible both for their world and their own lives.

Furthermore, a miracle-working deity improvises as life unfolds. A miracle-infested world is an unpredictable, sometimes chaotic place. If the laws that govern our lives can be set aside for divine intervention, nothing is stable or trustworthy. How to manipulate God for our own well-being becomes the ultimate religious goal. In the pursuit of that goal, insecurity abounds.

Perhaps even more interesting is the fact that a miracle-working deity is not necessarily moral. The supernatural God revealed in the Bible frequently appears to do immoral acts. Is it moral behavior to murder both infants and the elderly at the time of the great flood (Gen. 6:1–8)? Or to kill the firstborn male in every Egyptian household at the time of the exodus (Exod. 11:1–11)? Is that the act of a God the Egyptians could ever worship? What about the God who stops the sun in the sky to allow Joshua more daylight in which to slaughter the Amorites (Josh. 10:12ff.)? Is that a God the Amorites could ever acknowledge? Is a miracle-working deity who hates everyone his worshippers hate a moral deity? For those who seek to defend a miraculous deity, there are many questions and problems that must be addressed. The need to cling to the miraculous is not always an asset to faith, yet that remains the primary understanding of the God of the biblical story.

Despite the general impression that miracles are everywhere in the Bible, they are actually limited to particular narratives in the biblical story. In the Hebrew scriptures there are some miraculous elements in its opening narratives, the creation, the flood and the Tower of Babel. These involve miracles done by God. In addition, there are two cycles of stories dealing with miracles done by human beings acting on God's behalf. These stories feature the two people who may rank as the greatest of the heroes in the development of the religious system that came to be called Judaism. First, there are the stories that gathered around Moses, the clear founder of the Jewish sense of identity, the Jews' deliverer from bondage and their lawgiver. Second, there are the stories that gathered around Elijah, who is generally regarded as the father of the prophetic movement. Judaism even today is said to find its primary identity in "the law and the prophets"—that is, in Moses and Elijah.

When we analyze the miracles present in these two crucial parts of the Hebrew Bible, we find a number of similarities. Both Moses and Elijah appear to speak for God, to have received their power to do miracles from God and to be perceived as working on God's behalf. Yet no one attributed to either Moses or Elijah the status of a visiting deity; no one saw either person as being the incarnation of an external God. God worked through them, yes; but they did not become God. Many of the miracles attributed to Moses and Elijah are recycled in the Bible, later showing up in stories about their successors, Joshua and Elisha, who can do things remarkably similar to those done by their predecessors. Both Moses and Joshua, for example, split bodies of water to allow the Jews to walk on dry land (Exod. 14:21–22, Josh. 3:12–16). Both Elijah and Elisha were said to be able to manipulate the forces of nature (1 Kings 17:1ff., 2 Kings 6:1ff.), expand the food supply or the oil supply (1 Kings 17:8ff., 2 Kings 4:1–8) and even raise the dead (1 Kings 17:17ff., 2 Kings 4:18–37).

The deaths of Moses and Elijah were both shrouded in mystery. Moses, after viewing the Promised Land from the heights of Mount Nebo in the land of Moab, was said then to have died and to have been buried by God in the valley of the land of Moab. The burial place was meant to remain a secret, the Bible asserts, from that day to this (Deut. 34:1–8). Only God knew its location. It was not long, however, before the common assumption was that Moses had not died at all, but that God had taken him directly from life on earth to the presence of God in the heavens. Not having to pass through death itself was assumed to have been Moses' reward for his life of righteousness.

When Elijah came to the end of his life, we are told that he did not die, but was rather transported directly into the sky by magical fiery horses pulling a magical fiery chariot and aided by a whirlwind that propelled him back to God above the sky (2 Kings 2:1–12). His escape from death, like that of Moses, was also considered a reward for a life of service.

At the end of their lifetimes the power of God in both Moses and Elijah was passed on to their chosen successors, Joshua and Elisha, who as noted earlier carried out miracles similar to those of their predecessors. Moses laid his hands on Joshua to endow him with the spirit of wisdom as his chosen successor (Deut. 34:9), while Elijah not only chose Elisha, but at his own departure, which Elisha was privileged to witness, endowed Elisha with a double portion of his enormous (though still human) spirit (2 Kings 2:9). Elijah also left his mantle, which Elisha donned after tearing his old clothes into two pieces (2 Kings 2:13). The transference of power worked in both instances, for when Joshua was recognized as "full of the spirit of wisdom" through the act of having the hands of Moses laid on him, the people obeyed him and did as he had commanded (Deut. 34:9) and when

Elisha returned to his people after bidding Elijah farewell, the sons of the prophets said, "The spirit of Elijah rests on Elisha" and coming out to meet him, "they bowed to the ground before him" (2 Kings 2:15).

Just as there are scriptural similarities between the acts of Moses and Elijah and those of their successors, so also are there similarities linking the Moses/Joshua cycle with the Elijah/Elisha cycle. For example, the power to split a body of water to gain passage on dry land, cited earlier for Moses and Joshua, was shared by Elijah and Elisha (2 Kings 2:8, 2 Kings 2:14). Both Moses and Elijah were capable of expanding food supplies. While Moses was guided through the wilderness by a pillar of fire that linked heaven and earth, Elijah was endowed with the ability to call down fire from heaven both to demonstrate that God answered his prayers (1 Kings 18:20–35) and also to burn up his enemies (2 Kings 1:10ff.).

The miracles attributed to Moses, Elijah and their successors were always carried out in the service of the national interests of the Jews. God through Moses used miracles to soften up God's enemies, who not coincidentally always appeared to be Israel's enemies. That is what the plagues on Egypt were all about. God through Joshua used miracles to annihilate "the Canaanites, the Hittites,... the Amorites and the Jebusites" (Josh. 3:10), all of whom fell before the invading Israelites. God through Elijah used miracles to destroy the prophets of Baal on Mount Carmel (1 Kings 18:20–35). God through Elisha used miracles to bring she-bears out of the woods to tear up forty-two boys who had cursed him (2 Kings 2:23–25). These examples show that to possess miraculous power in the Bible was not always or necessarily to be counted moral, righteous or even civil. The issues are not nearly so clear as religious traditionalists like to believe.

In this study of miracles and the supernatural, we also need to face the issue of "theodicy," or the attempt to reconcile God's goodness despite the presence of evil. Once miraculous supernatural power is ascribed to God, then believers need an explanation for why God acts on some occasions and not others. If God has the power to answer the prayers of parents that their son or daughter might be spared death in a time of war, does the death of a prayed-for soldier mean that the parental prayers were ineffective, or perhaps that the victim deserved God's killing? Is either conclusion viable? If God has the ability to feed the hungry with manna from heaven or to expand the food supply so that hunger disappears, but instead allows deadly starvation to strike a land in a time of drought or blight, is God moral? If God had the power to defeat the enemies of the Jews and to destroy them at the time of the exodus, then why did God not intervene to stop the Holocaust? If one attributes to God supernatural power, then one has to explain why God uses it so sparingly—why there is so much pain, sickness and tragedy in human life. As the playwright Archibald MacLeish said in his play *J.B.*, based on the book of Job, "If God is God, he is not good. If God is good, he is not God."[1] The suggestion that God has and uses supernatural miraculous power finally produces a deity who is so capricious as to be immoral. The suggestion that God does not have supernatural power finally produces a deity who is so weak as to be impotent! That is the dilemma that theodicy must face. A deity who is immoral, impotent, or both does not have a very long shelf life.

I ask my readers to recognize the problems faced when we are not able to escape the literal attitude that has covered the Bible for so long. No matter how pious and sanctified our ignorance is, it is still ignorance; and as such it violates everything we know about rationality. Only a magical view of both God and life could cause anyone to think that stories and folk tales that gathered around a man named Abraham, who lived (if he lived at all) some nine hundred years before these stories achieved written form in what came to be called holy scripture, were passed on perfectly. Even the stories about Moses, who is generally dated around 1250 BCE, did not enter the sacred written text until some three hundred years after his death. Could stories about Moses pass through three hundred years of oral transmission and not lend themselves to the heightening of miracles and the exaggeration of details? Is it not the human tendency for such stories to grow in the constant act of retelling? When we come to Jesus and the gospels the oral period shrinks from centuries to forty to seventy years. Does that significantly lessen the problem? Are oral stories passed on without changes for forty to seventy years?

This principle is best illustrated by looking at the pivotal story in Israel's history, which depicts the moment of Israel's birth as a nation—a moment that is celebrated annually in the liturgy of the

Passover. The climax to that story is the huge miracle of the parting of the waters of the Red Sea (Exod. 14). Cecil B. DeMille implanted the picture of that event upon our minds in his dramatic, but not scholarly, motion picture entitled *The Ten Commandments*. It would surprise DeMille and many biblical literalists to learn that the great majority of biblical scholars today regard the Red Sea story as something that, if it happened at all, happened quite differently from the way the sacred scriptures suggest. This means that the major miracle story around which the beginning of the historic identity of the Jewish nation is organized, and which became the central episode in their sacred scriptures, is now regarded by scholars as suspect at best, and dead wrong at worst.

So what's wrong with this miracle story? First, if the Israelites literally went through the Red Sea, they went well out of their way. In addition, the Red Sea is about 120 miles wide at its narrowest point, so if they went through, even on dry land, in ten hours, as the book of Exodus states, they would have had to average twelve miles per hour, which means walking five-minute miles. This would be an amazing— yes, a miraculous—accomplishment, particularly for a motley crew of people of all sizes, ages and physical conditions! The biblical text in Hebrew, however, actually refers to the body of water that was crossed as Yam Suph. Those words, translated in scripture as "Red Sea," literally mean "sea of reeds." Today Yam Suph is identified not with the Red Sea at all but with a marshy swampland just north of what is now known as the Gulf of Suez. That area is covered with water little more than a meter deep, difficult but not impossible to navigate and less than twenty miles across. This knowledge alone causes us to suspect that the reality of that moment in history was quite different from the supernatural rendition that found its way into the sacred story of the Jews some three hundred years later.

Imagine, if you can, the terror present among those fleeing, unarmed slave people when they looked behind them and saw some miles away the cloud of dust created by the Egyptian army coming in hot pursuit of their escaping source of cheap labor. These slave people then looked ahead and saw a marshy swampland that would be difficult to navigate in the best of circumstances. There was no way they could escape the Egyptian soldiers in their iron chariots. They were on the brink of extermination, either by the sword or by drowning. It was a crisis without visible means of solution. To postpone death for as long as possible, they fled into the swamp.

As slave people fleeing their oppression, they traveled light. They had little but the clothes on their backs, so they made each step count as the distant Egyptians bore relentlessly down upon them. When the Egyptians reached the edge of the marsh, the Sea of Reeds, the Israelites were perhaps no more than a few hundred yards into it. Feeling supremely confident and sensing an easy victory, the Egyptians plunged into the marshland after the Jews. Burdened with iron carriages, heavy armor and swords and spears, the Egyptian army bogged down. The Hebrew slaves continued to step slowly but inexorably onward. Twenty miles is still quite a trip and it took a number of days before they finally reached firm soil. When they were at last through Yam Suph, with a note of enormous relief and exultant triumph they picked up the pace, walking boldly into the wilderness while the Egyptians sank deeper and deeper into the mire. It was a life-changing event. How could they not in this time in history proclaim that God had delivered them? Having nothing with which to defeat the Egyptians, they had nonetheless survived. Clearly the wonder of God's natural world had intervened to save them!

Some twelve generations went by before the story of that astounding exodus event was written down. Of course it grew in detail. Of course the miracle was heightened over the years, but the experience itself left an indelible imprint on the Jewish people. God had delivered them. God loved them. God must have a purpose for them. They were, from that day on, said to be God's specially chosen people, bound by their covenant with God and destined to be the nation through whom all the nations of the world would ultimately be blessed. God was ever after perceived to be one who is dominant over both water and nature. The Jews celebrated this truth in their liturgies and told and retold their epic. When this epic finally became the sacred Torah, the holy scriptures destined to be read in Jewish houses of worship, it was ultimately called the word of God.

In that process the central miraculous story of the Hebrew scriptures came into being. Did the miracles of Jesus come into being in a similar fashion? That is the question we must now consider. We need to keep the issues and the insights of this analysis in mind as we turn now to examine the miracles in the gospel story of Jesus. Perhaps they also are not literal events of history. Perhaps they are really external attempts to place a powerful internal experience into words. Can we unwrap them, dismantle them and even expunge them from the memory of Jesus without violating the Jesus experience? If we cannot, there will be no Christian future. If we can, there is a chance that Christianity will be able to live in our postmodern world. I think it is worth the effort. I invite you to walk with me now into one more area where ultimate truth must be separated from literal concepts.

6

NATURE MIRACLES: INTERPRETIVE SIGNS, NOT HISTORICAL EVENTS

I have come to a place in my Christian life where I no longer
need a miracle worker God to draw me into worship. Indeed,
such a God concept actually drives me out of my faith.

Clinging to the possibility of miracles meets something
deep in the human psyche. The manifestation of an
almost universal yearning, it finds expression in most religious systems.
It rises, I believe, out of the existential awareness of the trauma of self-
consciousness. The idea that human beings might be alone in the
universe, buffeted by natural forces over which they have no power or
control, gives rise to more fear than can be absorbed. That fear is
banked by the idea, which becomes a growing human conviction, that
there is a power far greater than that which human beings possess—a
power that watches over us and intervenes to help us.

It is so important psychologically for human beings to believe that a
supernatural power directs the affairs of life that people cling to irrational beliefs long after any apparent credibility of those beliefs has been
intellectually demolished. What else could account for such things as
the enormous resistance among religious people to evolution, which
seems to offer no place for an intervening deity? Even with DNA evidence showing our connections with other life forms and radiometric
measurements showing the date of the origins of planet earth, frightened

religious folk still seek to suppress this truth through the courts. One has only to think back on the 1925 Scopes trial in Tennessee, or look to the attempt to develop something called "creation science" and its own perfumed stepchild, "intelligent design." If evolution is true, then something called "natural selection" replaces divine purpose in the universe, and the primal fear of impotence in the face of the world's natural power, and loneliness in the face of the world's vastness, is all but overwhelming. Fundamentalism itself is another manifestation of this anxiety. Psychologists would call this denial. The idea that any religious institution is headed by one who possesses infallibility or that anyone's sacred scriptures are inerrant speaks only to human anxiety, not to human truth. Most people, however, do not raise these issues to consciousness. The lack of supernatural intervention remains hidden for them until they begin to question the efficacy of prayer.

The question about prayer is almost always the first one to which I have to respond when I am lecturing to audiences on topics like "The God Experience." When people begin to question how prayer works, they are raising to consciousness the ancient security system based on a supernatural deity who can deal with the powers of this world that frighten human beings so deeply. If miracles happen in response to our pleas, the skies are not empty. Our prayers are directed to a being not unlike ourselves, except with no human limitations—one who can come to our aid, grant us security, cure our illnesses, defeat our enemies, stop the floodwaters or the hurricane winds and keep us safe. The idea that miracles are recorded in the development of our faith story is an enormously supportive idea. To suggest, therefore, that these miracle stories might not be literally true engenders shock, is greeted with fear and not infrequently creates anger. That emotional response is sometimes mistaken for either zeal or firm conviction. It is neither. It is an expression of the primal anxiety of a self-conscious creature manifesting itself yet again, as the religious security system of yesterday begins its inevitable slide toward death.

If there are no literal miracles in the gospel narratives or if these accounts of supernatural activity begin to seem suspect, then clearly the foundations of our security system start to wobble. If there is no deity capable of protecting us with supernatural power, then the anxiety born at the dawn of human self-consciousness—our original loneliness—will once again overwhelm us. Yet despite all of these things, I think the time has come for rigorous honesty. I, for one, can no longer pretend that the supernatural theistic God of yesterday is still real, still waiting for an opportunity to intervene in human history in a miraculous way. As a result, I can no longer act as if there is some way in which the miracle stories that surround Jesus in the gospels can still be treated as events of history and thus as exceptions to the rules that govern all that we now know about the universe. In the world that I inhabit, miracles do not occur; supposed supernatural invasions to break the laws by which the universe operates are sheer delusion. The heavens do not open to pour down the Holy Spirit from the God who lives above the sky; water is not turned into wine to satisfy the thirst of wedding guests; epilepsy is not cured by expelling demons; deaf-muteness is not overcome by loosing the devil's hold on the victim's tongue; the dead are not raised back into the life of this world on the fourth day after burial (in the case of Lazarus), or even on the third day (in the case of Jesus), and finally, one does not exit this world by rising into the sky without jet propulsion.

If, in order to be a Christian, I must pretend that this premodern frame of reference is still valid, then for me integrity finally overwhelms faith. I can no longer be a believer, at least in this traditional sense. Yet, having said that, I remain a committed Christian. I am still convinced of the truth found in that ultimate reality that I call by the name God and I still see in Jesus the fullness of both God and humanity. This means that I have come to a place in my Christian life where I no longer need a miracle worker God to draw me into worship. Indeed, such a God concept actually drives me out of my faith. Having laid the groundwork for this discussion in the previous chapter, I now examine in specific detail the supernatural claims made for Jesus in the gospel accounts.

I begin by posing a very simple and yet revealing set of questions, the central theme of which can be asked in a variety of ways: Were the miracles that now appear in the gospels part of the original Jesus experience, or were they added later as part of the interpretive debate that swirled around him? Were these miracles viewed at their origins as events that literally occurred in history, or were they even then recognized as prophetic interpretive signs designed to address questions about the meaning experienced in Jesus' life? Is it possible that what first-century people thought of as a miracle would be to us today not a supernatural invasion at all, but an internal process of such deep integration within our selfhood that there was produced in our body, mind and spirit a new synthesis of wholeness? Does this synthesis have the power quite literally to expand our being, to overcome the dissonant static present in our bodies and even to call us into that "New Being" which, as German theologian Paul Tillich once said, comes to those who know themselves to be in touch with the "Ground of Being?"[1] Is it possible that the only real miracle associated with Jesus was a unique concentration of this power of wholeness? As we allow these new ideas and understandings to come into view, we turn now to look at the biblical data.

Miracles do not appear to be part of the earliest memory the church had of Jesus. As noted earlier, there are no miracles recorded in Paul, who had died before the first gospel was written. The only hint of a miracle in the writings of this first contributor to the New Testament's content is that he believed God had raised Jesus from the dead. Now certainly, one could argue that the resurrection represents a rather powerful miraculous claim that cannot be so summarily dismissed. A close reading of the Pauline material, however, reveals that for Paul the resurrection of Jesus had nothing to do with the later stories that portrayed Easter in terms of his physical resuscitation. Resurrection, for Paul, had to do first with God affirming Jesus' life (Rom. 1:1–4), and then with God opening the minds and eyes of the disciples to see who Jesus was—an experience that caused Paul to say, "Have I not seen Jesus our Lord?" (1 Cor. 9:1). Paul also said that God would raise us in the same way that God raised Jesus (1 Cor. 15:12ff.).

I will develop this line of thought much more fully when I come to the chapter on the resurrection. I mention it here only to free resurrection from the concept of miracles so that I can pursue the point that Paul did not seem to be aware of miracle stories attached to the life of Jesus. Paul does not even suggest that he himself had some kind of a supernatural conversion experience involving a vision on the road to Damascus. Never in the entire body of his epistles does he talk about seeing a heavenly light or being struck physically blind, nor does he report how that blindness was cured. He never mentions Ananias, who

Luke claims was supposed to have been the agent of that healing. All of these heightened details come into the Christian story only in the book of Acts, which was written thirty to forty years after Paul's death.

With no resort to the telling of supernatural miracle stories, Paul, nonetheless, seemed to be in touch with the experience that what he called God had somehow been met in the one he called Christ. That was for him both real and powerful. Paul's yearning to be open to this divine presence in Jesus was expressed in his description of the Christian life as life "in Christ." His sense that Jesus could best be explained as a kind of emptying of God into human life is spelled out in Philippians (2:5–11). None of this, however, ever seems to have led him to assume that what we call miracles ever occurred in Jesus' life. God and human life for Paul seemed to flow into one another. That at least opens to us the possibility that the tradition of miracles being connected with Jesus is a later development in the Jesus tradition and is not original. So I invite my readers to open their minds to entertain this possibility before we proceed.

Miracles make their first appearance in the recorded Jesus story in the eighth decade in Mark and in the ninth and tenth decades in the other gospels. So miracles appear to be a contribution of that time between 70 and 100 CE when the gospels came to be written. If we accept this dating process, as the ablest scholars in the world generally do, then we can properly ask why miracles were added to the Jesus story at that time, if they were not original to his memory or to the tradition that grew out of his life and ministry.

If miracles are a late-developing part of the Jesus story, then they, like so much else that we are discovering, might also be an expression, not of supernaturalism, but of the inadequacy of human language to be a vehicle for making rational sense out of an ultimate God experience. What we need to realize is that only a God language could be used to talk meaningfully about God, and we do not have a God language. Without a God language, human beings can talk about God only by heightening human events until they become supernatural realities similar to what we expect God and God's actions to be. That was clearly operative when the disciples of Jesus sought words big enough to describe the presumed divine life of Jesus—a life said to be able to set aside human limits and transcend human boundaries.

The supernatural activities attributed to Jesus fall roughly into three categories. First, there are what we call nature miracles; second, there are healing miracles, and third, there are the stories of Jesus raising the dead back to life. What the gospel writers are seeking to communicate about Jesus via miracle accounts appears to be slightly different in each of these three types of miracles, so I will address them separately, beginning with Jesus' power over nature, the main subject of this chapter.

The gospels are asserting that Jesus was endowed with power over the forces of nature when they relate such narratives as Jesus walking on the water, Jesus stilling the storm, Jesus calming the wind, Jesus expanding a finite substance like a loaf of bread until it can feed a multitude and Jesus cursing a fig tree to cause its immediate and un-natural death. My question when studying the nature miracles in the Bible is the same one I keep asking: What was it that people experienced in Jesus that caused them to surround him with these various supernatural nature stories?

When searching for valid conclusions, it is important first to recall that the gospel tradition was the creation of the Jewish people and as such it is steeped in their religious history and worldview. The Jewish faith story began in the assertion of God's power over nature. In the opening chapters of the Torah, God shaped the chaos into ordered life; created the sun, the moon and the stars; filled the oceans with fish, the sky with birds, and the earth with creeping things and mighty beasts, the greatest of which were the human male and female. God appointed these human creatures to exercise godlike dominion over all that God had made. Even after that initial creation, the God of the Jews was constantly perceived as entering the life of the world. That is a consistent theme in the stories of Adam and Eve, Cain and Abel, Noah, Abraham and Moses. The climactic moment in the exodus was described as a nature miracle, with the parting of the waters demonstrating God's power over nature. This power was ever afterward reasserted and celebrated in Jewish liturgies and was a theme repeated again and again by the psalmists and the prophets. God had the power to command and to raise "the stormy wind, which lifted up the waves of the sea" (Ps. 107:25), but God also had the power to deliver people from distress by making "the storm be still and the waves of the sea

[be] hushed" (Ps. 107:29–30). It was the prophet Nahum who wrote that God's way is in "the whirlwind and storm and the clouds are the dust of his [God's] feet." He went on to say that God "rebukes the sea and makes it dry" (Nah. 1:3, 4). Zechariah added that it is "the Lord who makes the storm clouds" (Zech. 10:1). These texts are illustrative of the Jewish understanding of the relationship between God and nature.

Knowing that Judaism perceived God as possessing power over nature, we can begin to see that the nature miracles in the gospels were shaped by the religious history of the Jewish people. In a variety of different ways the disciples of Jesus tried to put into words the conviction that they had encountered this God of the Jews in Jesus. Paul said God was in this Christ (2 Cor. 5:19). Mark said that the heavens opened and the Spirit of God descended upon this Jesus at his baptism (Mark 1:1–11). Matthew said his name was revealed to Joseph in a dream as "Emmanuel," which means "God with us" (Matt. 1:23). Matthew also had Jesus make the "Emmanuel" claim when he closed his gospel by recording the resurrected Jesus as saying, "Lo, I am with you always, to the close of the age" (Matt. 28:20). Luke says that Jesus not only came from God but also returned to God after his work was done (Luke 1:26–35, 24:50–53, Acts 1:1–11). John has Jesus assert in a variety of ways that he and God are one (John 1:14; 5:17, 20; 10:30; 17:1ff.).

This was the disciples' experience of Jesus. The problem was how were they going to talk about it? They solved the problem by searching the Hebrew scriptures for God language, and when they found it they wrapped it around Jesus—not because these words described things that actually happened, but because they were the only words big enough to make sense out of their experience. So the disciples turned the God who could make a path for God's self in the deep, the God whose footprints were upon the water (Ps. 77:19), into a narrative about Jesus walking on the water. When they portrayed Jesus as stilling the storm, they were saying that the God who could still the stormy winds and hush the violent waves of the sea was also present in Jesus. Sensing that God was somehow part of who Jesus was, the disciples used their narratives of the nature miracles to demonstrate the presence of God. These narratives were never intended to be accounts of something that actually happened in any objective sense, but were rather attempts to translate a powerful internal experience of God that they had with Jesus of Nazareth into the external language of their religious tradition. There is no language that describes an internal experience; external language is all we have available. Why cannot modern religious people recognize that difference? Why is it so necessary for them to literalize the limited external language when they seek to plumb the interior depths of our common humanity?

Another nature miracle attributed to Jesus was the ability to expand the food supply so that a few loaves of bread could fill the stomachs of a multitude of people. That story too, as an analysis of the Hebrew scriptures will attest, was similarly drawn from the Jewish tradition. It was a magnified Moses story. Moses was instrumental in feeding a hungry multitude in the wilderness by asking God to rain an unlimited quantity of bread upon them, which they gathered into countless baskets (Exod. 16:1–8). Elijah and Elisha were also said to have had the power to produce a food supply that never ran out (1 Kings 17:1–16, 2 Kings 4:1–7). The Jewish followers of Jesus, living in the latter years of the first century, took these themes from their religious heroes of the past and wrapped them around Jesus of Nazareth. A close reading of the miraculous feeding stories found in the gospels makes it clear that these writers were not describing history; rather, they were saying something about who they had come to believe that Jesus was. That becomes particularly clear when we examine the details about the two miraculous feeding stories that Mark and Matthew record. The first story involved five thousand people on the Jewish side of the lake who were fed with five loaves, after which twelve baskets of fragments were gathered up. The second one involved four thousand people on the Gentile side of the lake who were fed with seven loaves, after which seven baskets of fragments were gathered up. There has been much speculation as to what these various numbers and settings meant. Maybe, say some theorists, the twelve baskets represented the twelve tribes of Israel and the seven baskets were for the seven nations that were thought to be the number of Gentile nations with which the Jews were familiar. Whatever the significance of the details, these stories seem to say something about the ability of Jesus to feed the Jews and the Gentiles, with an ample supply of food left over in both cases. Perhaps it was an attempt in the earlier gospels to say objectively in a story what the gospel of John would later say about the person of Jesus: to know Jesus, said John, was to discover that he met the deepest hunger in the human soul, because he was the "bread of life." Jesus himself was said to have made that claim in John, and he coupled it with the name of God, "I AM," revealed in the burning bush episode in the Moses narrative (Exod. 3:13–22). So in John's version of the miraculous feeding of the multitude, Jesus says, "I am the bread of life" (John 6:35). John goes on to transform this story into a Christian Eucharist by saying that only by eating the flesh and drinking the blood of Jesus has salvation been made possible (6:54). After all, the Jews at the Passover meal also feasted on the body and blood of the lamb of God, and now they appear to be saying in these various versions of feeding the multitudes that there was a sufficient presence of this God in Jesus to fill the lives, not only of the Jews, but of all the Gentiles. As we look at how the story was used in John, as well as in Mark and Matthew, something very different from a simple miracle story emerges. When the miraculous elements in the story disappear, its ultimate Eucharistic meaning can step out of the shadows.

To complete the category of nature miracles in the gospels, I turn to what is surely one of the strangest episodes in the gospel tradition. Mark includes a narrative about Jesus laying a curse on a fig tree because it did not produce figs when he was hungry (Mark 11:12–26). The narrative says that this curse caused the tree to shrivel and die. Something other than a miracle is surely going on here and I will look at what that "something" is in more detail in a later chapter when I come to my analysis of Jesus understood under the symbol of the new Passover. Suffice it now to say that for Jesus to curse an unproductive fig tree, when as Mark says so clearly that "it was not the season for figs" (Mark 11:13), is literally bizarre. If one takes this story as history, however, it does seem to fall into the category of a nature miracle, but it also makes no rational sense. Even today, biblical commentators regularly omit it from their lists of miracle stories. It does not create energy even among fundamentalists, despite the fact that it portrays Jesus as having power over nature. It is interesting how people who think of themselves as literalists still pick and choose, avoiding that which is more than even they can intellectually digest.

My point in this chapter is to demonstrate that all of the nature miracles attributed to Jesus in the gospels are, to their authors, simply the means for interpreting, in a first-century Jewish setting, their Jesus experience. These nature miracle stories are not intended to be literalized and thus rendered both inconceivable and unbelievable. Nor are they designed to report on the supposed ability of Jesus to break the laws of the universe and thus to reveal a supposed supernatural identity. Rather, they are attempts by the disciples of Jesus to say that the same God who created this world, who controls the elements of wind and water, who fed our ancestors in the wilderness with heavenly food and delivered them from death at the Red Sea, has been encountered in a wholly new way in the human life of Jesus of Nazareth. As God was the source of their nation's deliverance, so Jesus too had become the source of their wholeness and a sign of their salvation. They had to stretch human language into the realm of God in order to make their words big enough to give expression to their God experience. The nature miracles in the gospels are not, I believe, about supernatural interventions at all; they are about communicating just what it was that the disciples believed they had met in Jesus of Nazareth. To read these accounts properly is not to literalize them, but to seek to enter the experience that created them. That is a vastly different matter.

7

HEALING MIRACLES: A VISION OF THE KINGDOM OF GOD

We believe in miracles in West Virginia, and we are still hoping for that miracle.
Governor Joe Manchin, January 4, 2006

May God bless those who are trapped below the earth and may God bless those who are concerned about those trapped.
President George W. Bush, January 4, 2006[1]

We turn now to examine those narratives in which the touch or the command of Jesus is said to bring physical healing. In these episodes the blind are made to see, the deaf to hear, the lame to walk, some malady is transformed into wholeness or some unclean or demonic spirit is banished. These stories have had a powerful impact on Christian practice throughout the centuries. Intercessions for healing probably still dominate the content of prayer for most believers. The phrase used so often in evangelical circles, "Thank you, Jesus!" when some restoration to wholeness is achieved is indicative of the lasting power that Jesus, as the source of healing, has had on the consciousness of the faithful. A God who answers prayers is the last aspect of the supernatural theistic deity that people are willing to surrender. People have developed a remarkable ability to rationalize the evidence and thus to explain why God did not intervene when the verdict goes the other way. God gets credit for the cure. Something else gets blamed for the death or unwelcome outcome.

This was powerfully and painfully revealed to this century's vast television audience when an explosion in a coal mine occurred in the town of Tallmansville, West Virginia. That explosion trapped thirteen miners some 260 feet below the surface in a long shaft that was more than two miles into the mine. The attention of the nation was riveted on the rescue effort. The hours dragged on as family members waited, knowing that each passing minute made it more likely that the decreasing supply of oxygen would snuff out the lives of their loved ones. Then against all odds the report rang out that twelve of the trapped miners had been found alive, while one was dead. The celebration was unrestrained in the Sago Baptist Church where the people had gathered. So was the religious rhetoric. The governor of West Virginia, Joe Manchin, pronounced it a "miracle" and exhorted the people from now on to "believe in miracles." One cannot help but wonder how this miracle-producing God singled out the one who was found dead, since he obviously had not been rescued. Perhaps this victim did not qualify for divine assistance, perhaps he was somehow decreed to be undeserving, perhaps it was his time to die in a strangely predestined world. Television cameras interviewed loved ones who almost universally attributed the rescue to divine intervention. "Thank you, God!" "Thank you, Jesus!" "Praise God!" were oft-cited refrains.

About two hours later, however, there was another announcement, this time ominously official, which said that the earlier report was incorrect. Only one miner had been brought out alive. He was unconscious, in critical condition, and the suggestion was that he might be seriously brain-damaged. The other twelve were dead. Suddenly the talk of miracles and God disappeared. The praises directed toward Jesus ceased and were replaced by expressions of anger and grief, filled with talk of lawsuits.

A life based on the expectation of miracles is seldom rewarded. The prayers of believers are unanswered far more often than they are answered. Nothing, however, seems able to destroy the hope that God, defined as a miracle-working deity beyond the sky, will intervene, that miracles are available to those who pray fervently and to those who deserve them, having earned divine favor by living well. Much of that hope appears to be rooted in the gospel stories, where again and again Jesus is portrayed as producing healing miracles.

In any study of the healing miracles in the New Testament, the first thing that must be embraced is that the way sickness was understood in the first century is light years from our understanding in the twenty-first century. First-century people knew nothing about germs, for example. That was a nineteenth-century discovery by the Frenchman Louis Pasteur. First-century people had never heard of a virus either. That was a twentieth-century addition to human knowledge. First-century people had no understanding of cardiovascular accidents, leukemia, tumors or cancer. Sickness in biblical times was primarily understood as God's punishment for human sinfulness. The question posed by the disciples to Jesus in John's gospel about the man born blind was in touch with that ancient common wisdom: "Rabbi, who sinned, this man or his parents, that he was born blind?" (John 9:2). The same idea was reflected when the critics of Jesus were so upset when he said to the paralytic, "Son, your sins are forgiven" (Mark 2:5–7). Their quarrel was not about sinfulness being the cause of the sickness, but rather with Jesus' claim, blasphemous to their ears, that he could be the source of forgiveness.

The New Testament attributed both mental illness and epilepsy to demon possession (Mark 1:25, 9:25). Deaf-muteness, the gospels indicated, resulted from the devil tying the tongue of the victim (Mark 7:35). Given that understanding of the cause of certain sicknesses, the prescription of prayer and sacrifices designed to placate God's wrath made perfect sense as an attempted cure. To attribute healing power to Jesus was actually to propose a definition of their claim of his divine status.

We, however, live in a world of medical knowledge that the minds of first-century people could never have imagined. Once germs were identified, modern medicine developed antibiotics and discovered that they worked just as well on sinners as they did on saints. Human research invented vaccines for various disorders from anthrax in sheep to polio in children and revealed in the process something about the interconnectedness of all life. Today medical technology can shrink tumors with radiation, attack them with chemotherapy, or excise them with laparoscopic or other surgical procedures. In the process modern medicine has removed God from sickness and secularized it completely. So deeply had the premodern interpretation of sickness entered both our religious minds and our psyches, however, that in my particular branch of Christianity, the Episcopal Church, the idea that sickness was punishment for sin did not get removed from our prayer books until the revision of 1979.[2]

Once we have accepted the wide differences between the way sickness and disease were understood in the first century and the way they are understood today, we need to embrace an additional cultural factor that makes the writers of the New Testament vastly different from the Western minds that shape Christian thinking today. The gospel writers were not just first-century people; they were Jewish people. Built into the Jewish consciousness was a context of hope and expectation that we need to recognize before any analysis of the healing miracles will be complete or understandable.

In that Jewish world there was a lively expectation that what they called the kingdom of God would dawn someday. This expectation, born out of years, even centuries of despair, focused on the uniquely Jewish hope that the messiah would come to inaugurate that kingdom. The signs of the kingdom were spelled out in many places in the Hebrew scriptures, but nowhere more beautifully than in chapter 35 of Isaiah, where the prophet described the things that would accompany the arrival of the kingdom of God:

> The wilderness and the dry land shall be glad,
>   the desert shall rejoice and blossom....
> They shall see the glory of the Lord....
> Then the eyes of the blind shall be opened,
>   and the ears of the deaf unstopped;
> then shall the lame man leap like a hart,
>   and the tongue of the dumb sing for joy. (Isa. 35:1–6)

Isaiah had struck a similar note earlier in his book when he wrote:

> In that day the deaf shall hear the words of a scroll,
> and out of their gloom and darkness
>   the eyes of the blind shall see.

The meek shall obtain fresh joy in the Lord,
  and the neediest people shall exult in the Holy One of Israel.
  (Isa. 29:18–19)

It is this clearly articulated Jewish expectation of the coming of the kingdom of God together with its accompanying signs that created for the gospel writers a different question that seems to drive us well beneath the level of literalism: Did Jesus actually do healing miracles, or were these added to the Jesus story as a way of assigning the status of messiah to him? Are the healing miracle stories another part of the developing tradition, and thus in the same category with the Bethlehem tradition of his birth? Are there hints in the New Testament that might lend credibility to this possibility? I think there are.

In both Matthew and Luke there is a similar story told at about the midpoint in their gospels that is, I believe, quite revealing (Matt. 11:2–6, Luke 7:18–23). In this story John the Baptist, who has not been heard from since the time of Jesus' baptism at the beginning of each of these gospels, is reintroduced for a cameo appearance. John, in prison, questions Jesus via messengers about whether or not Jesus is to be identified with the popular messianic expectation. Jesus responds by referring to the text just quoted from Isaiah 35, where the signs of the in-breaking kingdom of God are spelled out quite specifically. In order to see the power of this answer, I need to place it inside Jewish history.

To gain that context we go back to the Hebrew scripture's book of Malachi, titled not with a person's name but with a Hebrew word that means "my messenger." Malachi announces the coming of an anonymous messenger "to prepare the way" so that people will be ready when "the Lord whom you seek will suddenly come to the temple" (Mal. 3:1). When Mark, who does not include the above John-in-prison story in his gospel, introduces John the Baptist, he calls him a voice "crying in the wilderness (Mark 1:3). In that introduction Mark conflates the words from Isaiah with the words from the prophet Malachi.

There are many places in the gospels where the role of the nameless messenger of Malachi has been combined with the role of Elijah as the forerunner of the messiah, and then assigned to John the Baptist. John identifies himself overtly as that forerunner with such self-deprecating quotations as, "After me comes one who is mightier than I, the thong of whose sandals I am not worthy to stoop down and untie" (Mark 1:7). All of the other gospels echo this theme.

John, however, is also identified with the Elijah-type forerunner covertly, in that the clothes assigned to the Baptist—"a garment of camel's hair, and a leather girdle around his waist"—his location in the wilderness, and his wilderness diet of "locusts and wild honey" (Matt. 3:1–4) are all chosen to make his connection with Elijah obvious (2 Kings 1:8). Another covert hint comes with Luke's choice of Zechariah to be the name of John's father (Luke 1:5ff.). The biblical text of Zechariah, found as part of the larger "Book of the Twelve" (that part of the Hebrew scriptures sometimes called the minor prophets), is the immediate scriptural predecessor to Malachi. If John the Baptist is Malachi, the nameless forerunner of the messiah, then his father, and thus his immediate predecessor, must be named Zechariah. Don't ever assume that the names found in the gospels are chosen out of historic memory; as here, they are frequently chosen to proclaim specific themes.

So now back to Matthew and Luke and their accounts of John as he wrestles with Jesus' identity: John, the Elijah-Malachi figure, in prison where he is awaiting execution, is said in Matthew (11:2ff.) and in Luke (7:18ff.) to have sent messengers to Jesus specifically asking, "Are you he who is to come, or shall we look for another?" Jesus responds in a revelatory way, identifying himself as the messiah in a manner that could not be misinterpreted. "Go and tell John what you … see: the blind receive their sight and the lame walk, lepers are cleansed and the deaf hear, and the dead are raised up, and the poor have good news preached to them" (Matt. 11:4–5).

Luke adds here that generic miracle verse to which we have already referred. With no specific examples provided, he says, "In that hour he [Jesus] cured many of diseases and plagues and evil spirits, and on many that were blind he bestowed sight" (Luke 7:21). Then he repeats Jesus' words in the almost identical form that Matthew had used. Both lists add the phrase "the dead are raised up." Though that was not a messianic sign in Isaiah, it had become one in later-developing Jewish thought: it was expected that the dead would be raised for judgment on the last day.

In this episode all of the healing miracles are understood to be signs that Jesus is the messiah. That is a strong argument, I believe, that these narratives should not be treated as literal events that actually happened, but as messianic signs attached to the story of Jesus to identify him with the messianic role of ushering in the kingdom of heaven. They are, therefore, interpretive narratives far more than they are descriptions of supernatural events. The non-Jewish interpreters of the gospels, during what I call the Gentile captivity of the church (which lasted from about 100 CE until relatively recently), did not understand these Jewish references. Only when Christianity in the last half of the twentieth century finally began to recover its Jewish roots and to develop eyes that looked at the gospels from a Jewish perspective would these Jewish references be understood in their original context.[3] Miracles say little about history. They say a great deal about the specific interpretive images that were applied to Jesus in order to understand what it was that people actually experienced in him. Once the modern twenty-first-century reader understands that, then the story opens in fascinating ways.

Turning now to view the specific healing stories of the gospels from this new perspective, we note first that in Mark, the original gospel, there are two narratives in which the blind receive their sight (Mark 8:22–26, 10:46–52); two stories in which the deaf are enabled to hear and in which speech is restored to a mute who was thought in that day to be tongue-tied (Mark 7:32–35, Mark 9:17–27);[4] one in which a paralyzed man was enabled to walk (Mark 2:3–12); others in which unclean spirits are banished (Mark 1:23–26, 5:1–14, 7:25–30, 9:17–27), and two in which wholeness is restored—one involving a man with a withered hand, the other a woman with a chronic menstrual discharge (Mark 3:1–5, 5:25–34). All of the Isaiah predictions of what will accompany the in-breaking kingdom of God are covered!

A close analysis of these stories, however, reveals something even more than just a supernatural healing. The narratives are filled with hidden messages and code language. For example, in the account of the blind man from Bethsaida we are told that he was healed of his blindness in stages. Jesus is said to have taken him out of the village of Bethsaida and there to have placed spittle on his eyes, asking him, "Do you see anything?" The blind man looked up and said, "I see men; but they look like trees, walking." Jesus then laid his hands on him again, until the man and Jesus "looked intently" on each other; then the healing process continued until he "saw everything clearly." The story ends with Jesus sending this man directly home, saying, "Do not even enter the village" (Mark 8:22–26).

The immediate next episode, according to Mark, occurs in Caesarea Philippi, where Jesus asks, "Who do people say that I am?" The disciples respond with all of the possibilities: John the Baptist, Elijah, one of the prophets. Jesus then presses them on who *they* think he is, and Peter responds, "You are the Christ [that is, the messiah]." Jesus enjoins them to tell no one and begins to spell out the path that the Christ is destined to walk. What that path involves, Jesus says, is "that the Son of man must suffer many things, and be rejected by the elders and the chief priests and the scribes, and be killed, and after three days rise again." Jesus, the text tells us, "[says] this plainly." Peter then rebukes Jesus and is, in turn, rebuked by Jesus with the words, "Get behind me, Satan! For you are not on the side of God, but of men" (Mark 8:27–33).

I go into this encounter in such detail for two reasons. First, this is obviously not history. The precise prediction of the suffering, the crucifixion and the resurrection is a clear reading back into the historical life of Jesus the story of the climactic final events. Mark, the author of these words, was about to chronicle them in a dramatic narrative. Second, Peter is portrayed as one who presumed he understood, but whose subsequent words reveal that he did not. His "seeing" came by stages, Mark was saying. When we add to this detail the fact that we know from John's gospel that Peter came from Bethsaida (John 1:44) and that the giving of sight to the blind man from Bethsaida was said to have occurred in stages, with the final seeing accomplished only when Jesus and the blind man stare "intently" at each other, it begins to sound more like a parable of the life of Peter. When we next read the story of Peter's denial, we see the details of his lack of understanding at Caesarea Philippi. Luke seems to be referring to Mark's narrative about this blind man very specifically when, in his story of Peter's denial, he states, "The Lord turned and looked at Peter" (Luke 22:61). That intense stare, which gave the blind man from Bethsaida his full sight, in Luke's story causes Peter to remember and to weep bitterly. Reading this story as a simple healing miracle is clearly not what was intended.

There are two other restoring-sight stories in the gospels, one told by Mark but adapted by both Matthew and Luke, and the other told in John alone. Both of these stories offer similar possibilities for a non-literal reading. Mark tells us of Jesus restoring sight to a man named Bartimaeus (Mark 10:46–52), who is identified as a blind beggar and as the son of Timaeus. This is a strange designation, since Bartimaeus literally means son (*bar* = "son") of Timaeus, so one wonders what secret message is being sent to the first readers via these words. The story is repeated in Matthew (20:29–34) and in Luke (18:35–43), except that in Matthew no name is given, and thus the confusion avoided, but the single blind beggar of Mark has become "two blind men." When Luke repeats this story, he also omits the name, but like Mark he has only one blind man who is a beggar. In all of these stories the blind man calls Jesus by the messianic title "Son of David." He asks in all three accounts to receive his sight. All of the stories turn, however, on the struggle among the early disciples to see Jesus under the various symbols of the messianic titles "Son of man" and "Son of David" that were abroad, shaping the memory of Jesus, when the gospels were written. I will look more closely at these messianic titles in the next section of this book.

The final New Testament "sight to the blind" story is the pivotal narrative described by John in intimate detail as one of the "signs" that he says Jesus performed. In some ways the details in John's story (9:1–41) make it appear to be a coalescing of the two "sight to the blind" narratives in Mark. As with the blind man from Bethsaida, Jesus uses spittle in the act of restoration, and the healing is not instantaneous, but requires a further step of washing in the pool of Siloam. As in the Bartimaeus story, the blind man is a beggar by the gate. As in both earlier stories, the narrative turns on the messianic identity of Jesus. The debate is once more engaged in questions like these: Are you the Christ? Are you the Son of David? How can he be the Christ if he does not keep the sabbath? As this story is told in the Fourth Gospels, it includes the claim that to call Jesus the Christ is a sufficient reason in that moment in history to cause his followers to be "put out of the synagogue."

Included in this Johannine narrative of the man born blind is one of the "I am" sayings, peculiar to this gospel. "I am the light of the world" (9:5), Jesus is made to say, using the holy name of God, revealed in the book of Exodus to be "I AM," and providing to a blind world sufficient illuminating power to see. John concludes this episode by having Jesus say, "For judgment I came into this world, that those who do not see may see, and that those who see may become blind." When the Pharisees hear these words, they are made to ask the key question, "Are we also blind?" To which Jesus responds, "If you were blind, you would have no guilt; but now that you say, 'We see,' your guilt remains."

I hope it is now obvious that in each of these so-called miraculous accounts of Jesus giving sight to the blind, the stories are designed not to relate a supernatural event, but to focus the ongoing debate on the identity of Jesus. By reading them literally, we have in effect blinded countless generations of Christians from understanding the real meaning of these stories. Signs of the in-breaking kingdom of God are attached to the life of Jesus, who was said to embody that kingdom by opening the eyes of those who are blind so that they might see their deepest identity. It is in our humanity that we can claim to reveal the presence of the holy God.

We could also analyze the "opening of the ears of the deaf" stories, the "healing of the lame" stories, the "loosing of the tongues of the mute" stories, and discover in each of these categories that what is being communicated is once again not a supernatural event but a messianic sign. The gospels need to be read for what they are. They are not the chronicles of a remembered history, but the proclamations of a community of faith designed to say that the yearned-for kingdom of God has dawned in Jesus. The picture of human life made whole is at the heart of the Jesus experience. So wholeness appears to bear witness to who Jesus is: the blind see, the deaf hear, the lame walk and the mute sing. In the process of unlocking the meaning of the healing stories, we discover a new lens through which to look at Jesus. This human being was seen as acting out the messianic role of the mythological "Son of man." He opened people's eyes to see what life could be. That is the power of the Jesus experience. We need not pretend that we believe the supernaturally unbelievable in order to be Jesus' disciples. We need only see all that life can be—and in the ability of the human Jesus to open our eyes to this vision, a new sense of what it means to be divine begins to emerge.

8

DID JESUS LITERALLY RAISE THE DEAD?

JESUS: Your brother will rise again.
MARTHA: I know he will rise again in the resurrection at the last day.
JESUS: I am the resurrection and the life.
MARTHA: I believe that you are the Christ, the Son of God, he who is coming into the world.
John 11:23–27

If my readers want a one-word answer to the question posed by the title of this chapter, that word is a simple, straightforward no! Yet there are in the gospels three narratives about Jesus raising back to life a deceased person. Those resuscitated are: the daughter of Jairus, a ruler of the synagogue; a widow's son at Nain, and Lazarus. The first thing to note about these three episodes is that the raising of the widow's son is unique to Luke, the raising of Lazarus is unique to John and only the raising of Jairus' daughter is included in all three of the synoptic gospels—that is, Mark, Matthew and Luke. If such incredible events actually occurred, it is hard to believe that these phenomena would not have created such a sensation that accounts of them would have been narrated over and over again. In this chapter I will look at each of these stunning stories, which on the surface appear to be accounts of supernatural and death-defying miracles, but which, once we go deeply inside each of them, reveal interpretive clues that make it clear the gospel writers never meant them to be read literally.

We begin by noting that, contrary to the healing of various physical infirmities, the raising of the dead does not appear to be an original theme of Jewish messianic expectation. There is even serious question as to whether the resurrection of Jesus meant a return to the life of this world, but that is an issue I will address in detail in the chapter on the Easter stories. For now, let me seek to shed light on the three raising of the dead stories, beginning with the daughter of the synagogue ruler.

The three versions of this story share enough similarities to be recognized as the same story, but the differences are also significant. First, all three of the synoptic gospels identify the recipient of this miracle as the daughter of a ruler of the synagogue. Second, each version is told in two parts, interrupted by the account of the woman with the chronic menstrual discharge. Third, in all three accounts Jesus says of the child that she is not dead but sleeping (Mark 5:39, Matt. 9:24, Luke 8:52).

The differences found in each of the three versions are a bit more subtle. First, Mark and Luke say the ruler's name is Jairus, while Matthew omits the name. Mark and Luke have Jesus, accompanied by Peter, James and John, enter the child's room; in Matthew he is alone. Matthew omits that part of the story included in both Mark and Luke that Jesus was told before his arrival at the ruler's house that the child had already died. This means that Matthew can place a heavier emphasis than do the other two on Jesus' suggestion when he arrives that the child is not dead, but is only sleeping. He thus can also minimize the sense of amazement that both Mark and Luke record. So our first point is to say that Matthew does not seem to agree on the miraculous elements present in this story. That is unusual because, as we have noticed before, in other parts of his gospel Matthew displays a tendency to heighten miracles and even to add miraculous details.

Next we search for antecedents to this particular story in the Hebrew scriptures. Not surprisingly, the closest corollary is in the Elisha cycle (2 Kings 4:18–37). In both the Elisha story and this gospel story it is a child who is raised. In both stories the healers (Elisha and Jesus) are not immediately available but are journeying toward the destination. In both stories there is some conversation prior to the arrival of the healer about whether or not the child is really dead. In both stories there is physical contact between the healer and the child: Jesus takes the child by one hand, while Elisha stretches himself upon the child so as to give mouth-to-mouth resuscitation. This physical touching is of note, since according to the Torah, physical contact with the dead, even for a priest, leaves the person ceremonially unclean for seven days (Num. 19:11) and requires a cleansing action before the third day lest the uncleanness become even longer. In both stories the healer returns the child alive to his or her parents. In both stories the child's "spirit" is restored. This is symbolized in the Elisha story by seven sneezes and in Mark's story by the child getting up, walking and eating. There is clearly a connection between these two stories. The gospel writers are making use of the Elisha narrative to make a point. That means that the primary way this story should be read is not as a miracle account, but as an interpretive tale designed to reveal Jesus through the lens of Elisha, a hero from the Jewish past.

The second story of the raising of the dead, recorded only by Luke, is the account of Jesus raising the widow's son in the village of Nain (Luke 7:11–15). The first observation that we make about this story takes us back to the account that played so large a role in the previous chapter on understanding the healing miracles as messianic signs. As noted there, when the messengers for John the Baptist asked on his behalf whether Jesus was "he who is to come," Jesus responded by pointing to the messianic signs that Isaiah had said would accompany the in-breaking of the kingdom of God. Jesus, however, added two other signs, which are to be distinctive marks of the Christian community, but which were not on Isaiah's list. They are that the dead will be raised, and that the poor will receive the good news. The idea that raising the dead was a sign of the kingdom did not create a problem for Matthew, since he had already related his story of Jesus raising the daughter of the ruler of the synagogue. Luke, however, did not relate that episode until later in his gospel. So from Luke's perspective Jesus can hardly tell John that one of the messianic signs, which he should read as marking Jesus' life, is that the dead are raised if there has been no report of such an event in his text thus far. Consequently, Luke writes this narrative of the raising of the widow's son at Nain into his text immediately before the John the Baptist episode is related.

Following our regular procedure we next ask whether there are any equivalent stories in the Hebrew scriptures upon which the raising from the dead of a widow's son might have been patterned. Once again we discover that there is; not surprisingly, it too is in the Elijah-Elisha cycle, from which the gospels draw so heavily. This time, however, it is Elijah (1 Kings 17:17–24), not Elisha. The similarities between this Elijah story and Luke's account are many. In both stories the victim is the only son of the widow. In both stories the young man is stretched out on his funeral bed. In both stories the healer speaks, commanding God to act. In both stories the son is returned alive to his mother. In both stories the raising from the dead elicits a prophetic claim: in Elijah's case it is said that he speaks the words of God, while in the Jesus story it is said that a great prophet has arisen and God has visited God's people. Thus we come once more to what has, I trust, become a familiar conclusion: what is going on in these stories is not a narrative process in which a miraculous episode is chronicled to inspire awe, but an interpretive process designed to address the question of how it is that God is operating so specifically in Jesus. This gospel episode is no more than a narrative claim that in Jesus, the new Elijah is present. This is a dominant Lucan theme that he will develop from several other angles, which I will look at later.

This brings us to the final raising of the dead story in the gospels. It is by far the best known and yet it is still the most enigmatic—namely, the raising from the dead of a man named Lazarus (John 11:1–57). Once again we begin with some facts.

John's gospel identifies Lazarus as the brother of Mary and Martha. Mary and Martha had been introduced by Luke as two sisters who live in Bethany, a village in the Jerusalem area (Luke 10:38–41). There is in this earlier gospel, however, no mention of the fact that these sisters might have had a brother. That is a new idea introduced by the Fourth Gospel. The gospels contain a number of instances in which Bethany is referred to as a place where Jesus found lodging. It was in Bethany that Jesus and the disciples stayed during what has come to be called Holy Week (Mark 11:11–12). It was in a house in Bethany where he was anointed by the woman with the alabaster jar (Mark 14:3, Matt. 26:6). John later identifies that house as the home of Mary, Martha and Lazarus (John 12:1–3). It was from Bethany that Jesus made preparations for the Last Supper (Luke 19:29). It was in Bethany that Jesus was baptized (John 1:28). In this story about the raising of the deceased Lazarus, the setting once again is Bethany.

The details of this story, told only in John, are fascinating. John introduces the story with a reference to the fact that it was Mary, Lazarus' sister, who anointed the Lord with ointment and wiped his feet with her hair (John 11:3). The only trouble with this reference is that John's gospel does not tell us this story until the next chapter! In other words, it is a forward reference. In the narrative of Lazarus' raising, the sisters, Mary and Martha, send for Jesus because their brother is ill. Jesus waits deliberately for two days before responding to their urgent request, saying, "This illness is not unto death; it is for the glory of God, so that the Son of God may be glorified by means of it" (John 11:4).

Then Jesus begins his journey to Judea, despite his disciples' reminder that it was in Judea where his enemies tried to stone him. Jesus responds enigmatically by saying he will walk at night, implying that since he is the "light of the world," the darkness will not impede him. He then tells the disciples that Lazarus has fallen asleep and that he is going to wake him. His literal-minded disciples say that if he has fallen asleep, then he will surely awaken; that is, there is no need for Jesus to put himself in danger. Then Jesus clarifies the issue by saying, "Lazarus is dead" (John 11:14). Thomas, introduced here by John for the first time, says to the other disciples, "Let us also go, that we might die with him" (John 11:16).

They go. We are then told that by the time they arrive, Lazarus has been dead for four days. Martha goes out to meet Jesus prior to his arrival. She greets him with a note of resentment: "If you had been here, my brother would not have died" (John 11:21).

Jesus responds, "Your brother will rise again." "I know," says Martha, "that he will rise again in the resurrection at the last day." To this Jesus responds with one of the "I am" sayings: "I am the resurrection and the life; he who believes in me, though he die, yet shall he live, and whoever lives and believes in me shall never die" (John 11:25–26). Martha responds with the full messianic designation "I believe that you are the Christ, the Son of God, he who is coming into the world" (John 11:27).

They then walk together until they arrive in Bethany, two miles from Jerusalem, where a crowd of mourners has gathered. Mary then comes out to Jesus with resentful words almost identical to Martha's: that if he had come quickly, this tragedy could have been averted. Jesus asks to be pointed to the burial spot, where he weeps. People observe his love for Lazarus and wonder why, with his power, he could not have kept him from dying.

Jesus then orders the stone to be removed from the tomb. Martha objects, claiming that since Lazarus has been dead four days there would be an odor—or, as the King James Bible says so overtly, "by this time he stinketh" (John 11:39, KJV). Jesus prays at the entrance to the tomb, and then he calls forth Lazarus. The dead man arises and comes forth replete with the burial bandages. Both his hands and his feet are bound and his face is wrapped in the burial cloth. Jesus directs the mourners to unbind him and let him go.

Some people, says John, believed in Jesus because of this miracle. Others, however, went to the Pharisees and told them what Jesus had done. This, according to John, was the catalyst that made the crucifixion inevitable. Code language fills the text from this point on. If the people follow this man, the chief priests and Pharisees say, the Romans "will come and destroy both our holy place and our nation" (John 11:48). The Romans would actually do exactly that about forty years after this episode was supposed to have occurred. When John wrote, however, that destruction was already about thirty years in the past. Caiaphas, the high priest that year, declared, "It is expedient ... that one man should die for the people, and that the whole nation should not perish" (John 11:50). This episode then concludes with the words: "So from that day on they took counsel how to put him to death" (John 11:53). John then moves his narrative into the Passover, the setting in which he said the crucifixion happened.

Contrary to what we discovered in the other two raising of the dead stories in the gospels, there are no connections in the Hebrew scriptures with this story of Lazarus. However, this episode does seem to have many similarities with a parable in Luke's gospel about a man named Lazarus who also dies (Luke 16:19–31). Scholars have long noted a number of additional connections between Luke and John, sufficient to suggest some dependency of John on Luke or at least to

suggest that John and Luke might have had a common source. I suspect that John knew the work of Luke. Only in these two gospels does
the woman anoint the feet of Jesus and wipe them with her hair. Luke
appears to have added that detail to this story found originally in Mark.
Matthew does not contain that detail, but rather appears to have
copied this story exactly as Mark related it (Mark 14:3–9, Matt.
26:6–13). John, however, does include Luke's addition (Luke 7:36–50,
John 12:3–8). Both Luke and John attribute to Judas, as the motive
for his betrayal, the fact that Satan or the devil had entered him (Luke
22:3, John 13:2). Neither Luke nor John uses the word "Gethsemane."
Both Luke and John have two angels at the tomb on the day of the
resurrection. Finally, there is this connection between the two Lazarus
stories.

I think it quite possible that John has in his Lazarus story simply
historicized Luke's parable of Lazarus and the rich man, the latter
sometimes called Dives. Not only do the two episodes have the name
Lazarus in common, but the theme of Luke's parable is identical with
what John says actually results from the miracle he describes. In Luke's
story Abraham says that if the people do not "hear Moses and the
prophets, neither will they be convinced if someone should rise from
the dead" (Luke 16:31). In John's story that is exactly what happens
with the raising of Lazarus.

The details of the raising of Lazarus story in John's gospel seem to
reflect a contrast as well as a similarity with the themes that will appear
in John's own Easter narrative. Lazarus had been dead for four days. In
some Jewish thought the soul or spirit was believed to hover near the
grave until the third day, when it finally departed; thereafter, the de-
caying process of death was thought to be irreversible. Three days
was the limit that is observed in the Jesus story. At both the graves of
Lazarus and Jesus a woman named Mary was present weeping (John
11:33, John 20:11). Lazarus' grave, like Jesus' grave, had a stone seal-
ing its entrance (John 11:38, 20:1). In the Lazarus story Jesus orders
the stone removed (11:39). In the Easter story Mary Magdalene finds
the stone already removed (John 20:1). Lazarus comes forth still
bound in his grave clothes (John 11:44). Simon Peter and the one
called the beloved disciple discover the grave clothes of Jesus lying in
distinct piles, as if he had simply risen out of them (John 20:6–7).

John appears to be painting a contrast in these two raisings. In the case of Lazarus it was a physical resuscitation that brought a dead man back into the life of this world. Lazarus was still bound by the clothes of death that would inevitably bind him at some later point when he died again. In the Easter story John says that Jesus was lifted out of his grave clothes, suggesting that they could never bind him again. Paul had observed that "death has no more dominion over [Christ]," and that "Christ being raised from the dead will never die again" (Rom. 6:9). The raising of Lazarus was quite physical, while the raising of Jesus was a transformation into a body that could ascend to the Father (John 20:17) and thus was no longer bound by the laws of the physical universe. He could now walk through walls (John 20:19), breathe the Holy Spirit on the disciples (John 20:22) and appear at will beside the Sea of Galilee (John 21:4).

That completes our study of the three episodes in the gospels where Jesus is portrayed as having the power to raise the dead. One appears to be the retelling of an Elisha story, one the retelling of an Elijah story and one the historicization of a parable found in Luke's gospel. This study convinces me that a literal supernatural reading of the gospels would be a violation of the original intent of the gospel writers. Jesus did not raise the dead in any literal sense. Rather, he was portrayed in these episodes as one who was greater than Elisha or Elijah, the prophets who were said to embody the very power of God. People experienced in him a life force, a transcendent power and a sense of the timeless eternal God. They struggled in the language and concepts of their first-century Jewish world to make sense out of their experience that in Jesus they had met the presence of the holy God, bounded neither by the exigencies of human life nor by the limitations imposed on our humanity of such things as time, space and mortality.

Miracles in the New Testament are, time after time, simply a literary device to enable the gospel authors to talk about the in-breaking kingdom that is available to those who have the eyes to see. Miracles are part of the vision of wholeness that inspires us human beings to press the limits of our humanity in an eternal search for the transcendence that we feel is our destiny. Jesus is a human life whose capacity to live, to love and to be, opened the eyes of those who were touched by him to enter an unbounded life, to experience an unbounded love, to participate in an unbounded being. He had nothing to do with breaking natural laws, doing supernatural miracles, whether healing the sick and infirm or raising the dead. Miracles represented the only way first-century Jewish people could stretch human language sufficiently to allow them to communicate what they believed they had encountered in Jesus.

Today that first-century supernatural language not only blinds us to the meaning of Jesus, but actually distorts Jesus for us. It either leads us to a hysterical defensiveness in which the indefensible must be protected lest we sink into a bottomless pit of nothingness; or it causes us to think that traditional God language is irrational and meaningless, which in turn forces us to reject the religious viewpoint and to embrace the emptiness of a godless world. Perhaps if we can break Jesus out of religion, free him from creeds, doctrines and dogmas, we can once again hear his invitation to enter the God experience known in the fullness of life. That is the Jesus I seek. He neither was nor is a miracle worker. He did not walk on water, heal the sick, or raise the dead. Rather, in his radical humanity, he lived out the meaning of God and caused those who glimpsed his life or felt his power to exclaim, "God was in Christ," and thus God, the gospel writers assert, can also be in you and in me.

We turn next to watch life transform death in this story of Jesus. There, as we watch divinity unfold in the human Jesus, we will learn that divinity is not something different from humanity.

9

THE CRUCIFIXION NARRATIVE: LITURGY MASQUERADING AS HISTORY

For I delivered to you as of first importance what I also received, that Christ died for our sins in accordance with the scriptures, that he was buried.

1 Cor. 15:3–4a (the totality of the only written story of the cross that Christians had until the eighth decade CE)

If, as I suggested in the earlier chapter on the twelve disciples, Judas—said to have betrayed Jesus to the authorities and thus to have led to his death—is not a person of history, then how much history is in the rest of the story of Jesus' crucifixion? That is now our question.

The earliest written record we have of the death of Jesus is so sparse as to be chilling. There are almost no details. All of those things from the gospel stories that regular worshippers hold on to as familiar details of the crucifixion were actually developed at least forty years after the death of Jesus! There is no evidence that they were original. A search for authentic early data on the details of the crucifixion—that is, data that are earlier than the eighth decade—comes up far emptier than people expect. Let me review the facts briefly. Paul, in the earliest New Testament writing we have, asserts that Jesus was crucified. In fact, he refers to the cross of Jesus at least eight times, to Jesus' act of being crucified nine times and to the death of Jesus numerous times.

Usually these are single references with few details, as if the fact of the crucifixion and death of Jesus was simply assumed by Paul and was thus beyond either debate or doubt. The most complete account that Paul gives of the crucifixion occurs in 1 Corinthians 15, written in the middle years of the sixth decade of the Common Era, or about twenty-five years after the event itself. However, even this source reveals very few details (vv. 3–11).

Paul introduces this narrative with these words: "I delivered to you as of first importance what I also received," after which he recites what he calls the formative events of the Christian story. What he says about the crucifixion fills literally just one line: "Christ died for our sins in accordance with the scriptures." That is all Paul seems to know. There is no account of the betrayal, no visit to the Garden of Gethsemane, no arrest and no trial before the chief priests. There are none of the familiar details that grace the passion stories of the gospels. There is no mention of Pilate, no recollection of the accusations made against Jesus and no record of the pressure from the Jewish crowd to have him executed. There is no story of his being beaten, no mention of a crown of thorns, no narrative of his having to bear his own cross and no mention of a hill called Calvary. There is no account of the soldiers who drove the nails, or of the thieves who were said to have been crucified with him. There is no mention of the darkness at noon and no reference to any word Jesus was said to have spoken from the cross to anyone. Paul did assert that the death of Jesus had a saving purpose: it was, he said, "for our sins," to which he added the notion that it was also "in accordance with the scriptures." There is, however, no description of Jesus' agony. He died. That is all Paul said.

Paul continues his narration of the events that follow the crucifixion, but once again the details are very sparse. Paul covers the burial of Jesus with three words: "He was buried." In this first story of the death of Jesus that we have in the Bible there is no mention of a tomb, no burial sheet, no spices, no garden and no Joseph of Arimathea. Paul's burial text is almost matter-of-fact. When people die, they get buried; nothing else is mentioned. That is the sum total of what the Christian church had in writing about the death and burial of Jesus until the eighth decade (or some fifteen or so years after Paul's writing), when the first gospel, Mark, was written. The question that expositors raise when they read this primitive Pauline text is: Did Paul know more than this, or was this the sum of the details that were passed on to him?

We might better be able to answer that question if we could find out who it was that passed this tradition on to Paul. In searching the Pauline corpus for clues, we discover in the epistle to the Galatians, written in the early fifties, that three years after Paul's conversion he went to visit Cephas (or Simon Peter) and remained with him for fifteen days (Gal. 1:18). Is it not reasonable to assume that this was the source of his information? Then we have to ask whether this is all that Paul remembered of what Peter had told him, or whether it was all that Peter knew and thus all that he passed on. Had the story of the cross, as we have come to understand it, simply not been composed by this time? Most people never ask these questions, but they cry out to be explored if our task is to get behind the myth to the human life and to get behind the explanation to the experience.

Between the writing of 1 Corinthians and the appearance of the first gospel in the early seventies, many things happened. Both Paul and Peter apparently died. The Jews had become involved, by their own aggressive choice, in an unfortunate and losing war against the Romans that lasted from 66 to 73 CE. The climactic battle of this war was fought in the year 70, when the Roman legions under a general named Titus breached the defensive walls around Jerusalem and proceeded not only to conquer but also to lay waste to the city, even destroying the sacred temple. When the war ended, there followed a period of intense hostility toward the Jews on the part of the Romans. This negativity was directed particularly against the Jerusalem religious leadership, the chief priests and the temple hierarchy, who were held by the Romans to be responsible for starting the war. It was in this context that Mark's gospel was written. He was deeply aware of the tragedy that had befallen both the Jewish nation in general and the Jews in Jerusalem in particular. This is true even though Mark does not appear to have been a resident in that city at the time.

Mark introduced two things into his narrative that in the next decade were included by both Matthew and Luke, serving to cement them deeply into Christian consciousness. First, he located the story of Jesus' crucifixion in the season of the Jewish observance of Passover.

That allowed Passover connections to shape the crucifixion narrative, which they have obviously done. Second, he sought to elucidate Paul's assertion that the death of Jesus was "in accordance with the scriptures," by using the scriptures of the Hebrew tradition to fill in the details in the narrative that purported to describe just how it was that Jesus died. The traditionally unasked questions that need to be faced in this inquiry in order to drive it as far as possible are these: Is this narrative of the cross composed of the remembered history of eyewitness observers, or is it a liturgical drama, created well after the fact and designed not to describe actual events but rather to help worshippers understand who Jesus was and why his death had a special meaning? To put it slightly differently, but more boldly: How many of the details of Jesus' crucifixion really happened? Are the details of his death grounded in tradition and interpretation rather than in fact, as are the details of his birth, the number and identity of his disciples and the historicity of the miracle stories? By and large these are issues that institutional Christianity has never raised. I do not plan to dodge them in this quest for the truth about Jesus.

When Mark put quill to scroll to create the first gospel in Christian history, he weighted his story heavily toward the final events in Jesus' life. The cross was clearly the focus of his account. Only eight verses of this gospel, for example, were dedicated to Mark's version of Easter, while over a hundred describe the final twenty-four hours of Jesus' life. Beyond that, just over a third of this gospel addresses the events of the final week of Jesus' life. Mark's gospel has been described as the story of the crucifixion with a long preface. It is very clear from a study of this gospel text where the emphasis is to be placed when seeking to embrace Mark's understanding of the meaning of Jesus. The death of Jesus was the central reality.

The next thing that literally leaps out at the reader is that the crucifixion is not only placed into the context of the Passover, but (as I will show below) it is made to parallel the story of the Jewish people's exodus from Egypt, of which the Passover was the liturgical expression. As these things enter our consciousness, the whole central narrative of our faith story begins to feel as if it is more interpretive than historical. Consider for a moment the following connections. Both the crucifixion and the exodus were the founding moments in the stories of these two communities of faith, the Christians and the Jews. Both were designed to convey the idea of deliverance from bondage. In the exodus story it was deliverance from the bondage of slavery in Egypt, while in the crucifixion story it was deliverance from "the bondage of sin." Both accounts portrayed that deliverance as a journey from death to life. In the exodus story the death was a symbolic drowning in the waters of the Red Sea followed by a divine rescue, as God parted the waters to open the possibility of new life in a Promised Land. In the crucifixion story it was death on a cross, which was transformed by the promise of the new life of resurrection in the eternal Promised Land of the kingdom of God, of which Jesus was the first illustration. Both narratives enjoined upon future generations the demand to remember this founding moment by reenacting it liturgically inside the faith community that this event in history brought into being. In the exodus story the Jews were told, "This day shall be for you a memorial day, and you shall keep it as a feast to the Lord; throughout your generations you shall observe it as an ordinance forever" (Exod. 12:14). Paul had Jesus say in his version of the Last Supper that they were to reenact this meal "in remembrance of me" (1 Cor. 11:24). Finally, both the story of the exodus and the story of the crucifixion focused on the death of one who was called the "lamb of God." In the exodus story it was the unblemished young male lamb from the Jews' flocks. In the passion story it was the unblemished young male representative of his people, who would be called by John the Baptist in John's gospel the "lamb of God" (1:36). In both deaths it was said that the shed blood of the liturgical lamb was the symbol that broke the power of death so that the lamb became the "agent of life." We should certainly become quite suspicious of the historicity of the story of the crucifixion when we find that these clearly shaped ideas that purport to describe the death of Jesus are in fact based upon the liturgical observance of the earlier Jewish faith story.

Our suspicions increase when we look at the words that Mark used when he wrote the first narrative account of the death of Jesus and when we discover that it is organized in a twenty-four-hour cycle, neatly divided into eight three-hour segments. That makes the story of the crucifixion begin to look less and less like history and more and more like liturgy. The Passover of the Jews was normally a three-hour ritual that revolved around a common meal. In the Christian story of the cross it appears that the three-hour liturgy of the Jews has been stretched by the followers of Jesus into a twenty-four-hour observance that also revolved around a common meal.

When Mark originally composed his story of the cross, he noted that it began "when it was evening" (14:17). In this ancient world, living without electricity, that would mean when the sun went down, or approximately 6:00 p.m. Mark, as a Jew, knew that the normal duration of the Passover meal was three hours and that it was concluded with the singing of a hymn. So at the end of his first segment he notes right on cue, "And when they had sung a hymn, they went out to the Mount of Olives" (14:26). It is obviously now about 9:00 p.m. The Passover meal was complete, and it had been reinterpreted as symbolic of Jesus' broken body and the blood of a new covenant "which is poured out for many" (14:22–25). Jesus was about to become, in his death, the new paschal lamb.

Mark then has Jesus and the disciple band go to the Garden of Gethsemane, where, we are told, his closest disciples, Peter, James and John, are not able to remain awake. "Could you not watch one hour?" (14:37), Jesus asked. The process was repeated two more times. The disciples could not watch one, two or three hours. Mark's sense of liturgy is exquisite! It was now 12:00 midnight, and the second phase of the twenty-four-hour liturgical drama is complete.

The act of betrayal comes next, described quite poignantly as occurring at the stroke of midnight, so that the event that this author viewed as the darkest deed in human history could occur at the darkest moment of the night. Mark then described the arrest, noting that at this moment "*all* [not *some* but *all*, referring to Jesus' disciples] forsook him, and fled" (14:50). Jesus would face this final ordeal quite alone. Next, Jesus is led away for a trial before the high priest of the Jews, the other senior priests and the elders. The evidence they need to accomplish his inevitable death is extracted. "Are you the Christ, the Son of the Blessed?" Jesus is asked. Jesus answers, "I am; and you will see the Son of man sitting at the right hand of Power, and coming with the clouds of heaven" (14:61–62). This governing body then judges him, on the basis of his messianic claim, to be worthy of death. It is now 3:00 a.m. Before proceeding, we need to note here that it was the tradition of the Jews, in compliance with the Torah, not to sit in judgment except in the light of day. This is another hint that we are not dealing with historical memory.

In that society the watch of the night between 3:00 and 6:00 a.m. was called cockcrow. Into this time slot in his drama, Mark now inserts the story of Peter's threefold denial of Jesus (14:66–72). Presumably Mark understood Peter's behavior to be another act of apostolic unfaithfulness. Peter, James and John have shown that they could not watch one, two or three hours. Now Peter, the apostolic leader (who, to indicate his loyalty, is portrayed as following the arrested Jesus into the courtyard of the high priest), enacts the final sign of apostolic abandonment, denying Jesus, we are told, three times—once each hour until the cock crows, marking the end of that phase of the night. That would make it 6:00 a.m.

As if primed to assert that the pattern of eight segments of a twenty-four-hour vigil is exactly on target, Mark announces that the action continued "as soon as it was morning" (15:1)—that is, at the dawn of a new day, or 6:00 a.m. The condemned Jesus is led by the chief priests, scribes and elders to Pontius Pilate, the head of the Roman government. Here, Mark suggests, the Roman part of Jesus' trial occurs. It involves a form of plea-bargaining. Pilate is portrayed as seeking a way out. He says, in effect, "I find no fault in him. How about Barabbas?" Nothing works. The death of Jesus is inevitable. The crowd, we are told, is out for the blood of this one man, Jesus. We listen to their cries, angry cries, calling for his death. Then in rapid succession we are told of the predeath torture, the mocking and the scourging. Jesus is dressed in a purple cloak like a king, a crown of thorns is placed on his head and a broken reed is placed in his hands, as if a scepter of power. Then, the cruel games over, Mark says that "they led him out to crucify him" (15:20).

Even in the midst of the journey to the cross Mark does not fail to remind his readers once again that this drama has been shaped liturgically, for he announces, "It was the third hour," or 9:00 a.m., "when they crucified him" (Mark 15:25). He gives us only a few details about the actual crucifixion. The cross, says Mark, is first carried to Calvary by one named Simon of Cyrene. Wine mingled with myrrh is offered to Jesus before his crucifixion and that of the two robbers. The passing crowd derides Jesus; the chief priests mock him. The two robbers in Mark are only silent observers.

Then, says Mark, "the sixth hour had come" (15:33)—that is, it was now 12:00 noon—and at that moment, as if on cue, darkness covered the whole earth. It was the apocalyptic darkness such as that which was expected to accompany the end of the world. How long did it last? For three hours, Mark states, in order to carry the drama to 3:00 p.m., at which time Jesus utters the words known as the cry of dereliction: "My God, my God, why hast thou forsaken me?" (15:34). This cry, we are told, was mistaken by the crowd to be a call for Elijah to come. We once again meet this gigantic figure in Jewish thinking, Elijah, who is yet another apocalyptic symbol.[1] Jesus then "uttered a loud cry," the content of which Mark does not describe, "and breathed his last" (15:37). At that dramatic moment Mark inserts two additional powerful messianic symbols into the story. The veil in the temple that separates the Holy Place, in which people could gather, from the Holy of Holies, God's very dwelling place (from which the people were prohibited), was torn from top to bottom (15:38), signifying that access to God had been opened in a new way. Next a Gentile, a Roman centurion, interpreted the drama by identifying the deceased person as the "Son of God"—that is, one in whom God had been dramatically present (15:39).

The last watch in the disciples' vigil observance, the time from 3:00 to 6:00 p.m., had now arrived, to complete the twenty-four-hour observance. In that time slot Mark puts the burial of Jesus. The figure of Joseph of Arimathea, who asks Pilate for the body of Jesus, is introduced for the first time in Christian history. The tomb is readied. The body is wrapped in a linen shroud and placed inside the tomb, which is then sealed by rolling a stone against its door. All of this work is accomplished before the sun goes down. That brings us to 6:00 p.m. on Friday evening. The holy sabbath had arrived.

That long narrative in Mark's gospel represents the first dramatic telling of the story of Jesus' death. It is clearly presented in a liturgical format. Its twenty-four-hour structure is quite visible, with its eight three-hour segments appropriately announced. Its form makes it very obvious that when this drama was first described, it was not history but liturgy that was the driving force. How Jesus actually died was not being described. Instead, the death of Jesus was being interpreted. That becomes even clearer when we recognize that *none* of the actual words or details used to describe the crucifixion come from the memory of eyewitnesses. They come rather from the ancient words of the Hebrew scriptures, used almost verbatim. Mark, taking seriously Paul's assertion that Jesus died "in accordance with the scriptures" (1 Cor. 15:3), uses scripture to relate the central moment in the Jesus story. To that narrative we turn next.

10

THE CROSS:
TOLD "IN ACCORDANCE
WITH THE SCRIPTURES"

They [the disciples] all forsook him, and fled.
Mark 14:50

He died ... in accordance with the scriptures.
1 Cor. 15:3

The desertion of the disciples is surely one of the most certain historical memories of the early Christian movement. Not only was it counterintuitive, but it also constituted a negative recollection about the actions of people who, when the gospels were written, were regarded as larger-than-life heroes. A movement does not tend to introduce negative stories about its founders, but it is also unable to suppress a searing historical memory that is so vivid it is incapable of being forgotten. In that latter case, what usually happens is that an exonerating explanation is developed to temper the recollection.

That is exactly what one finds in Mark's original and thus primary narrative of the crucifixion, quoted above. Not only are the disciples portrayed in the surrounding text as having been unable to watch with Jesus, but all are said to have forsaken him and fled; and one of them, no less a person than the chief of the apostles, Simon Peter, actually denied that he had ever known Jesus. So bitter was this memory that an explanation exonerating the disciples was developed at a very early stage in the first gospel narrative. It was placed into the story of the cross to introduce the second three-hour segment of Mark's liturgical drama. As the disciples departed from the upper room for Gethsemane after concluding the Passover celebration with a hymn, Jesus said to them, "You will all fall away; for it is written, 'I will strike the shepherd, and the sheep will be scattered'" (14:27). The quotation is from Zechariah (13:7). What Jesus is made to say, according to Mark, is that the apostolic desertion was necessary, inevitable and even predicted by Jesus. Mark was saying that this desertion had to occur, that it was part of the divine plan. The disciples could have done nothing else. One does not provide so perfect a "divine justifying explanation" for something that never occurred. History was clearly present in this story. That desertion, however, forces upon us another realization—namely, that Jesus died alone. We need to embrace that reality no matter how uncomfortable it makes us feel. No one was there either to witness the death of Jesus or to record it.

We need next to realize what is surely a fact: that what we are reading in the earliest story of the crucifixion is not remembered history. Before we can fully articulate what it was, however, we need to take one further interpretive step into understanding what the gospel writers were looking to accomplish. Examining Mark's original passion narrative, we seek to identify the sources of that narrative, which has now become for us a set of very familiar details. If we can understand how its author originally crafted his narrative, then we will be able better to discern his purpose and intention, and by traveling this route seek to enter the experience that demanded his explanatory narrative. The clue that unlocks this quest is found, I believe, in the words of Paul in 1 Corinthians to which I have previously alluded. When Paul wrote his sparse account of the crucifixion, he asserted that the death of Jesus was "in accordance with the scriptures."

A careful study of the story of the crucifixion as Mark described it reveals a heavy dependence on two major passages from the Hebrew scriptures, which in turn serve as springboards to other passages that are used to fill out the details of the story of the cross. The major passages are Psalm 22 and Isaiah 53. To pull these two crucial sources into our consciousness and to trace how they triggered other recollections of additional texts to complete the story is therefore our next step in the interpretive process.

The most obvious clue that directs us to Psalm 22 is the cry of dereliction that Mark places onto the lips of Jesus as his only distinguishable words from the cross (15:34). Mark records the cry both in Aramaic and in Greek. It translates, "My God, my God, why hast thou forsaken me?" It is of interest to note that both Luke and John omit this cry from the cross, replacing it with words that seem much more confident and victorious. Mark, however, makes this cry the climax of his crucifixion drama. In this he is followed in an identical manner by Matthew. Expositors through the centuries have struggled with what this cry means, since it appears to run so counter to the image of Jesus as the invading deity that was to dominate theological formulas for the first five hundred years of Christian history. Whatever else they sought to make of this cry, they had to recognize that it is quoted directly from the first verse of Psalm 22. The entire psalm had, I suspect, been used to interpret this portrait of Jesus' death long before Mark's writing. The passion narrative has all the marks of a developing tradition and the influence of this psalm on shaping it is undeniable. Let me point out the rich connections.

Psalm 22 says, "All who see me mock at me, they make mouths at me, they wag their heads; 'He committed his cause to the Lord; let him deliver him, let him rescue him, for he delights in him'" (vv. 7–8). Compare this with Mark's words: "And those who passed by derided him, wagging their heads, and saying, 'Aha! You who would destroy the temple and build it in three days, save yourself, and come down from the cross!' So also the chief priests mocked him to one another with the scribes, saying, 'He saved others; he cannot save himself. Let the Christ, the King of Israel, come down now from the cross that we may see and believe'" (15:29–32). Matthew makes the connection with Psalm 22 even more explicit when he adds to Mark's statement the words, "He trusts in God; let God deliver him now, if he desires him" (Matt. 27:43).

Psalm 22 goes on to say, "I am poured out like water, and all my bones are out of joint; ... my strength is dried up like a potsherd, and my tongue cleaves to my jaws" (vv. 14–15). That is the passage that created both the crucified image of a dangling body held to the cross only by spikes and ropes and the sense of thirst that tormented the victim. Mark's account suggests that those near Jesus filled a sponge full of vinegar and put it on a reed to quench this thirst (15:36). John would later heighten this story by having Jesus say the words, "I thirst," before the sponge, filled with vinegar, was lifted to his lips. John added that this was done "to fulfill the scripture" (19:28–29). He was obviously referring to Psalm 22.

This psalm continues: "They have pierced my hands and my feet—I can count all my bones" (vv. 16–17). The image of crucifixion seemed obvious here to Mark. Once again John heightens this narrative about the bones of Jesus by demonstrating that Jesus' legs were not broken, so that once again the scriptures might be fulfilled (19:33). John also develops the "pierced" aspect of this story by suggesting that one of the soldiers, upon finding Jesus already dead, "pierced his side with a spear," expanding the narrative to include a reference from Psalm 34, "He keeps all his bones; not one of them is broken" (v. 20), and adding a note from Zechariah, "I will pour out on the house of David and the inhabitants of Jerusalem a spirit of compassion and supplication, so that, when they look on him whom they have pierced, they shall mourn for him, as one mourns for an only child, and weep bitterly over him, as one weeps over a first-born" (12:10).

Later in Psalm 22 we find these words: "They divide my garments among them and for my raiment they cast lots" (v. 18). Mark incorporates this verse almost verbatim when he writes, "And they crucified him and divided his garments among them casting lots for them, to decide what each should take" (v. 24). Once again John expands this storyline with more imaginative details: "When the soldiers had crucified Jesus they took his garments and made four parts, one for each soldier; also his tunic. But the tunic was without seam, woven from top to bottom, so they said to one another, 'Let us not tear it, but cast lots for it to see whose it shall be'" (John 19:23–24). Then John adds, "This was done to fulfill the scriptures" (v. 24b), and he proceeds to quote Psalm 22:18. The story is being told so that it conforms to this Hebrew psalm and to the scriptures that are clearly open before the writers. It is not the other way around.

With the dependence on Psalm 22 clearly established, we turn now to Isaiah 53. The earliest interpreters of Jesus leaned heavily on all of the "Servant Songs" of Second Isaiah, of which Isaiah 53 is a part. In the next section of this book, I will examine the whole of Second Isaiah (chapters 40–55, written by an unknown prophet and added to the text of Isaiah) much more fully; but for our purposes here, I will concentrate on that part of Second Isaiah that seems to have been crucial to the writers of the story of the cross and especially to Mark, who as the original creator of a passion narrative would be the shaping influence on all of the others.

Isaiah 53 describes the way the death of the "servant" affected the lives of others and this clearly laid the groundwork for the various theories of atonement that were developed to put flesh on Paul's words that "Christ died for our sins." "Surely he has borne our griefs and carried our sorrows; yet we esteemed him stricken, smitten by God and afflicted. But he was wounded for our transgressions, he was bruised for our inequities; upon him was the chastisement that made us whole, and with his stripes we are healed. All we like sheep have gone astray; we have turned every one to his own way; and the Lord has laid on him the iniquity of us all" (53:4–6).

Isaiah 53 then says, "He was oppressed, and he was afflicted, yet he opened not his mouth; like a lamb that is led to the slaughter, and like a sheep that before its shearers is dumb, so he opened not his mouth" (53:7). Mark incorporates this note into his story by writing, "And the high priest stood up in the midst, and asked Jesus, 'Have you no answer to make? What is it that these men testify against you?' But he [Jesus] was silent and made no answer" (Mark 14:60).

Isaiah 53 stated that the servant "made his grave with the wicked" (53:9), and later that he "was numbered with the transgressors" (53:12). Mark incorporates these notes into the narrative by saying, "And with him they crucified two robbers, one on his right and one on his left" (15:27). The two robbers say nothing in Mark; they are simply part of the scenery. They were, however, destined to grow. Matthew says of these robbers that they "also reviled [Jesus]" in the same way as the crowd (Matt. 27:44). Luke then turns one of them into a penitent thief so that Jesus can assure him of his intercession on that thief's behalf: "Today you will be with me in Paradise" (Luke 23:39–43). Luke's addition was in response to yet another line in Isaiah 53, where it is written that the servant "made intercession for the transgressors" (53:12). In a similar manner, to fulfill the same textual expectation, Luke alone has Jesus intercede for the soldiers: "Father, forgive them; for they know not what they do" (Luke 23:34).

Finally, Second Isaiah wrote that the "servant" was "with a rich man in his death" (53:9). This inspired, I am now quite convinced, the story of Joseph of Arimathea, who was described in Mark as a "respected member of the council" (15:43), and therefore a man of means, who provided the tomb for Jesus' burial. Matthew expands this story very specifically to identify Joseph with the text in Isaiah by introducing Joseph as "a rich man from Arimathea" (27:57).

When it suddenly becomes obvious that the story purporting to describe the crucifixion of Jesus has been built on narratives from the Hebrew scriptures, scholars must recognize that the passion story is not based on the eyewitness accounts of those who saw the crucifixion, and that the event therefore probably did not actually happen as described. The passion story is, rather, a highly stylized interpretive portrait designed to lead the person reading or hearing it into an understanding of who Jesus was. The story was written without eyewitnesses because there were no eyewitnesses! The story was crafted to identify Jesus with messianic images familiar to the readers of the Hebrew scriptures. As I sought to demonstrate in the previous chapter, the crucifixion account was designed for liturgical use. This means that anyone seeking to discover the meaning of Jesus today must be prepared to acknowledge that this story of the crucifixion is not history. While Jesus was undoubtedly crucified by the Romans, the familiar details that accompany the story of the cross are not literally true and did not actually happen. There was no actual dialogue ever recorded with the high priests, or with Pilate, or even with the crowd. There were no words of Jesus spoken from the cross that we know. There were no thieves crucified with him, penitent or otherwise. There was no tomb in which he was laid and no Joseph of Arimathea who presided over his burial. The disciples had fled when Jesus was arrested, so Jesus died alone. The familiar narratives which purport to describe how he died were designed to help people discern what his followers had come to believe about him—namely, that his death was not a tragedy without meaning, but the fulfillment of the scriptures and therefore an event of sacred and saving significance. That does not make the gospels' interpretation wrong, but it does mean that even the story of the cross is not a literal story. If there had been eyewitnesses, then surely the story would not have been created based on ancient Jewish texts!

Church leaders have always known about this linkage with Hebrew scriptures, but, unable to face its implications, they devised another explanation. They applied a magical interpretation to the Hebrew scriptures and began to suggest that God had led the authors of those scriptures, the prophets in particular, to a vision of the messiah who was to come. This vision supplied them with the exact words that Jesus would say (or would cause to be said by others) and predicted the deeds that Jesus would someday perform. This in turn, they agreed, would be the sign that would demonstrate for all to see that Jesus was the expected one.

It was an ingenious solution, so long as the world believed that God actually wrote the scriptures and could plant hidden clues within its sacred pages that would find fulfillment in a specific God-filled life hundreds of years later. Of course, this would also mean that this intervening God would have to micromanage the world in order to guard those scriptures from distortion or destruction as they journeyed through history. Their secret and hidden predictions would need to be protected from external forces. Those forces could be foreign enemies who might defeat the Jewish nation and, with that defeat, destroy the Jewish sacred writings, a fate that sooner or later appeared to be the destiny of the great majority of nations. Those external forces might also include natural disasters like floods that might destroy both an entire nation and its sacred artifacts. It also meant that this ever-invasive God would have to guide the hands of the scribes who preserved the sacred texts, so that in that period of hundreds of years in which these words were hand-copied, no mistakes would be made, no words would be added or omitted. This meant also that God had to make certain that when these writings were translated into Greek the original clues were in no way compromised. In short, this point of view required a supernatural heavenly guardian guiding those sacred prophetic texts through the centuries, lest their magical secrets be lost and the messiah go unrecognized.

This perspective, which requires a superstitious way of reading the scriptures, was ingenious but hardly credible or realistic. Yet it still prevails in fundamentalist circles. Matthew encouraged it more than most with his formula "This took place to fulfill what the Lord had spoken by the prophet" (1:22), a phrase he used in a variety of forms many times in his text. John repeats this formula again and again when he writes, "For these things took place that the scriptures might be fulfilled" (19:36). That is, however, not the way it occurred.

The earliest Christians, all of whom were Jews seeking to interpret the power they had found in the life of Jesus, feverishly explored the sacred writings of their people, searching for a way not only to understand what the sources of his power were, but also, and more importantly, to make sense out of the fact that the one in whom they believed they had experienced the meaning of God had actually been executed on a cross. As they processed this internal debate, they found consolation and affirmation in their sacred writings, so that these writings began to shape their memory of Jesus. They fitted his life into this emerging scriptural portrait. Far from Jesus fulfilling the expectations of the people of Israel for a messiah who was to come in some programmed way, they simply told the story of Jesus so that he fitted into this scriptural pattern. Of course, Jesus could be seen magically to have fulfilled the scriptures if the early Christians began with those scriptures and forced their memory of Jesus to fit those expectations. It was particularly easy to do this since there were no eyewitnesses. The Jesus story could be created out of scriptural whole cloth. Surely, he died "in accordance with the scriptures." I suspect that the story of his death was first composed homiletically—that is, by church leaders preaching on these texts in the synagogues—and then it was gradually transmuted into liturgical forms as Christians devised a worship tradition to expand and even to replace the Passover, a tradition in which this biblical reconstruction of the final events in Jesus' life would be repeated year after year as part of the liturgy of Holy Week.

The Jesus experience was real. However, the gospels' explanation of that experience, even the explanation of his death, was anything but remembered history. The story of Jesus' death was told in a manner similar to that of his birth: both were filled with mythical characters that fired the church's imagination and later altered the church's memory as these dramatic personae began to be thought of as real. Among these nonhistorical characters from the story of the cross were the thieves crucified with him, the crowd that taunted him and Joseph of Arimathea, who provided the tomb for his burial. Among the mythical words that Jesus was said to have spoken were the sayings from the cross, every one of them.

The reality is that Jesus was executed by the Romans. The reality is that the common method of execution by the Romans was crucifixion. The reality is that his death cried out for explanation because it countered everything that the disciples experienced about God through the life of this Jesus. Yet neither the way he died nor the events and the people who filled the story of the cross are historical. All are part of a magnificent interpretive portrait. Jesus had opened doors into the disciples' souls that cried out for understanding. They were caught between the transforming memory of his life and the chilling reality of his death. They lived in that valley of despair until they resolved this conflict. At some point something happened to them that transformed his death into another expression of his life-giving love. That is what enabled them to see his death as being a part of the fulfillment of God's plan. I will return to this conflict in my final chapters. For now I simply introduce these themes and let them begin to bubble!

We now turn to that moment of transformation and explore its dimensions. It is called Easter.

11

THE ETERNAL TRUTH INSIDE THE MYTHS OF RESURRECTION AND ASCENSION

To literalize Easter has become the defining heresy of traditional Protestant and Catholic Christianity. That transforming mystery has given way to propositional truths.

We come now to that crucial moment that made Christianity possible. We celebrate it at Easter. We call it resurrection. Was it real? If the resurrection is not real, then there appears to be nothing left to Christianity that is sufficient to elicit any interest. That is certainly what Paul appeared to believe when he wrote, "If Christ has not been raised,... we are of all people most to be pitied" (1 Cor. 15:17–19). Our quest to discover the Jesus of history now comes up against this final test. Here myth must be separated from reality and a decision made. The issue is usually posed by saying that either resurrection is real or Christianity was built on an illusion and will not endure. I do not believe it is quite so simple.

I understand the concern and even the anxiety that many feel when they reach this ultimate crossroad in our faith story, but we cannot avoid it. The question that needs to be addressed is, What is it to which we must say yes or no? In other words, What is resurrection? I can, with absolute honesty and with deep conviction, say that I believe the resurrection of Jesus was real. To support that assertion I can point to data that reveal in very objective ways that something of great and significant power happened following the crucifixion of Jesus, something that had dramatic and life-changing consequences. Those resulting changes are easy to document. That which caused the changes is not.

In an earlier context we noted what seems to be the absolutely historical fact that Jesus faced apostolic abandonment when he was arrested. We have documented the overwhelming probability that Jesus died alone. What we need to look at now is the equally real fact of history that after the crucifixion some experience of great magnitude brought Jesus' disciples back, empowered them and gave them the courage to take up the cause of this Jesus in the face of persecution and martyrdom. They never wavered. The strength of their conviction was such that no threat or fear could now separate them from the God they believed they had met in Jesus. When they began to give content to this transforming experience, the words they used were "Death cannot contain him," and "We have seen the Lord." Something must have accounted for this dramatic change in their lives.

Simultaneously, we can also document the fact that the way the disciples understood God was changed by whatever that Easter experience was. The heart of Judaism was voiced in the declaration of faith known as the Shema: "Hear, O Israel: the Lord your God is one." As affirmed in the Shema, a Jew must never bow his or her head to anything other than the holy God. After the death of Jesus, however, these same Jewish disciples had their understanding of God transformed to the place where they no longer saw Jesus apart from God. Jesus of Nazareth had become for them the human face of God.[1] The Jewish Thomas was made to say to the Jewish Jesus, "[You are] my Lord and my God" (John 20:28). Something had to account for this dramatic change.

A third new reality was born when whatever the resurrection experience was got identified with the first day of the week and gave birth to a new holy day. Within a single generation the Christian Sunday began to rival the Jewish sabbath for supremacy, even among the Jewish disciples of Jesus.

People do not change or even expand sacred traditions easily. For that reason, the fundamental changes named above, among other things, compel me to assert that whatever it was that the early Christians came to call Easter is real. Stirring shifts in consciousness, along with dramatic changes in character, theology and worship, gripped the followers of Jesus at some point following the crucifixion. These data cannot be dismissed as trivial, for they are in fact quite substantial and quite real. None of these data, however, tells us what happened—only that *something* happened.

What the Easter experience was is an altogether different question. When we go to the details of the resurrection as found in the gospels, we are confronted with a host of assertions that are contradictory, confusing and baffling. Most traditional believers have never faced these realities in their faith story. For example, it is a fact that it was the ninth decade of the Christian era before a single written source suggested that the dramatic changes I have described were actually caused by Jesus walking physically out of his tomb, as a resuscitated body ready to take up life again in this world. Paul does not say that. Mark has no story of a physical appearance of a risen Jesus. Matthew is ambivalent: of his two resurrection narratives, the first, involving the women at the tomb, appears to be physical, but the second, involving the disciples in Galilee, is more like a vision. Only when one gets to Luke and John, the last two canonical gospels to be composed (which take us to the late ninth and to the tenth decades), does the interpretation of Easter begin to involve stories of the physicality of the resurrected body of Jesus walking out of the tomb. In time, certainly from the second century on, when creeds began to take shape, this quite obviously late-developing tradition would literally overwhelm the earlier nonphysical tradition and begin to form the now common understanding of Easter.

The next thing that a serious student of the New Testament must embrace is that, even though these books have been called by the church "the word of God" and claims have been made for them through the ages as the source of ultimate authority, there is still substantial disagreement in these texts about almost every detail in this central moment of the origins of Christianity. Let me point out a few inconsistencies briefly. Was there a tomb in a garden where Jesus was buried? While the gospels make much of a tomb, Paul appears never to have heard of one (1 Cor. 15:1–11). The book of Acts seems to imply that Jesus was buried by the same people who killed him (Acts 13:29). We know from our study of this period of history that in conquered Judea an elaborate burial for the body of a convicted and executed felon (which is what Jesus was) was all but unknown. Normally, the victim would be placed into a shallow grave along with the other executed criminals of that day, covered over to prevent offensive odors, and soon forgotten. Wild dogs scavenging during the night feasted on the victims' bodies under cover of darkness, and whatever was left decomposed quickly in that climate.

Next the gospels tell us that a group of women went to the tomb on the first day of the week. Paul has no mention of this tradition. The gospels all do; however, they do not agree on exactly who the women were or what their number was. Mark has three women, Matthew two, Luke five or six and John only one. No gospel writer agrees with another on this minor detail. Did these women see the risen Lord on that first Easter morning? Mark says no; Matthew says yes; Luke says no; John says yes. The gospels also disagree on who the messenger was who announced the resurrection. It was a young man dressed in a white robe, says Mark (16:5). It was a supernatural angel who came out of the sky and who possessed sufficient supernatural power to put the guards to sleep and roll back the stone from the door of the sepulcher, says Matthew (28:2–4). It was "two men in dazzling apparel" and thus presumably angels, says Luke (24:4). When one comes to John, it is still two angels, but one of them seems to morph into Jesus himself (20:11–18).

The New Testament writers do not agree on who was the first witness to the resurrection. It was Cephas, says Paul (1 Cor. 15:5). Mark has no first witness, since he provides only the promise that the disciples will see Jesus when they return to Galilee. Matthew says the first ones to see the resurrected Jesus were the women in the garden (28:9). Luke says it was Cleopas and his traveling companion (24:13–35). John says it was Mary Magdalene (John 20:11–18). The gospels do not even agree on where the disciples were when the Easter experience broke in upon them: It will be in Galilee, says Mark (16:7). It was in Galilee on top of a mountain, says Matthew (28:16–20). It was never in Galilee, says Luke; it was only in Jerusalem or in the Jerusalem area (24:36, 49). It was in Jerusalem first and much later in Galilee, says John (20:1ff., 21:1).

The gospels do not agree on the order in which the experiences we now call resurrection, ascension and Pentecost actually happened. Resurrection and ascension were the same thing, says Paul (Rom. 1:1–4). Between Jesus' appearance to the women in the garden and the appearance of Jesus to the disciples on the mountaintop, Jesus entered a heavenly realm, says Matthew (28:16–20). It was a three-fold action over fifty days, with resurrection on Easter, ascension forty days later and Pentecost ten days after that, says Luke (Luke 24, Acts 1, 2). It was resurrection on Easter morn, ascension on Easter day following Jesus' appearance to Magdalene alone, and Pentecost on Easter evening, when Jesus "breathed on [the disciples]" and they received the Holy Spirit, says John (John 20:1, 17–23).

Suddenly we are forced into an awareness of the complexity that is present in understanding that revelatory moment which stands at the very center of Christianity itself. Embrace this reality consciously. First these are powerful data, which scream that something of great significance happened after the crucifixion of Jesus that had the capacity to transform the disciples from fleeing cowards into unflinching persons of enormous strength, to change the way they conceptualized God and to give birth to a new holy day. Second, there is the undisputed fact that almost every detail that became part of the disciples' explanation was in conflict and in disagreement with another account. Finally, it is an observable fact that the later the narrative, the more obviously supernatural and miraculous it becomes. These are the issues that we must address if we are to enter the confusion that surrounds the birth of Christianity.

I now begin this probe by the observation that what the disciples experienced in Jesus compelled them to go beyond the limits of their own humanity. Whatever Easter was, it called them beyond fear, as the heroic post-Easter behavior of the disciples reveals; it called them beyond tribal identity, as the story of the Holy Spirit giving them the ability to speak the language of their hearers makes clear (Acts 2); it called them beyond the limits of their religion, as the creation of a new holy day proclaims, and it called them beyond their sense of their own mortality, as their resurrection language illustrates. So what these followers of Jesus did was exactly what the Jews did in the revelatory moment of the exodus: they began to express their experience through liturgy. The content of the resurrection narratives in the gospels, like the content of the crucifixion story, has a liturgical form about it.

Indications that the explanations of Easter are being conveyed by the language form of a worship setting are plentiful in the gospels. The Jewish Passover with its common meal is a liturgical reenactment of Jewish origins, and it is also the context in which the gospel writers assert that the resurrection is first known. This resurrection is observed on the new liturgical holy day of the Christian movement, the first day of the week. Its content reflects time and again the liturgical language of its eucharistic context—for example, Luke notes that Cleopas and the other man on the road to Emmaus reported that "[Jesus] was made known to them in the breaking of the bread" (Luke 24:35). Finally, it is couched in the language of a return to one's roots, one's homeland: "He is going before you to Galilee; there you will see him" (Mark 16:7). Matthew fills in the details: the disciples went to Galilee, "and when they saw him they worshipped him" (Matt. 28:17). None of this means that the transforming experience we call Easter was not real. It does mean that it was like an ecstatic moment breaking in upon their consciousness from another realm, another reality before which they were awestruck and to which they could respond only with worship. As noted earlier, the followers of Jesus had no God language through which to talk about this profound God experience, so they reverted to the best thing that they did have, which was the language of liturgy, in which human beings believe themselves to be united in spirit with whatever they think God is. Any attempt to literalize this liturgical language of worship is to miss completely the meaning of the resurrection experience.

The resurrection language of the gospels is literal nonsense. Earthquakes do not announce earthly events. Angels do not invade time, space and history to roll back a stone, to make a historic resurrection announcement. A resuscitated Jesus does not walk out of his tomb in some physical form that can eat, drink, walk, talk, teach and expound on scriptures. This "raised" bodily person does not appear and disappear at will, walk through walls, or invite the doubters to feel his wounds. He cannot be the agent who accomplished the miraculous catch of fish on the Sea of Galilee, or the one who departed from the disciples by defying gravity and rising up into the sky of a three-tiered universe. All of these things are interpretive tales employed in the process of human explanation in which a life-changing inner experience was enabled to be communicated in the language of history by the use of external symbols. That is what liturgy is.

We need to trace the Easter story developmentally. It was first, above all else, an ecstatic experience. Second, that ecstatic experience became the subject of exclamation, an ecstatic cry without details. Only in the third stage does the exclamation get turned into an explanatory narrative. In the Easter moment the ecstatic experience was the dawning realization that death could not bind the God presence the disciples had met in Jesus of Nazareth. The ejaculatory exclamation was, "Death no longer has dominion over him" (Rom. 6:9)—that is, death cannot contain him. The explanation then evolved into the narrative of an empty tomb, a grave and grave clothes, all symbols of death that were unable to contain or to bind Jesus.

One should note that the later stories of Easter were all developed from Mark's original narrative, in which no one sees the risen Christ. In Mark's gospel the women followers simply stare into a tomb that has not been able to contain him. By the time we get to John's account, some thirty years later, Thomas seeks to feel the nail prints. That is quite a journey.

"Death cannot contain him" is finally a negative claim. There is also a positive exclamation, however. The positive claim is that the disciples' eyes have been opened so that they can say, "I have seen the Lord." It is the explanatory side of this positive explanation that finally produces accounts of sightings of Jesus. To see him "raised," however, does not necessarily mean to feel his flesh; it means to embrace his meaning.

Paul, writing to the Corinthians in the midfifties, provides us with not a single descriptive detail; he says only that "Christ was raised" (1 Cor. 15:4). Mark, likewise, never describes an appearance of the risen Jesus. Matthew says he appeared out of heaven. Luke says he was known in the breaking of bread. John says Jesus forbade Mary to touch him because he had not yet ascended to his Father. All of these episodes are filled with the language of a revelatory encounter; they describe a different kind of seeing. It is more like the seeing of insight, or second sight. It is not the language of physical sight and literal history.

The resurrection was not and is not a photographical phenomenon. Yet the words "We have seen the Lord" finally, and I suspect inevitably, give way to graphic explanations that portray Jesus as still inside the only realm of existence in which human language can work, because we have no other way to use the words of our own creation.

The fact that "the third day" came to be thought of as the day of the resurrection, or Easter, is one more sign that the context for the earliest interpretation of Jesus was liturgical, not literal. Three days in the Bible means a short time, just as forty days in the Bible means a longer time. That is, it is a reference not to a specific time, but to an imprecise measure of time. Three days is used in a variety of nonliteral ways, as a quick look at a biblical concordance will reveal. Even more telling is the way this three-day symbol dances around in the gospel story. Was it "after" three days, as Mark has Jesus predict on three different occasions (8:31, 9:31, 10:34)? Or was it "on the third day," as Matthew and Luke assert, deliberately editing Mark's numbering system in their gospel accounts (Matt. 16:21, 17:23, 20:19, Luke 9:22, 18:33)? That is not the only variable. Matthew later has Jesus refer to the "three days and three nights" that he would be in the midst of the earth, emulating the time that Jonah was in the belly of the whale (Matt. 12:40). Adding additional confusion to this time factor, Mark says that Jesus will meet his disciples in Galilee, and Matthew says that that promise was fulfilled. If the resurrected Jesus was seen in Galilee, such a literal sighting could not possibly have occurred either on or after three days, because Galilee would have been a seven- to ten-day journey from Jerusalem in those days. Luke, writing in the book of Acts, stretches the appearances of Jesus over the familiar forty-day time span, culminating his narrative with the story of Jesus' ascension (Acts 1). When John adds the appendix to his gospel (chapter 21) to provide an account of a Galilean resurrection appearance, his text reveals that a long period of time has elapsed since the first Easter Sunday. This means that John is suggesting that resurrection appearances continued for quite a while, perhaps even months, before finally coming to an end.

What makes the power of the three-day symbol even more intriguing is that it serves to locate the founding moment of the Christian story on the same day that the faith community gathered to reenact the liturgy of its origins. What the Passover did for the exodus in interpreting the beginning of Judaism in the Red Sea, the Eucharist did for Christians in the description of their origins in the moment of resurrection. It should also be noted that Paul had earlier written that this eucharistic action, derived from the Last Supper, was the clue to understanding or interpreting the meaning of Jesus' death: "For as often as you eat this bread and drink the cup, you proclaim the Lord's death until he comes" (1 Cor. 11:26). The Christian Eucharist and the resurrection both became signs of the coming of the kingdom of God. Mark makes that theme obvious when at the Last Supper he has Jesus say, "I shall not drink again of the fruit of the vine until that day when I drink it new in the kingdom of God" (Mark 14:25). That was clearly a messianic claim. Matthew repeats Mark's words almost verbatim. Luke suggests that this meal is the clue to an understanding of Jesus' suffering. In the Passover, the Jews had to endure the symbolic death in the Red Sea in order to arrive in the Promised Land. The church made Jesus' death a symbolic death for all people and his resurrection was the sign of being born again to the new life of the spirit. Similar themes were wrapped around the church's initiation rite of baptism. John omits the Last Supper from his gospel altogether, but he transforms the appearance of Jesus to Peter and the disciples by the sea in Galilee into a Eucharist. In this narrative, however, John has Jesus only "take" and "give" the bread (John 21:13), whereas in earlier accounts of the eucharistic meal all of the eucharistic verbs—"take," "bless," "break" and "give"—are recorded. John has in the body of the gospel identified Jesus already as the bread of life, which means that because his body was blessed and broken on the cross, those actions need not be repeated literally when Jesus eats with his disciples by the lake in Galilee. The fact is, however, that everywhere one turns in the resurrection narratives of the New Testament, one finds the language of liturgy, of ecstasy, of transcendent breakthrough. It is not the language of time, space and history. It is not to be literalized and bound by our human limits any more than the Jesus about whom this language was originally used can be bound by human limits and especially by the limits of mortality.

Over history the resurrection stories of the various gospels have flowed together in the common mind until their differences have become totally blurred and their content blended into a kind of harmony that a careful reading of these texts will not sustain. I have tried to separate them, but in order to make the story complete I need to point to a uniquely Lucan narrative which many people confuse with the resurrection. I refer to the story of Jesus' ascension into heaven. Why Luke needed to develop the ascension story is itself noteworthy. More than any writer before him, Luke transformed the resurrection into a physical, literal account of a resuscitated body. When Luke has Jesus appear to the disciples for the first time, they think they are seeing a ghost. To counter this nonphysical interpretation, Luke has Jesus invite them to touch his hands and feet. Ghosts or spirits do not have flesh and bones, he argues. It is a very physical claim. Then this risen, non-ghostlike Jesus asks for food. He is provided with a piece of broiled fish, which he eats, thus demonstrating that his gastrointestinal system is working fully. Then he does for them what he had previously done for Cleopas in Luke's first resurrection narrative—he "open[s] their minds to understand the scriptures" and provides the disciples with their missionary marching orders: "Repentance and forgiveness of sins should be preached ... to all nations, beginning from Jerusalem." He then commands the disciples to stay in the city until they are "clothed with power from on high" (24:44–50). Only then does Jesus part from them (v. 51).

Where did Jesus go at that point? Luke had portrayed him as physically resuscitated back into the life of this world, as we just saw. That presented Luke with a problem, since normally the only way to get out of this world is to die. Jesus had tried that; but if resurrection means, as it appears to Luke to mean, physical resuscitation back into the life of this world, then death did not provide him with an exit. This necessitated the development by Luke of a different exit strategy for Jesus. That is exactly what he provides in the opening chapter of the book of Acts: Luke has Jesus rise into the sky, with two men dressed in white robes interpreting his departure and predicting his second coming. His disciples, plus the women and the mother of Jesus and even his brothers, then return to an upper room to await the empowerment that was to come at Pentecost.

Clearly the story of the ascension is not history. When one rises into the sky, one does not get to heaven. One either goes into orbit or escapes the gravitational pull of the earth and drifts into the infinity of space.

When we search for Hebrew antecedents of the story of Jesus' ascension, our attention is drawn once again to the familiar cycle of Elijah-Elisha stories. Elijah also ascended into heaven. Elijah also bestowed his spirit on his successor disciple. A careful reading of that story reveals that Luke simply magnified Elijah's ascension to create his story of Jesus' ascension (2 Kings 2).

Elijah needed the help of a fiery chariot drawn by magical fiery horses to propel him heavenward. He was also assisted by a God-sent whirlwind to provide additional thrust into the sky. Jesus, the new Elijah, ascends on his own. Elijah poured out a double portion of his enormous but still human spirit on his single disciple, Elisha. Jesus poured out the power of God's Holy Spirit on the gathered Christian community in sufficient measure to last through all the centuries. Luke takes the fire from Elijah's horse-drawn chariot and turns it into the tongues of fire that dance on the heads of the disciples without burning them and he takes the propelling whirlwind from the Elijah story and turns it into the "mighty rushing wind" that filled the upper room.

We are not reading history; we are watching the gospel writer paint a portrait drawn from the Hebrew scriptures, designed to present the Jesus experience as an invitation into oneness with God; and in that portrait he uses the only language he has available, the magnificent language of his religious tradition.

We need to embrace the fact that even at the central moment in the Christian story, there was originally something moving and profound, something which transformed life, but it was something that human words could not fully embrace. To literalize Easter, both the story of the resurrection and the story of the ascension, has become the defining heresy of traditional Protestant and Catholic Christianity. That transforming mystery has given way to propositional truths that no twenty-first-century mind can still embrace.

The Jesus story, including the narrative of the resurrection, is an invitation to journey beyond human limits, beyond human boundaries, into the realm of that experience we call God, who is not above the sky, but rather is found in the depths of life. To enter the Christian story we must have our eyes opened to see things beyond the limits of sight, and our ears unstopped to hear music beyond the human range of sound. Our tongues then become loosed so that we can utter the sounds of ecstasy and life itself becomes opened until it is no longer bounded by death. That is the journey which the Christian faith bids us begin. So we hear Jesus' invitation, "Come to me, all who labor and are heavy laden, and I will give you rest" (Matt. 11:38), and we listen to Jesus' promise, "I have come that they may have life and have it abundantly" (John 10:10).

The first stage of our faith journey, the clearing out of distortions in the way we view the Jesus story, is now complete. The literalness of centuries of misinterpretation of the Jesus story has been broken open. The pieces lie before us in frightening array. Jesus was born in a perfectly normal way in Nazareth. His mother was not the icon of virgin purity. His earthly father, Joseph, was a literary creation. His family thought he was out of his mind. He probably did not have twelve male disciples. He had disciples who were both male and female. He did not command nature to obey him. He did not in any literal sense give sight to the blind, hearing to the deaf or wholeness to the paralyzed and infirm. He did not raise the dead. There was no stylized Last Supper in which bread was identified with his broken body and wine with his poured-out shed blood designed to symbolize his final prediction of death. There was no betrayal and no romance connected with his death, no mocking crowd, no crown of thorns, no words from the cross, no thieves, no cry of thirst and no darkness at noon. There was no tomb, no Joseph of Arimathea, no earthquake, no angel who rolled back the stone. There was no resuscitated body that emerged from that tomb on the third day, no touching of the wounds of Jesus, no opening by him of the secrets of scripture. Finally, there was no ascension into a heaven that exists above the sky.

All of these narrative details were the creation of a community of people who individually and corporately had an experience that they believed was of God in the human life of one Jesus of Nazareth. Their way of explaining their experience has now run its course. It makes assumptions we cannot make. It uses categories of thought we cannot use. The traditional explanation of the Jesus experience is dying. For many, it is already dead. Traditional Christians have committed the fatal error of identifying the truth of the Jesus experience with the literalness of their explanations of that experience. That never works. Every explanation dies when its time dies. The death of the explanation, however, does not mean the death of the experience. Our task is to separate the eternal experience from the time-bound and time-warped explanations. To that task we now turn. It will take us behind, perhaps underneath, the biblical story to a place where traditional Christians have been loath to go. There is no alternative. The journey must continue until we see a new light that ignites a future hope.

Part 2

THE ORIGINAL IMAGES OF JESUS

INTRODUCTION: EXPLORING THE ORIGINAL IMAGES OF JESUS

I seek a Jesus beyond scripture, beyond creeds, beyond doctrines, beyond dogmas and even beyond religion itself. Only there will our gaze turn toward the mystery of God, the mystery of life, the mystery of love and the mystery of being.

There are some who are so attached to the traditional religious formulas of the past that, when they discover that these formulas are no longer working and indeed are no longer believable, they want nothing more to do with what has become for them disillusioning Christianity. I am not one of those people. I see the decline and death of yesterday's religious understandings as an opportunity to grow, to step into a new consciousness, to explore new ways to talk about the experience of God. I find an exhilarating freedom in the recognition that the virgin birth is not about biology, the miracles of the New Testament are not about supernatural intervention, the resurrection is not about physical resuscitation and belief in the "divinity of Jesus" cannot be identified with the invasion by an external deity into human existence. I am pleased to discover that theism is not about who God is any more than atheism is a denial of who God is. I am elated to discern that theism is nothing more than a human definition of God and that atheism is simply the denial of that human definition. I do not believe that God is served by a defensive clinging to the time-warped explanations of the past. My conviction is that the setting aside of the literal understandings of yesterday offers an amazing opportunity to explore the Christ story today and I am eager to be about that task.

It is because I care so deeply about reviving the ultimate truth and reality I find in Christianity that I invite my readers to have the courage to let their dated explanations go, in order to commence a new journey into the heart of the Christian story. My promise to you is that there is much more to be learned on such a journey than you have yet imagined.

Attempts to reform the way modern men and women understand the Christ story have been initiated inside Christianity before, but fear has thus far always beaten them back. Then more rigid defenses have developed around the old symbols with the hope that these new ecclesiastical Maginot lines would protect us from harm for at least a few more years. Sadly, they too have turned out to be illusory.

On the Roman Catholic side of church history there was in the mid-twentieth century one brief and beautiful attempt to escape the ghetto of traditional thinking and to engage the real world. It occurred during the papacy of John XXIII (1958–63). Sensing the magnitude of the issues confronting his increasingly irrelevant church, Pope John convened the Second Vatican Council (also called Vatican II) and allowed yesterday's faith understanding to interact with today's learning. The result was salutary. The winds of change and reform began to blow through the cobwebs of this ancient institution. It was a glorious and hopeful moment. It did not last, however. As soon as Catholicism's traditional and badly dated understandings began to be challenged publicly, fear grew among the faithful until it was rampant. Threatened institutional leaders began to feel the loss of their power, and "defenders of the faith" rose in a mighty chorus to beat down this potentially life-expanding reform effort.

With the death of John XXIII the movement collapsed. Every pope since John XXIII has been dedicated to battening down the hatches of antiquity and to reasserting traditional authority. One has only to trace the successive occupants of that papal office to see this precipitous retreat from reality. After John XXIII, the Catholic Church installed Paul VI, who halted all theological initiatives and reversed all progress on family planning. Next they chose John Paul I, who lasted only a few months. Then John Paul II took the throne of the Vatican and began systematically to oppress all creative thought in the Catholic community. Finally the mantle fell on Benedict XVI, who had been John Paul II's chief enforcer of orthodoxy. Indeed, it was this present pope, the former Joseph Cardinal Ratzinger, who was the power behind the destruction of that band of Catholic scholars who had helped to make the Second Vatican Council possible in the first place. Under his direction, eminent Catholic thinkers like Hans Küng, Edward Schillebeeckx, Charles Curran, Leonardo Boff and Matthew Fox were removed from teaching posts, harassed, laicized or silenced. A whole generation of scholars was muted when its leading thinkers and creative scholars were attacked, with the result that today Roman Catholic scholarship has all but disappeared from the priestly ranks. That church's leadership has made the critical mistake of identifying its explanations of truth with truth itself and of seeking to deny the relativity of all propositional statements. The idea that the ultimate truth of God can be reduced to creedal or doctrinal formulas is both ludicrous and spiritually suicidal. The result of this is that Catholic Christianity is tragically more irrelevant to the world today than it has ever been before.

On the Protestant side of Christianity a similar movement of reform occurred during the same time frame. An English bishop named John Arthur Thomas Robinson posed the issues facing Protestant Christianity powerfully in a popular book entitled *Honest to God*, which was published in 1963.[1] Translated into almost every language of the world, this small book calling on Christians to rethink their image of both God and Christ sold millions of copies. Robinson was joined in his reformation efforts by James Pike[2] and a group of fellow American scholars who called themselves "the death of God" theologians: William Hamilton, Thomas J. J. Altizer and Paul Van Buren. They had soul mates in other places—among them, John Hick and Don Cupitt in the United Kingdom, and Lloyd Geering in New Zealand.[3] It was a feisty, promising time during which Christianity was debated in the public media and even featured in cover stories in *Time* magazine. Alas, however, this movement ultimately amounted to little more than an expression of hidden hope, because the frightened Christian institutions of Protestantism struck back as Catholicism had done. Robinson and Cupitt were marginalized in England. Hick was threatened by his judicatory. Pike was tied up like a modern-day Gulliver. The American scholars were caricatured by an audience made up of defensive traditionalists on one side and those members of the increasingly secular society who cared very little about anything religious on the other. In New Zealand the Presbyterian Church put Lloyd Geering on trial for heresy and almost committed institutional suicide in the process. Like Vatican II, this movement was soon little more than a footnote of history. Repressed thought doesn't disappear, however; it simply goes underground and waits for a more propitious time to reappear.

Will my new efforts in this direction fare any better? I wish I could answer that, but only time will tell. I know only that I can keep silent no longer. The secular society has grown dramatically since the 1960s. Today the religious community, both Catholic and Protestant, has become more out of touch, more traditional, more aggressively defensive and even more hysterical in its stance. My sense is that neither Vatican II nor the radical Protestant theologians went nearly far enough to reach their goals. Unable to escape their criticism of what Christianity had become, they never got around to spelling out what Christianity might evolve into being. My hope is to move to that place where they were not able to go. I am too deeply drawn to the mystery of God not to do so.

So, in Part 2 of this book, I seek to reveal the roadmap that I hope can now be followed into Christianity's future. My first task is to open the door on what is called the oral period of Christian history, that time before any memories or words of Jesus were written down, to search for clues that will illumine that primary Christ experience and help us in our quest today. This journey will inevitably take us very deeply into the Jewish world out of which Jesus emerged. It will carry us into a knowledge of Jewish scriptures, Jewish liturgies and Jewish expectations. It will lay bare what Gentile misunderstandings of Jewish concepts have done to the Jesus story.

To see Jesus in his original Jewish context is not, however, our ultimate goal. There can be no stopping there. It is but another important step on our timeless quest. That quest must finally go deeply into our own humanity, where perhaps we can see Jesus apart from religion or, as I have entitled this journey, where we can see a "Jesus for the Non-Religious." I seek a Jesus beyond scripture, beyond creeds, beyond doctrines, beyond dogmas and even beyond religion itself. Only there will our gaze turn toward the mystery of God, the mystery of life, the mystery of love and the mystery of being. We will also and inevitably turn in this process toward the mystery of our own humanity, the mystery of self-consciousness and the mystery of transcendence; in that endeavor we will feel ourselves being pushed deeply toward that eternal human quest for wholeness. For even Jesus, I submit, is not an end in himself, as Christians have so mistakenly assumed. Jesus is but a doorway into the wonder of God. The first followers of Jesus were not called Christians, as if knowing Christ was their goal; rather, they called themselves "the followers of the way,"[4] as if Jesus was himself but part of their journey. The Christ path was a path toward wholeness, a journey into that which is ultimately real and for which no words have yet been devised. All religion must ultimately flow into this same mystical reality. Jesus is not the end of that journey, but a means toward that end.

We start in the Jewish world that produced Jesus of Nazareth.

13

THE ORAL TRADITION: WHERE WAS JESUS REMEMBERED?

The life of Jesus and the message of Jesus are located in the memory of the gospel writers time after time in the center of Jewish worship. Long before the Jesus story came to be written in the gospels, it had already been interpreted through the Jewish scriptures.

There are people who think that prior to the writing of the gospels the memory of Jesus was passed on in what is called the oral period in a personal, desultory way—that is, by parents relating Jesus stories to their children or people discussing Jesus with their neighbors over the back fence or in the marketplace. Nothing could be further from the truth. An analysis of the gospels themselves makes that obvious.

When Mark wrote the first gospel in the early seventies, he opened his narrative with the words "the beginning of the good news [or gospel] of Jesus Christ" (1:1, NRSV). That single verse is packed with references to the Jewish Bible. The phrase "good news" is lifted out of Second Isaiah, who used it in three different places (40:9, 52:7, 61:1). Mark employs this key phrase once more a few verses later, when he has Jesus himself speak it (1:14–15). Mark then moves immediately to relate this "good news" to the sources on which he was surely leaning. They are all found in the Hebrew scriptures. "As it is written in the prophet Isaiah" (1:2a, NRSV), he says, quoting his source quite literally. Actually, in this passage Mark conflates two prophetic announcements, though he credits only Isaiah. His first words, "See, I am sending my messenger ahead of you" (v. 2b, NRSV), come from the book of Malachi (3:1), with echoes from Exodus (23:20). Only then does he add the words about "the voice of one crying out in the wilderness: 'Prepare the way of the Lord, make his paths straight'" (v. 3), which do come from Isaiah (40:3). Thus the very first verses of the first gospel are replete with several layers of reference material that point us to the Hebrew scriptures. This should be a hint that before the gospels ever came to be written, the Jesus story had already become deeply intertwined during the oral period with the sacred writings of the Jews.

Matthew, in writing the second gospel in Christian history, introduces his story of Jesus with a list of his Jewish antecedents, in which are included references to such obscure characters in the Jewish scriptures as Tamar, Rehab, Boaz and Uriah (Matt. 1:2–16). Only someone deeply aware of the sacred story of the Hebrews would understand the message Matthew was seeking to convey. Matthew later acts like a country preacher quoting proof texts as he develops his narrative. In his story of Jesus' birth he uses a variation of a particular formula, "All this took place to fulfill what was spoken by the prophets," no fewer than five times (1:22–23; 2:5–6, 15, 17–18, 23). Matthew answers every question about the birth of Jesus with the authority of Jewish scriptures. Why was Jesus born of a virgin? Because the prophet Isaiah had predicted it (Isa. 7:14). Where was Jesus born? In Bethlehem, for thus spoke the prophet Micah (Mic. 5:2). Why did Joseph, Mary and the baby Jesus flee to Egypt? Because the prophet Hosea had said, "Out of Egypt have I called my son" (Hosea 11:1). Why did Herod kill innocent children? To fulfill the scriptures which speak of Rachel weeping for her children who had been lost to the Assyrians (Jer. 31:15). Why did the family of Jesus settle in Nazareth? To fulfill the prophecy that he would be called a Nazarene.[1]

When Luke opens his gospel story, some time after Matthew, he seeks to show that Jesus observed every Jewish ritual assigned to a male child. He was circumcised on the eighth day (2:21) and presented in the temple on the fortieth day (Luke 2:22) as part of a purification ritual. His name, "Jesus," is simply the Greek spelling of the Hebrew name Joshua, who was one of Israel's great deliverers (Luke 1:31). Luke closes his infancy narrative with the account of Jesus' parents taking him, when he was twelve years of age, to Jerusalem for the festival of the Passover. That story of the visit to the temple is replete with connections to the biblical account of the boy Samuel, who was taken to the temple by Hannah, his mother (1 Sam. 2). Even the Magnificat that Luke has Mary sing was shaped by the Song of Hannah, sung in celebration of Samuel's birth and his dedication to the service of God.

John's gospel, the last written of those included in the canon, is also filled with references to the Hebrew scriptures. Its first chapter is a play on the first chapter of Genesis, and it includes in the body of this text constant references to the name of God, "I AM," which was taken directly from the book of Exodus (3:14). In one place John has Jesus say, "Before Abraham was, I am" (8:58). There is obviously a deep connection between the memory of Jesus and the Hebrew scriptures that far precedes the gospels. The question this realization makes obvious for us is: What was the setting in which this connection occurred?

A second insight, building on this one, comes with the realization that there are many references in the gospels to Jesus being related to the centers of Jewish worship. His life is framed by the temple, at least in Luke's gospel. He is presented in the temple to the old priest Simeon when he is forty days old, and he reclaims the temple just before his crucifixion. There are also twenty-three separate references in the gospels that place Jesus specifically in the synagogue. That was clearly a major part of the disciples' memory of him. Jesus was said to have visited the synagogue regularly—or, in Luke's words, "as his custom was" (4:16). I include a sample of those references from each gospel just to allow my readers to feel their cumulative impact:

[Following his baptism, Jesus] entered the synagogue and taught. (Mark 1:21, NRSV for all)

On the sabbath he began to teach in the synagogue. (Mark 6:2)

[Jesus] went throughout Galilee, teaching in their synagogues and proclaiming the good news of the kingdom. (Matt. 4:23)

He left that place and entered their synagogue. (Matt. 12:9)

He came to his hometown and began to teach the people in their synagogue. (Matt. 13:54)

He began to teach in their synagogues and was praised by everyone. (Luke 4:15)

On another sabbath he entered the synagogue and taught. (Luke 6:6)

Now he was teaching in one of their synagogues on the sabbath. (Luke 13:10)

He said these things while he was teaching in the synagogue at Capernaum. (John 6:59)

Jesus answered [the high priest], "I have spoken openly to the world; I have always taught in the synagogues and in the temple, where all the Jews come together. I have said nothing in secret." (John 18:20)

As these examples show, the life of Jesus and the message of Jesus are located in the memory of the gospel writers time after time in the center of Jewish worship. The same thing was true of his disciples after his death. In the book of Acts Peter is portrayed as speaking immediately after the Pentecost experience in Jerusalem, where the temple is the center of his activity. In his first address he quotes the prophet Joel and sprinkles verses from the Psalms and Isaiah liberally throughout the balance of his sermon (Acts 2:14–36). His second address is said to have been delivered from the temple's portico. There he talks about Abraham, Isaac, Jacob, Moses and Samuel (Acts 3:11–26). When arrested by the temple authorities, Peter addresses the religious leaders with words drawn from both the Psalms and Exodus (Acts 4:8–12). When Stephen is portrayed defending himself before the synagogue leader, his speech relates Jesus to the history of the Jewish people as recorded in their scriptures, and he touches all of the familiar Jewish bases (Acts 7). Paul is depicted over and over again as being present in the synagogue on the sabbath day, talking about Jesus (Acts 13:14, 14:1, 17:10, 18:4, 18:19). In Acts 17:1–2, attending the synagogue on the sabbath is referred to as Paul's "custom." The story of Jesus was, according to both the gospels and the book of Acts, centered in the places of Jewish worship.

What actually happens in Jewish worship also appears to be common knowledge in the early church, since those patterns are described without comment from time to time in the book of Acts and references to Jewish holy days can be found in the texts of the gospels themselves. Luke notes in the book of Acts, for example, that in every city for generations past, Moses has had those who proclaim him, "for he is read every sabbath in the synagogues" (15:21). Luke was obviously familiar with the custom in that period of Jewish history that "Moses"—that is, the so-called five books of Moses, or the Torah (Genesis, Exodus, Leviticus, Numbers, Deuteronomy)—was required to be read aloud in its entirety over the course of the sabbaths during every single year in the worship life of each synagogue.

Long before anyone had taken up the task of writing the gospels, Jesus had already been interpreted through the Hebrew scriptures and in that process the Jesus story was shaped, probably more than most of us have even yet imagined, by the Jewish story. These facts lead me to the assertion that it could only have been in the synagogue that the Jesus story was recalled and shaped during the oral period. This location was neither an accidental nor a happenstance occurrence. A movement that began inside Judaism and that traced its origins to a man who was regularly in the synagogue would not have left that environment when its leader departed. There was also no other place in which the memory of Jesus could have become so deeply identified with and wrapped inside the Jewish scriptures. To understand the full weight of this insight, we need to place ourselves in the world of first-century Judea for just a moment.

People in that day did not own personal Bibles. There was no Gideon Society to put the scriptures in hotel rooms and conference centers. The books of the Bible were on scrolls that were cultural and community treasures. These scrolls were preserved by the very expensive process of hand-copying. Only in the synagogue, where scripture study was a community function on the sabbath, did people have access to these sacred texts. The synagogue was, therefore, the setting of the oral period. It could not have happened anywhere else. That is a firm conclusion.

Though this fact should have been obvious, throughout most of Christian history evidence supporting it has seemed to be invisible. A magical view of the gospels was developed which asserted that instead of the Hebrew stories shaping the Jesus story, the events of Jesus' life simply fulfilled biblical expectations and prophecies in some miraculous and preordained way. Jesus, however, did not live out the prophetic expectations. Indeed, this bizarre and false idea has served to hide from us the fact that the Jesus story was actually composed with the Hebrew scriptures open and the memory of Jesus was actually adapted to conform to biblical expectations. In the process both history and objectivity were compromised. We must, therefore, enter the synagogue interpretive process if we are to discover the Jesus of history.

The next step in unraveling the mystery of the New Testament properly is to learn something about the liturgy of the synagogue that so obviously and so decisively shaped the Christian memory. Most Christians, unfortunately, are so totally uninformed about the shape of synagogue worship that they do not know how to recognize its influence even when they are reading it in the pages of the gospels.

There is a reference, hidden away in the book of Acts (13:13–16), that comes to our aid in this interpretive task. In these verses, Luke outlines the form that liturgy took in a first-century synagogue in which Paul was preaching. It is a little interpretive jewel that literally leaps out of the text and into the lap of those of us who seek a key to unlocking the hidden years between the crucifixion and the writing of the gospels. Liturgical forms change very slowly. It is a safe assumption that the liturgy of the synagogue that Luke described in the early nineties would have been quite similar to the liturgy of the synagogue from the thirties to the seventies, when the Jesus story was being carried orally.

Paul, says Luke, went with his companions to Antioch in Pisidia. On the sabbath day they went into the synagogue and sat down for worship. The service progressed in a regular fashion. The first note Luke offers us on the synagogue liturgy is the phrase "after the reading of the law." The five books of Moses, Genesis through Deuteronomy, were called "the law." Each book, written on a scroll, was read each sabbath from the point where the reading had stopped on the previous sabbath. One cannot skip around on a scroll! To accomplish the mandatory reading of the entire Torah annually, this lesson from "Moses" or "the law" had to be equal to five to six chapters of our present texts of these books. The Torah reading, however, was the most sacrosanct part of the weekly liturgy. It was rigidly followed and consistently observed, despite its length.

Luke then said that after the reading of "the law," the liturgy of the synagogue continued with a reading from "the prophets." In first-century Judaism there were two groups of prophets. The first group, called the early prophets (Joshua, Judges, 1 and 2 Samuel and 1 and 2 Kings), told the story of Jewish history from Joshua's conquest of Canaan in the thirteenth century BCE to the defeat of the Jews at the hands of the Babylonians in the sixth century BCE. This material also introduced such prophetic figures as Samuel, Nathan, Elijah and Elisha, each of whom made powerful contributions to the unfolding drama of biblical religion.[2] This second lesson was read, but without the same mandate to conclude it within a specific time frame. It was therefore a shorter lesson and was regarded as not being of the magnitude or having the same gravitas as the Torah.

The second group of prophets was called the latter prophets. Their writings produced a burst of energy that began with First Isaiah in the eighth century, then continued through Jeremiah in the seventh and Ezekiel, who worked into the sixth century BCE. Included among these major figures was a group of prophets who produced books so small that they were put together on a single scroll and referred to as the "Book of the Twelve." In our Bibles today these are what we call the minor prophets, encompassing the books of Hosea through Malachi. These figures represent Jewish voices that began in the eighth century and continued into the fifth century BCE. The single scroll containing the "Book of the Twelve" was read in the synagogue as one book. So the term "latter prophets" referred to these four prophetic works: Isaiah, Jeremiah, Ezekiel and the Book of the Twelve.[3] Each of these four works was about the same size in length and tended to be read one prophet a year over a four-year cycle.

It was after these readings of the law and the early and latter prophets, interspersed with psalms of praise and prayer, that Luke says the officials of the synagogue sent Paul and his companions this message: "Brothers, if you have any word of exhortation for the people, give it!"

(13:15, NRSV). So Paul rose, accepting the invitation, and began to preach.

His sermon, like all the others as the book of Acts recreates them, roams through Jewish history from their deliverance from Egypt, through their time in the wilderness, to their conquest of Canaan, a period of history, Paul said, that lasted some 450 years. He then wanders through the judges and the rise and fall of the monarchy, ultimately concluding his story with John the Baptist. Next he relates how Abraham's descendants did not recognize the one to whom John pointed, the one of whom the prophets "who are read every sabbath" spoke. Then he covers the crucifixion and God's action in raising Jesus. He quotes Psalm 2 (v. 7) for evidence to support the resurrection. Then he quotes Isaiah 55 (v. 3) and Psalm 16 (v. 10) as he builds toward his great crescendo. Finally he quotes from the prophet Habakkuk (1:5) in a passage that anticipates the Jewish rejection of Jesus. If this sermon is an indication or model of early Christian preaching, then clearly it was against the readings of the sacred scriptures of the Jewish people that the story of Jesus was recalled and refashioned.

It was this very same pattern, I believe, that happened in synagogue after synagogue throughout the Jewish world during the forty to seventy years between crucifixion and gospel writing. Followers of Jesus came to synagogues as worshipping Jews and, sabbath after sabbath, year by year, they heard the scriptures read, remembered the words of Jesus and opened their eyes to the Jesus experience as it was illumined by both scripture and liturgy. They processed their memories through the various elements of their corporate worship until the Jesus experience fit and made sense to them.

The only way, therefore, that we today can ultimately understand the power of the Jesus experience is to stand where they stood, to probe the images they applied to Jesus, to open the symbols they used to understand him and to seek the God they met in Jesus. The questions we must take to the gospels are, therefore, quite different from the bankruptcy of the questions of our present world. Today people ask, "Did these things really happen?" to which the only response is a yes or a no answer, a dichotomy that ultimately makes us either literalists or dropouts. The proper question by which to enter the study of this ancient tradition is: "What was there about Jesus of Nazareth that caused his earliest followers to wrap the sacred history of their Jewish past around him and to expand the stories of their religious heroes until they were big enough to communicate what it was that they experienced in this Jesus?" That question leads to many others: Why did those early followers see in Jesus the fulfillment of the traditions of the Jews? Why did they come to believe that Jesus had transformed those traditions? Why did their words about Jesus suggest that the things that bound their lives always faded before the power present in his life? Why did his death come to be seen as nothing but a prelude to an expanded life? What was there about his humanity that opened their eyes to God in a new way? It is the Jesus who inspired these reactions that we seek in this study, and we will not stop until our goal is reached.

JESUS UNDERSTOOD AS THE NEW PASSOVER

To see the crucifixion drawn into the orbit of the Passover and to embrace the fact that Jesus was understood after the analogy of the paschal lamb is to step into a whole new dimension of the meaning of Jesus and into a whole new dimension of what it means to be human.

It is very difficult to push aside the fact that most of us were taught to read the gospels as literal accounts of things that actually happened, but push we must. Rather than literal accounts, the gospels are instead interpretations of Jesus filtered through the worship life of the Jews in which the story of Jesus was remembered and recalled for two to three generations before the gospels were written. The gospels are filled with images familiar only to Jewish worshippers and are all but nonsensical to those of us who are outside the knowledge of that faith tradition, which has caused us in our ignorance to accommodate ourselves to gross misunderstandings. Then we literalized our misunderstandings! The gospels point to a life that was lived in history, but it was not that physical life which really mattered to the gospel writers; it was what Jesus meant and what it was that they believed they had experienced through him. Paul, paving the way for the gospel writers, articulated this when he wrote of Jesus in the mid-fifties: "We regard no one from a human point of view; even though we once knew Christ from a human point of view, we know him no longer in that way" (2 Cor. 5:16, NRSV). The reason for this, says Paul, was that "if anyone is in Christ, there is a new creation: everything old has passed away; see, everything has become new" (2 Cor. 5:17, NRSV). That was a description not of a physical knowing, but of an ecstatic, mind-opening experience. It was, therefore, not to record the details of the life of Jesus that the gospels were written, but to interpret the Jesus experience. That distinction must be grasped, or we will never escape the meaningless battle that tears the contemporary Christian church apart between the literalizers of the gospel texts on one side and those who reject those literalized texts as unbelievable on the other.

Of course, there are echoes of a real person of history behind the gospel passages. Those echoes can be isolated and looked at. The primary focus of the gospel writers, however, is on the death of Jesus and whatever the experience was that transformed the meaning of his death from despair to the hope for new life. So, almost inevitably, our search for the meaning of Jesus must start with the description of these final events.

The biblical evidence itself makes it clear that the meaning of the crucifixion was the crucial linchpin in the Jesus story and that his death was interpreted from a very early time against the background of the Passover. This connection was not necessarily a connection of history, however, so our inquiry must begin by challenging the literalness of the idea that Jesus was crucified at the time of the Passover. If we can demonstrate that this connection was neither historical nor original, then that fact will give us insight into the way the death of Jesus was first understood. To do this we once again seek to find a way to go beneath the literal words of the New Testament.

Mark, Matthew and Luke locate the death of Jesus at the time of the Passover by identifying the Last Supper with the Passover meal. The Fourth Gospel, John, also makes this connection, but it does so by suggesting that the day of the crucifixion was the day on which the paschal lamb was slaughtered, which means that for John the Last Supper was not the Passover, but a preparatory meal anticipating the Passover.

Before looking at the details contained in the crucifixion narratives, we need to embrace the fact that the gospels assert that it was the Passover which drew Jesus and his disciples to Jerusalem. The whole story of the cross is told as a part of the Passover observation. The band actually entered the holy city, according to the gospels, the week before.[1] That entry is still celebrated today as the first day of what Christians call Holy Week. If we probe these stories carefully, however, we discover hints of a different time frame for the crucifixion and symbols that appear to be lifted quite literally out of another Jewish celebration that was far removed in the calendar from Passover.

Mark, writing first, says that a crowd, accompanying this triumphal procession from the Mount of Olives to Jerusalem, waved leafy branches and laid down their clothing before him while they shouted, "Hosanna, blessed is he who comes in the name of the Lord" (Mark 11:9). Since the Passover was observed on 14–15 Nisan, it would fall in our calendar in late March or early April. The story of Jesus' entry into Jerusalem, celebrated by Christians today as "Palm Sunday," was said, at least by Mark, Matthew and Luke, to have occurred a week earlier, which would place it as early as mid-March. The problem this dating reveals is that there was little chance that there would have been leafy branches in that part of the Middle East so early in the spring. Mid-April to early May would have been when the leaves began to appear. This story then offers us our first hint that the crucifixion narrative may have been originally set in a different season of the year. If that could be established, then the question for us would be why such a coupling of the crucifixion with the Passover was deemed to be essential.

This hint becomes more credible when we see what Matthew and Luke, both of whom are dependent on Mark and copy him extensively, do when this inconsistency dawns on each writer's consciousness. Matthew, writing some ten years after Mark, comes to the reference to leafy branches and drops the word "leafy" from his text. In Matthew the crowd spreads or waves only "branches" (Matt. 21:8). Ordinarily, of course, one does not speak of "spreading" or "waving" sticks; those words are better suited to leaves. The case builds as we note this minor editing. It continues to build when we turn to Luke, writing still later, and discover that he also seems to sense a problem: he omits both Mark's leafy branches and Matthew's bare branches, relating only the account of the people laying down their garments in the path of the procession (Luke 19:36). Even the garment story, however, suggests a warmer season of the year than late March. One does not normally lay down one's outer garment in the cold of that time of the year.

When John's gospel was written in the last years of the tenth decade, he could hardly have been unaware of these earlier gospels, though his purpose was so different that he did not lean on them for much. However, he solved the leafy branch problem by saying that the crowd waved "branches of palm trees"—that is, the leaves of an evergreen tree (John 12:13). Most people are not aware that the branches carried in this procession did not become palm leaves until the last canonical gospel to be written, since we now call the day Palm Sunday and we mark it with the carrying of palms in procession. These gospel variations about waving leaves do not constitute a determinative argument. They are more like an opening wedge that begins to shake the old consensus. I file them for your consideration and move on.

The next hint suggesting a forced identification of the crucifixion with the Passover comes once again in Mark. Mark says that at the end of the Palm Sunday entry into Jerusalem, Jesus went into the temple, saw the moneychangers and then retired to Bethany for the night, where he and his disciples seem to have been headquartered. The next morning Jesus and his disciples journeyed the short distance back to Jerusalem, where Mark will next relate the episode we know as the cleansing of the temple. On this journey Mark informs us that Jesus was hungry and seeing a fig tree in the distance, he went to it seeking figs. It was, however, as Mark notes, "not the season for figs" (Mark 11:13). Nonetheless, Jesus, finding no fruit, laid a curse on this tree. That is, to say the least, a very strange story, as we saw in the earlier discussion of nature miracles—in fact, a story that, if taken literally, is rather un-Jesus-like. Some things are just not in the realm of the possible, not even the supernatural possible. The group and Jesus then went on to Jerusalem, entered the temple, threw out the moneychangers and the sellers of animals and reclaimed the sanctity of the temple (Mark 11:15–19). The work of that day now complete, they returned by the same route back to Bethany. When they got back to the fig tree, Peter called attention to it. The tree had shriveled all the way down to its roots. "Master, look! The fig tree which you cursed [this morning] has withered," Peter exclaimed. The curse clearly had taken! Jesus responded with some words about the efficacy of prayer that do not appear to be at all related to the context (Mark 11:21–25).

It is interesting to note again how both Matthew and Luke deal with this Marcan story when they come to write their gospels. Matthew collapses Mark's two-part story into a single episode, not separated by the cleansing of the temple narrative (Matt. 21:18–22). It is as if Matthew recognizes the problem and wants to get rid of it as quickly as possible. Luke, on the other hand, simply omits it. It appears to show up in Luke in another place as a parable about a fig tree that produces no figs and thus risks being destroyed by the owner (Luke 13:6–9).

Once again there is in this fig tree narrative a hint suggesting that perhaps the original context of both the triumphal procession into Jerusalem and the fig tree story were in a different time of the year, when branches have leaves and when fig trees produce figs. This reinforces our suspicion that perhaps the Passover was not the literal or original setting of the crucifixion.

That possibility is encouraged when we look at the Jewish eight-day fall celebration of the harvest, known as Sukkoth, also called the Festival of Tabernacles or Booths. This observance, which attracted huge numbers of pilgrims to Jerusalem, was probably the most popular holiday among the Jews in the first century, although its only mention in the New Testament comes in John (7:10). There are, however, several telling features to this fall festival that are of particular importance to my attempt to demonstrate that the crucifixion did not originally happen during Passover. In the observance of Sukkoth, worshippers processed through Jerusalem and in the temple, waving in their right hands something called a *lulab*, which was a bunch of leafy branches made of willow, myrtle and palm. As they waved these branches in that procession, the worshippers recited words from Psalm 118, the psalm normally used at Sukkoth. Among those words were "Save us, we beseech you, O Lord." "Save us" in Hebrew is *hosianna* or *hosanna*. That phrasing was typically followed with the words "Blessed is the one who comes in the name of the Lord" (Ps. 118:25, 26, NRSV). One immediately recognizes that these Sukkoth traditions have been shifted from the fall to the season of the Passover and have been adapted to the Palm Sunday story, to meet the interpretive needs of the gospel. So the destabilization of the connection between the crucifixion story and the Passover begins to hit firm ground.

The final clue suggesting that the connection between Passover and crucifixion was more liturgical than historical is in the realization, previously developed in Chapter 9, that Mark's original story of the crucifixion reveals a liturgical format of eight three-hour segments. That story does not present itself as an eyewitness account at all, but rather as the fulfillment of the messianic images drawn from Psalm 22 and Isaiah 53.

Christian liturgical practice simply expanded the original Passover observance into a twenty-four-hour liturgy as the way to observe the passion of Jesus. Both narratives—that of the Passover and that of the crucifixion—were designed to give a timeless dimension to the founding moment in each faith story. Vestiges of that twenty-four-hour liturgy are still present today in Christian practice among the more liturgically oriented traditions. Note the following elements:

The Maundy Thursday reenactment of Jesus' final supper with his disciples is patterned after the Passover, with the symbolic elements of the bread being identified with Jesus' broken body on the cross and the wine with Jesus' blood shed in the crucifixion. When that portion of the liturgy is completed, the altar is stripped and the worshippers are invited to keep watch with Jesus through the final hours of his life, and then to walk with Jesus the way of the cross. Sometimes churches are kept open all night for the meditations of the worshippers. In the morning of the next day, which has come to be called Good Friday, the liturgy is resumed with what is called "the Mass of the presanctified host," referring to Communion administered from the reserved sacrament rather than from a new celebration (for celebrations are deemed to be too festive for this solemn occasion). At noon, the three-hour watch by the cross begins, a liturgy designed to place the modern worshipper quite literally at the foot of the cross to watch with Jesus during his final moments. This portion of this worship activity ends with the announcement that Jesus "breathed his last"—or, in that lovely Elizabethan phrase, that he "gave up the ghost" (Mark 15:37, KJV). Then the worshippers leave the church in quiet reverence to wait for the sun to go down, which marks both the end of the vigil and also the end of the Lenten fast. Saturday is then spent in anticipation of the

Easter vigil and the lighting of the Easter fire after sundown that welcomes the day of the resurrection. What we must remember, however, is that this liturgy was designed not to recall what happened so much as it is to enable disciples in every generation to meditate on the death of Jesus, who, like the paschal lamb, broke the power of death.

The story of the crucifixion was literally shaped to make the death of Jesus appear to be analogous to the death of the Passover (or paschal) lamb. That was an interpretive decision obviously made before any gospel was written. It also introduced into Christian history the title "lamb of God," and contributed mightily to making this title the most popular image of Jesus.

Before one can understand the full meaning of this image and, therefore, of this connection to the paschal lamb of God, one must first understand the teaching of Passover that was enshrined in the Torah and mandated to be observed by the people (Exod. 12, Lev. 23). The Passover entered the Jewish tradition as accompaniment to the last of the many plagues that were said to have been visited upon the Egyptians by the God of the Jews, all of which were designed to force the pharaoh to free the people of Israel from the bondage of slavery (Exod. 7:14–11:10). When none of the previous plagues accomplished that purpose, God, in consultation with Moses, decided to strike again in the most terrifying of ways. God in some form, perhaps as the "angel of death," would pass through all the land to kill (should it not be called divine murder?) the firstborn male in every household, from the pharaoh down to and including the flocks (Exod. 11:6). In order to make sure that this plague of death fell only on Egyptians, the Jews were instructed by God, again through Moses, to form themselves into extended family groups, making sure that all single, elderly and widowed persons were included (Exod. 12:4). Smaller families were to join together with their neighbors. Then each group would take a lamb from its flocks to be sacrificed, placing blood from this slaughtered lamb on the doorposts of all Jewish homes. When God, or God's "angel of death," came to a home that had a bloody doorpost, the "angel" would "pass over" that house—hence the name, Passover. This magical bloody doorpost would guarantee that only Egyptians were the victims of this plague. The blood of the paschal lamb thus had the power to dispel, to break or to drive away the presence of death. It was a primitive, superstitious and blatantly tribal memory, but it was, nonetheless, a powerful story.

The carcass of the slaughtered lamb was then cleaned, dressed and roasted to become the main dish at the celebratory Passover meal. That is, the Passover meal was observed by the family gathering around the table of the Lord, to eat the flesh of the body of the "lamb of God." One can begin to see how the various themes of Eucharist and Passover have intermingled. This was the way that the Passover became the means for celebrating the central truth that the early Christians found in Jesus—namely, that in his life even the power of death appeared to yield its terror before him.

I suspect that the first connection between the crucifixion of Jesus and the slaughter of the paschal lamb was not, therefore, the historic memory that the crucifixion occurred at the time of the Passover. Rather, it developed as an ongoing interpretive process, inspired perhaps by the fact that Paul called Jesus "our paschal lamb" (1 Cor. 5:7). I would wager that an early Christian preacher in a synagogue service, perhaps anticipating the observance of Passover, used Paul's reference as a text to develop a Jesus sermon designed to reinterpret the Passover in the light of the Jesus experience. If I had to recreate that homiletical effort, I would suggest that its content included these points of similarity:

- Jesus and the Passover lamb were both sacrificed.

- The blood of one was placed on the doorpost of Jewish homes; the blood of the other was placed on a cross that was suspended between earth and heaven and stood as a kind of doorpost to the world.

- The blood of each had the power to banish death.

The preacher's approach was probably something like this: "Those of us who approach God, protected by the blood of this new Passover sacrifice, now discover that the fear of death has been broken in our lives. Jesus has called us into the eternity of the living God. That which Paul had once called the last enemy to be defeated has now been overcome. Death has no more dominion over him, nor does it have dominion over those of us who have been covered by the blood that marked his death. He lived unto God and so can we."

In this manner, the crucifixion came to be interpreted through the Passover experience. When the story of the crucifixion was finally written, it was then said to have occurred at the time of the Passover. The concern of the gospel writers was not to record what happened in history, but to probe the experience that people had with Jesus, which caused them to see in his death a power sufficient to destroy death and to free our humanity to enter another realm of consciousness. That is apparently what the Jesus experience did.

The gospels were written to invite us into the Jesus experience of new life, one not bounded by death; and a new humanity, one that reaches toward transcendence. To see the crucifixion drawn into the orbit of the Passover and to embrace the fact that Jesus was understood after the analogy of the paschal lamb, is to step into a whole new dimension of the meaning of Jesus and into a whole new dimension of what it means to be human. It is also to open a door into a new Christianity.

15

JESUS UNDERSTOOD UNDER THE SYMBOLS OF YOM KIPPUR

The details of the crucifixion are not history. There was no moment when the legs of Jesus escaped being broken, no crowd that cried for the death of Jesus and no drama of Barabbas being set free.

The synagogue-worshipping disciples of Jesus found their experience with Jesus constantly interpreted through and illumined by the liturgies of the Jews. Thus, seeing Jesus through the lens of the Passover, as we did in the previous chapter, is the first building block in our attempt to get behind the myth to the man. It is, however, not to be the last. With our eyes newly sensitized, we now move on to see once again that prior to the writing of the gospels, the Jesus memory had been dramatically shaped by another special day in the Jewish liturgical calendar, known as Yom Kippur, or the Day of Atonement. Indeed, the word "atonement," borrowed from this Jewish observance, was destined to become the name of a major doctrine that would form a cornerstone in Christian theology, shaping everything from baptism to the Eucharist with a particular understanding of Jesus as redeemer. Many people have no idea of how that word entered the Christian tradition. In this chapter I hope to illumine that connection.

As soon as Jesus was identified with the sacrificial lamb of the Passover, it was perhaps all but inevitable that he would soon be identified with another sacrificial lamb used in another Jewish holy day. Yom Kippur offered that opportunity. The connections were both consistent and obvious. The Passover lamb and the lamb of Yom Kippur were both killed. Both of them were thought to offer a form of "salvation" through the shedding of blood. The Passover lamb's blood addressed the human anxiety of death. The blood of the sacrificial lamb of Yom Kippur addressed the perceived human yearning to be at one with God as well as the realization that this oneness had been subverted by alienation, guilt and sin. Both of these liturgical practices became the means whereby the Jewish people saw in an animal's liturgical death a doorway through which they might symbolically pass in their journey to a new understanding of what it means to be whole. We now bring Yom Kippur into our focus, seeking to embrace just why it was that the early disciples of Jesus thought it appropriate to process the meaning they found in him through the lens of this Jewish observance.

Human beings all live with an experience of separation, aloneness and alienation born, I believe, in the trauma of self-consciousness. It is manifested as the anxiety of meaninglessness that accompanies the external human drive to discover and appropriate ultimate meaning for human life in its transitory existence. It feeds our sense of guilt and fear. It constitutes a major piece of what it means to be fully human. No one escapes this reality, and every religious system has some way of addressing it.

To the Jews these aspects of human need and human life were spoken to liturgically with an annual rite of corporate penitence in which their sense of separation from the source of life was symbolically overcome. That is what Yom Kippur was all about. When followers of Jesus began to connect Jesus to Yom Kippur, new insights opened into the meaning that they had experienced in their relationship with Jesus. It is a complex story, for there are many aspects to this Jewish Holy Day.

The connection between Jesus and Yom Kippur begins once more, I believe, with Paul, who, writing to the Corinthians in the midfifties, penned the first written sentence we have that was designed to interpret the crucifixion. He claimed there to be reflecting the earliest tradition about Jesus that had been handed down to him (1 Cor. 15:1–11). He tied the crucifixion of Jesus, I suspect knowingly, to Yom Kippur when he wrote that Jesus died "for our sins," expressing the idea that the death of Jesus had some very specific effects on all people in the salvation drama. This was a claim that the death of Jesus was not random or without ultimate meaning. It was, rather, purposeful, perhaps even divinely appointed. We examine, therefore, just what it was that Paul meant when he claimed that the death of Jesus was related to our sins, which is the central teaching associated with the sacrificial lamb in the liturgy of Yom Kippur.

First of all, this is a major Pauline theme that occurs over and over in his writing. In Romans Paul says that Jesus was "a sacrifice of atonement by his blood, effective through faith" (Rom. 3:25, NRSV). He quotes Psalms (32:1) about the blessed one whose "sins are covered" (Rom. 4:7). He quotes Isaiah (59:20, 21) about a deliverer who will take away the people's sins (Rom. 11:26, 27). He refers to Jesus as the one "who gave himself for our sins to deliver us" (Gal. 1:4). This idea is not tangential for the Jewish Paul; it is a deeply crucial part of his thinking and closely related to the powerful echoes found in his observance of Yom Kippur.

While Paul may well have been the originator of this Yom Kippur connection, later writers surely built on it and it became part of the general Jesus understanding very early. By the time Mark's gospel was written, this Pauline idea had been developed significantly. Mark suggested that the death of Jesus had been a "ransom" required in order to free human beings from the bondage of sin (Mark 10:45). Matthew repeated this Marcan idea verbatim, without any comment (Matt. 20:28). The one to whom that "ransom" was paid is not clear in the text of either gospel and Christian theology has through the ages debated as to whether this ransom was paid to God or to the devil. In either case the implication found in this interpretive word is that a ransom was necessary, since human life has been captured by a sense of separation, a quest for meaning and the unrelievable guilt of being. The strong suggestion is present that somehow human life was in bondage, having no power with which to extricate itself from these sources of anxiety. The word "ransom" suggests that human life was not capable of paying the price, so a substitute had to step in. The substitute needed, however, to be deemed capable of assuming the cost of the ransom. This idea, when it was freed from its Jewish origins, would have an interesting and quite destructive history as religious systems literalized its symbolic meaning.

By the time the Fourth Gospel was written, the connection between Jesus and the sacrifice of Yom Kippur had become complete and the interpretation of Jesus under the symbols of Yom Kippur was fixed. The first time John the Baptist sees Jesus of Nazareth in John's gospel, he is made to utter a phrase that was lifted in its totality out of the liturgy of Yom Kippur in order to articulate his understanding of who Jesus was: "Here is the Lamb of God who takes away the sin of the world!" (John 1:29, NRSV).

Behind these images was the Jewish mythology that told of the origin of human guilt. It was caused, said the ancient Jewish legend, by the fact that human beings in the Garden of Eden had by an act of disobedience been banished from God's presence. Eden, that place for which we had been originally made, was a place of oneness with God. Because of that primal disobedience the new and inevitable destiny of human beings was to live "east of Eden,"[1] or in a state of separation from God. This view of human life as estranged from God answered many human questions. Why do men have to struggle against the elements to eke out their daily bread? Why do women have to endure the pain of childbirth? Why do we all yearn to go back to Eden? It was all because of our separation and alienation, resulting from our banishment from oneness with God in the mythical Garden of Eden. Human beings were created to be immortal; our original status meant that we could walk with God in a state of perfection. That glory was now, however, permanently closed off to us. In that Jewish myth an angel with a drawn sword guarded the entrance to Eden to ensure that we could never return to our original status (Gen. 3:24). We had to live our lives in the pain of existence with our immortality removed and with death being the final punishment for our sinfulness. Salvation in this view of human life was a vision of a future time when our alienation would be overcome. Guilt was the one constant symbol of alienation—human life suffered the guilt of inadequacy, the guilt of not being what we were created to be; so salvation was portrayed as forgiveness and restoration. Salvation was the moment in which oneness with God would be reestablished. Atonement thus became a prime theological word.

Since that was the Bible's earliest definition of human life, it should surprise no one to discover that those scriptures were filled with what might be called divine initiatives aimed at achieving atonement, or "at-one-ment." At the very least this is the way the Bible came to be interpreted, especially in later Christian circles, when the doctrine of atonement became a dominant theme. There was first the story of Noah and the flood, in which God's despair over the evil present in God's good creation led God to the dramatic act of destroying all human life save for a single righteous family that consisted of a man, his wife, three sons and their wives. That story suggested that God felt that redemption of the world was impossible, since human evil had become so great. Destroying humanity and starting again with this one righteous family was thus the new divine plan. The rest of creation, this story suggested, would discover salvation through Noah, who made the preservation of every species of animal in the world possible by having a pair of each accompany him on the ark. Of course, this myth of the flood has thousands of rational problems, but most myths when literalized do. The story, however, drives to its relentless conclusion that human life has been infected with evil that separates us from God, creating a chasm that human beings cannot transcend. We cannot ultimately save ourselves.

However, the great but violent divine experiment of a flood to purge humanity of its sinfulness also did not work. Noah was not ultimately righteous or incorruptible. No sooner had the waters of the flood receded and the dry land emerged anew than Noah succumbed to the seemingly natural human propensity for evil. He became drunk on new wine and one of his children broke the code of conduct by staring at him in his naked, inebriated state (Gen. 9:21–28). The evil that distorted the human soul was too deep to be destroyed even by a flood. It had become an ineradicable part of our human nature. To bring about atonement, to overcome the sin of the world, God would have to adopt a more comprehensive and a longer-range program of redemption.

It was said that this understanding of the divine quest for salvation led to the call of Abraham and the creation of a chosen people whose task would be to become the people through whom all the nations of the world would finally be blessed—that is, they were to become the people through whom human atonement would finally be achieved (Gen. 12:3). Atonement thinking was beginning to dominate religious consciousness.

There were other steps in this developing quest for atonement in Jewish history. One was the giving of the law at Mount Sinai. If the law could be kept in its totality, salvation would come to the earth. That did not happen, of course. Another step was the rise of the prophetic movement inside the Jewish religion. The prophets were not predictors of the future, as so many people now seem to assume; they were those who were understood as having been specifically raised by God to call the Jewish people (and through them all human beings) back to their unbroken relationship with God expressed in God's original covenant. The story of the prophets also ended in failure. The prophets regularly met with the typical prophet's fate: they were banished or killed. The alienation between God and the people was so total that even the holy God was unable to overcome it. So deeply was this understanding part of what it meant to be human that finally the Jewish people placed this reality into the li-turgical life of the synagogue.

In the liturgy of Yom Kippur this human yearning for wholeness, completion and at-one-ment found expression. One day a year was to be designated the "Day of Atonement." On that day liturgical acts would be performed that would symbolically overcome the alienation, restoring the people to the wholeness, the oneness that was originally theirs. Atonement would thus be experienced, if but for a moment, at least liturgically. Yom Kippur would stand as a symbol of the atone-ment for which human life was ultimately destined when the kingdom of God dawned. So when Yom Kippur was born, it was placed in the Jewish calendar on the tenth day of the month of Tishri, just after the celebration of Rosh Hashanah, the Jewish New Year (when the people gathered to pray for the coming of the kingdom), and just before Suk-koth, the harvest festival that marked the end of the agricultural year. Yom Kippur's institution and how it is to be observed is described in the book of Leviticus (chapter 23). It was to be a deeply penitential day, consistent with the acknowledgment of the human situation of alienation and evil.

In preparation for this day, the people were told to gather in solemn assembly. Two animals were to be chosen from out of their flocks to be the sacrificial symbols through which this liturgical act of reconciliation with God would occur. These two animals could be either sheep or goats; tradition, however, has tended to understand one as a lamb and the other as a goat. Both were required to be young, healthy and male, reflecting the patriarchal mentality and value system of the ancient world. Both were to be free of blemishes, scars, scratches and broken bones. They were to be meticulously examined by the high priest to ascertain their physical perfection. One could not offer to God an imperfect offering. Then by lot one of the animals was chosen to be the sacrifice; the other one was designated to be the sin-bearer.

The lamb chosen for sacrifice was thought to be the perfect creature to achieve reconciliation with God. Not only was this male lamb judged to be physically perfect, but it was seen as morally perfect as well in the developing tradition: living as lambs do beneath the level of human freedom, it could not choose to do evil, and thus never sinned. If the sinfulness of the people kept them from God's presence, then perhaps by coming to God through the sinlessness of the physically and morally perfect lamb of God, the yearned-for reconciliation might at least symbolically be accomplished in this liturgical action. The people prepared for this sacred moment by adopting appropriate behavior. They fasted and denied themselves anything that might signify a lack of self-judgment. They made an offering of a cleansing fire; they refrained from work for the entire day and practiced an ostentatious penitence (Lev. 23:26–32).

When the people's preparation was complete, the lamb of God was ceremonially slaughtered. Its blood was placed on the mercy seat in the Holy of Holies, that part of the temple thought to be the very dwelling place of God. The high priest could enter the Holy of Holies only on this one day of the year and only after rigorous ceremonial acts of cleansing. Sometimes, as a way of bringing the people into the meaning of the sacrifice, the blood of the perfect lamb of God would also be sprinkled on the people, who could thus claim that they had been "washed in the blood of the lamb of God." Covered with the blood of the lamb, they were thought to be, at least for that moment, cleansed of their sinfulness, acceptable, even at one with God.

When that first part of the liturgy of Yom Kippur was complete, the Jewish worshippers next moved to the second animal, which was then brought to the high priest. This creature, remembered typically in the tradition as a young goat but not necessarily having to be, was also physically perfect and presumed to be sinless, since it was also unable to choose to do evil. The high priest, taking the horns of this goat, would begin the rhythmic prayers of penitence, confessing in the name of the people all of their sins and evil. The sins of the people were symbolically pictured as rising out of the people and landing on the head and back of this creature. The sinless goat became the bearer of the sins of the people. With their sins now transferred to the sin-bearing goat, the people were assumed to be both cleansed and sinless. Then, in their new moral perfection, they pronounced curses on the goat and demanded its death. One carrying that much sin ought not to be allowed to live. The liturgy of Yom Kippur, however, did not call for the goat's slaughter; it called rather for this goat, carrying all the people's sins, to be banished to the wilderness. A space in the assembly was opened and the sin-laden goat was driven from the people's presence, leaving them pure and at one with God, at least for one symbolic day.

This creature came to be called the scapegoat, the one who bears the punishment for the sins of others; the one who saves us from the punishment that is our due. The sacrificed lamb was thus said to have "died for our sins." The sin-bearing goat had "taken away the sins of the world." These phrases were all originally associated with Yom Kippur, yet they were destined to become the words by which the death of Jesus on the cross would finally be interpreted. Most Christians, unfortunately, have no sense of the origins of this liturgical language, or of the concept of the saving efficacy of blood. Yet nothing shaped the Christian understanding of Jesus more than Yom Kippur. As Christianity moved more and more into a Gentile world, these ideas left the context of liturgy and began to be thought of as a kind of legal contract. The door for a Christianity of guilt and fear, confession and absolution, reward and punishment had been opened.

There is no question that the Jesus we meet in the gospels had already been shaped by a Yom Kippur understanding of atonement. Recall the story told us in John's gospel that at the cross the legs of the two thieves were broken to hasten death, lest they defile the sabbath that arrived at sundown. Coming to Jesus, John's gospel says, they found him already dead, so they did not break his legs (John 19:33). The symbol was preserved: the lamb of God sacrificed at Yom Kippur had to be physically perfect, with no broken bones. John went on to say that this action fulfilled the words of the prophets. Psalm 22, which we have previously met, had stated that the victim "knew" all his bones, an idea that was supplemented by the note in Psalm 34, "He keeps all his bones; not one of them is broken" (v. 20). Both of these references from Psalms were originally references to the lamb of Yom Kippur, but when quoted in the gospels, they have clearly been transferred to Jesus. The Torah referred to the Passover lamb similarly by saying, "You shall not break a bone of it" (Exod. 12:46). Symbolic sacrifices had to be perfect. The symbols of Yom Kippur, like the symbol of the paschal lamb, were quite clearly incorporated into the Jesus story in the oral period, which means that the Jesus we meet in the gospels had already been interpreted through the liturgy of Yom Kippur.

There is a second place in the gospels where this identification appears to be shaping the narrative. In Mark's gospel, when Jesus is being led to his death, he appears as a victim before Pilate. In the language of the liturgy of Yom Kippur, Pilate, with the symbolic sin-bearing figure of Jesus standing before him, asks the crowd, "What do you wish me to do with the man you call the King of the Jews?" The crowd responds, "Crucify him!" Jesus is being portrayed as the sin-bearer worthy of death. Pilate then asks the question that could just as easily have been asked by the high priest with a scapegoat, loaded down with the sins of the people, as the crowd demands its death: "Why, what evil has he done?" To which the crowd before Pilate shouts even louder, "Crucify him!" (Mark 15:12–14, NRSV). If this Jesus is bearing the sins of the world, he is sufficiently evil and he must die. Then Pilate delivers Jesus to be taken outside the city and killed. The sacrificial lamb and the scapegoat of Yom Kippur have been combined. That combining, which occurred in the oral period, became a means for interpreting the purpose of the death of Jesus.

Similar echoes are found in Luke (23:21), where Pilate is portrayed as trying to release Jesus, but the crowd keeps calling for his death, and in John (19:13–16), where the words "Away with him!" are inter-spersed with the cries for Jesus' death. These narratives have the marks of Yom Kippur all over them. They are not historic remembrances. They are liturgical interpretations.

Finally, there is an enigmatic figure introduced into the crucifixion story in all four gospels whose name is Barabbas (Mark 15:7ff., Matt. 27:16ff., Luke 23:18, John 18:40). In the passion narrative he is the figure who is released instead of Jesus. Mystery surrounds Barabbas, who is never mentioned either before this moment or after. He is de-fined in Mark as one who "committed murder during the insurrec-tion" (15:7). His evil seems to increase as the later gospels pick up his story. He is "notorious" in Matthew (27:16), a bandit in John (18:40, NRSV).

Once I escaped the lifelong training that had caused me to think literally when reading the Bible, I found that the figure of Barabbas intrigued me. The first reason for this fascination was that Pilate as-serted there was a custom of releasing a prisoner at the time of the Passover. He asked the crowd to choose between Jesus and Barabbas. My research turned up no evidence that such a custom ever existed. The second source of fascination was his name. *Bar* is one of two Hebrew words that mean "son."[2] We met this word earlier in the story of blind Bar-Timaeus (Mark 10:46). Matthew refers to Peter as Simon, Bar-Jonah (16:17), or son of Jonah or Jonas, presumably the name of Peter's father. A magician, identified as a false prophet, is called Bar-Jesus, the son of Jesus, in the book of Acts (13:6). The other half of the name of Barabbas is "Abba," the word used for God or father. "Abba" appears to be Jesus' name of preference for God (Mark 14:36), and it is also used by Paul (Rom. 8:15 and Gal. 4:6). In other words, Bar-Abbas means nothing less than "son of God."

I perceive here another oblique reference to the Jewish Day of Atonement that only those who were familiar with the Yom Kippur liturgy would ever be able to see. Just as in Yom Kippur there are two animals—one that is sacrificed, the lamb of God; and one that is set free, the scapegoat—so in the story of the cross there are two sons of God—one who is sacrificed, Jesus; the other who is set free, Barabbas.[3] More than most of us have imagined, the liturgy of Yom Kippur has shaped the story of the crucifixion. The tragedy is that for so long the only way we thought it proper to read the story of Jesus' crucifixion was to presume that each of its details accurately recorded actual events when in fact the story of the cross is liturgy shaped by the synagogue, seeking to find words big enough to enable the reader to enter the meaning of Jesus.

The details of this story are not history. That must be said again and again. There was no moment when the legs of Jesus escaped being broken, no crowd that cried for the death of Jesus and no drama of Barabbas being set free. Perhaps now we can begin to understand that in the gospels we are dealing with interpretive data, developed during the oral period and used to help people process the meaning they found in Jesus. Once again our real questions become: What was there about Jesus of Nazareth that caused people to liken him to the creatures in the liturgy of Yom Kippur, whose roles were to bring the people and God together, to overcome that human sense of alienation, separation, guilt and anxiety that mark all human life? What was there about Jesus that caused people to believe that in him oneness with the source of life itself was possible, that guilt and alienation do not have to be our daily bread? For that is what the Jesus experience seems to have done. In Jesus these old things have passed away and all things have become new. In Jesus we are a new creation. Consider yourself, said Paul, "dead to sin and alive to God" (Rom. 6:11). "We do not live to ourselves," wrote Paul. "If we live, we live to the Lord" (Rom. 14:7–8, NRSV). "Whether we live or die," he concludes, "we are the Lord's." Paul strikes a similar note when he writes, "It is no longer I who live, but it is Christ who lives in me" (Gal. 2:20, NRSV). The disciples of Jesus are known by their love, their ability to give themselves away. All of these proclamations are said to be the result of the death of Jesus. All of them use the language of Yom Kippur, the Day of Atonement. How is it that we experience oneness and wholeness in Jesus? That is the question that continues to drive us beyond literalness, beyond theology, beyond mythology, beyond ancient images and even beyond religion. There is something about the Jesus experience that opens our eyes to what it means to be at one with God, at one with each other, at one with ourselves. When we arrive in this place, we are a step closer to our goal. The journey, however, is not yet complete.

16

JESUS AS THE SON OF MAN

Son of man, stand upon your feet, and I will speak with you.
Ezek. 2:1

I saw in the night visions, and behold, with the clouds of
heaven there came one like a son of man, and he came to the
Ancient of Days and was presented before him. And to him was
given dominion and glory and kingdom, that all peoples, nations
and languages should serve him; his dominion is an everlasting
dominion, which shall not pass away, and his kingdom one that
shall not be destroyed.
Dan. 7:13–14

Do you believe in the Son of man?... Who is he, sir, that I may
believe in him?... You have seen him, and it is he who speaks
to you.
John 9:35–37

We noted and examined earlier the claim made by the
writers of the gospels that Jesus was a worker of miracles.
We discovered that this claim was associated with a particular view of
the messiah called the "Son of man." It was a title obviously applied to
Jesus in the oral period, since references to this image permeate the
gospel stories. What does it mean and what did it communicate about
Jesus when he began to be designated the "Son of man" by his followers? Those are now my questions.

"Son of man" is probably the oldest and the most popular title developed for the one who was to fulfill the messianic expectations of the Jewish people. It is a phrase that began simply enough, but it kept growing until it included claims of otherworldly power and came to be filled with divine, miraculous connotations. As such, it is one more doorway through which we can walk in our search to understand the dimensions of the original Jesus experience.

The phrase "Son of man" entered the tradition of the Jews primarily through the sixth-century work of Ezekiel, the major prophet of the exile. Ezekiel used the phrase "Son of man" more than ninety times, but always simply as the title by which God addressed him—for example, "Son of man, stand upon your feet, and I will speak with you" (Ezek. 2:1). The words "Son of man," literally *ben adam* in Hebrew, seem to mean little more than "human being," *ben* being a second Hebrew word for "son" and *adam* a Hebrew word for "humankind" (or "mankind," as our patriarchal language once assumed to be the proper translation). The New Revised Standard Version of the Bible regularly translates *ben adam* as "mortal." It was originally little more than a designation of Ezekiel's status as a child of Adam and thus a human being.

Throughout the book of Ezekiel one gets the impression that this author believed that God was directing God's prophet, so that the prophet would see what needed to be seen and do what needed to be done. Ezekiel's life was lived in a very critical time in the Jewish history of defeat, exile and survival. Ezekiel, probably more than any other single person, was instrumental in keeping the Jewish people both intact and separate during the generations of the exile known as the Babylonian captivity. He helped form the Jewish people into a tightly knit entity, capable not only of enduring the exile, but of retaining the will to return later in successive generations to reclaim their homeland and reestablish their identity as a living nation. He was also probably the dominant player in that group of people who came to be called the priestly writers—those who, during the exile in Babylon, rewrote the Torah, doubling it in size and filling it with liturgical details such as the ones we find in the book of Leviticus, and who were finally responsible for searing quite literally onto the Jewish soul such practices as sabbath day worship, kosher dietary rules and the physical mark of male circumcision. Each of these signs of Jewish distinctiveness served the purpose of keeping the Jews separate from their neighbors. They became the very marks of Judaism, the things that made the Jews different. Jews would not work on the seventh day, Jews ate a peculiar diet, which had to be prepared in a special kitchen, and Jewish males had cut into their bodies the physical sign of their Judaism. Those were the gifts of Ezekiel, the prophet whom God is described as calling simply by the name "Son of man."

After the writing of Ezekiel the name or title "Son of man" did not appear again in the Jewish scriptures for about four hundred years, re-emerging in the book of Daniel, a text of the second century BCE, in a radically transformed concept. By this time the circumstances of the Jewish people had deteriorated significantly and with that deterioration the loss of hope among the Jews had become increasingly real. The Persians, who had allowed the exiles in Babylon to return to their homeland, had been replaced by the Macedonians as the dominant power in the region. With the death of Alexander the Great, the Macedonian Empire had fallen apart and little Judah then had fallen under the rotating domination of either Syria or Egypt. The Jewish hope for real freedom and for a place in the world's sun began to burn dimmer and dimmer until it finally died. Then the Jews turned their attention toward something that came to be called apocalypticism, in which they ceased to think of deliverance from bondage as something that would eventually come to them inside history and began to dream of a deliverance and a destiny that could be achieved only beyond history. This was the doorway through which apocalyptic or "end of the world" thinking entered Jewish life. In the great apocalyptic wonder that would accompany the end of history, the Jews began to dream dreams about a messiah who would come as the agent of God. At the end of the world this messiah would preside over the final judgment, after which God's everlasting kingdom would be established on earth. As these images were attached to the Jewish messianic hopes, the nature of what "messiah" meant slowly changed. More and more the expected messiah was portrayed not just as the heir who might restore the throne of David, but also as a heavenly figure possessing supernatural power. It was this transformed figure wrapped inside Jewish dreams who rode into Jewish consciousness in the writings of Daniel.

Though clearly borrowing from Ezekiel, Daniel used the title "Son of man" with a vastly different meaning. In an almost direct relationship to the hopelessness lived out in Jewish history, this new, mythological and supernatural image of the messiah quickly gained popularity.

The author of the book of Daniel introduced this "Son of man" figure into his narrative as part of a dream or vision. Dreams in that time were thought to be the means through which divine messages were received. In his dream Daniel was allowed to see the throne of heaven in all its splendor. Seated on that throne, he said, was one called the "Ancient of Days," translated in the New Revised Standard Version simply as the "Ancient One." This God figure was depicted as having clothing that was as white as snow; the hair on the divine head was like pure wool. The throne of the "Ancient of Days" was made of fire and wheels of fire turned incessantly around it. Indeed, fire streamed out of this "Ancient of Days" constantly, even as angelic beings, numbering more than ten thousand times ten thousand, served the Holy One (Dan. 7:9–10). In this setting, Daniel asserted, the final judgment would emerge, bringing human history to an end. This passage is a prime example of the way human beings magnify human language and human images when trying to find words big enough and majestic enough to describe the experience of God. To be aware of this fact that human language is all we have frees us, however, from the temptation to literalize it.

Next in Daniel's vision, another figure comes to the throne of the "Ancient of Days," riding on the clouds of heaven. This figure Daniel described as "one like a son of man"—that is, *ben adam*, or "the human one." Yet to call this character "a human being" was a bit surreal, since he did not appear to be human at all. Daniel's description of the "Son of man," who was next presented to the "Ancient of Days," was fascinating. To this figure, he wrote, "was given dominion and glory and kingdom, that all peoples, nations and languages should serve him." The dominion of this figure was said to be an "everlasting dominion"—that is, one that was beyond time, and the kingship that this figure would exercise was "one that shall not be destroyed" (Dan. 7:13–14).

When Daniel begins the process of interpreting this vision, he speaks of the rise and fall of those kingdoms that would dominate

God's holy people. They were four in number, but the fourth kingdom would be the most terrible, and when that kingdom was destroyed, all the greatness of all the kingdoms would be given to "the holy ones of the Most High" (Dan. 7:22, NRSV). In other words, the greatness of those kingdoms would accrue to the defeated and downtrodden people of the Jews, who were, they claimed, God's elect. The "Son of man" had thus become a heavenly figure, possessing supernatural power, and had been assigned the task of bringing about the end of the world, the judgment and the eternal reign of God on earth.

Once more it is interesting to note that Paul, who died before any of the gospels were written, appears to have had no concept of Jesus having been shaped by this image. By the time the gospels came into being, however, this "Son of man" image had clearly become a primary lens through which Jesus was interpreted. Like the image of the new paschal lamb of Passover and the sacrificial lamb and sin-bearing scapegoat of Yom Kippur, this image was now wrapped around Jesus and it shaped people's memory of him during those hidden years between his death and the writing of the gospels. It was during that crucial decade of the sixties—the years after Paul and before Mark—that these interpretive portraits became so influential.

So the idea of Jesus as the "Son of man" offers us yet another window of opportunity through which we can travel in our desire to reach out toward whatever the original Jesus experience was. Our question, however, remains the same: What was there about Jesus of Nazareth that made it seem appropriate for people in that day to apply this "Son of man" image to him? What was it that caused people to begin to see him as a supernatural being, who came from heaven to do the work of the "Ancient of Days"?

My first task in unpacking this symbol is to examine the gospel texts in which "Son of man" is applied to Jesus of Nazareth. Mark first uses the phrase in the story of the healing of a paralytic early in his gospel. Jesus did the act of healing using these words: "My son, your sins are forgiven" (Mark 2:5). To be able to forgive sins was clearly a divine claim and it was immediately challenged by Jesus' critics, who asked, "Who can forgive sins but God alone?" (Mark 2:7). Jesus responds, however, by saying, "So that you may know that the Son of man has authority on earth to forgive sins,... I say to you, stand up, take your mat and go to your home" (Mark 2:10–11, NRSV). The "Son of man" in the book of Daniel, in the role of one who would preside over the last judgment, had the power to bind and to loose the sins of people. Jesus was clearly being viewed through this newly applied image.

The last time Mark uses this "Son of man" phrase is on the final day of Jesus' life, when he is on trial before the high priest. The high priest asks, "Are you the Christ [the messiah], the Son of the Blessed?" (Mark 14:61). As used in this question, the phrase sounds very much like a supernatural designation. Whether or not the question was provocative in this sense, however, certainly Jesus' answer is: "I am," he says; "and you will see the Son of man sitting at the right hand of Power, and coming with the clouds of heaven" (14:62). Between these two uses at the beginning and end of Mark's gospel, the phrase "Son of man," as a title for Jesus, is employed on twelve other occasions. It is very clear that by the time Mark wrote in the early seventies, this image from Daniel had been incorporated into the memory of Jesus. Mark simply assumed what had become common wisdom: that, among believers at least, Jesus had come to be thought of as the supernatural "Son of man" who would come from God to inaugurate the kingdom of God.

Matthew expands this identification of Jesus with Daniel's image of the supernatural "Son of man" by using this phrase twenty-seven times. Some are almost casual, a kind of self-bestowed title, as when Matthew has Jesus say, "The Son of man has nowhere to lay his head" (Matt. 8:20). Others are clearly infused with much more of Daniel's meaning. Jesus, in Matthew, is said to have sent his twelve disciples out on a mission with these instructions: "You will not have gone through all the towns of Israel, before the Son of man comes" (Matt. 10:23). When Matthew has Jesus state that the destiny of the "Son of man" has been set by the scriptures (Matt. 26:24), the primary source to which he was referring was surely the book of Daniel.

Matthew adds to his gospel two other narratives about Jesus that are unique to Matthew and in which he enhances the identification of the "Son of man" with Jesus in inescapable ways. The first is the parable of the judgment, in which at the end of time the nations of the world are separated one from another in a way similar to a shepherd separating the sheep from the goats. In this parable the "Son of man" comes in his glory, accompanied by angels, to judge the world on the final day.

The sheep this judge calls to himself. The goats he orders into the "eternal fire prepared for the devil and his angels" (Matt. 25:31–46). The second overt reference to Daniel's "Son of man" image comes in Matthew's treatment of Jesus' resurrection. Matthew has the risen Christ speak only once to his disciples (28:16–20). In that appearance Jesus comes out of heaven possessing, says Matthew, "all authority in heaven and on earth"—that is, he is clothed with the symbols of the "Son of man." Matthew has prepared his readers for this claim by having Jesus tip them off in advance: in chapter 16, Matthew portrays Jesus as saying, "For the Son of man is to come with his angels in the glory of his Father, and then he will repay everyone for what has been done" (Matt. 16:27, NRSV). It was yet another reference to the judgment role applied to the messianic figure by the book of Daniel. Matthew saw resurrection in that context.

Luke, writing even later than Matthew and oriented away from Jewish expectations toward the more cosmopolitan world of dispersed Jews and Gentile proselytes, nonetheless still uses the phrase "Son of man" twenty-seven times. His most striking uses are found in his references to the end of the world (chapter 17 and 21), where the figure who appears to mark the end of history will be the "Son of man," an identity that Luke clearly has Jesus claim for himself.

John uses the phrase "Son of man" only thirteen times, but the most striking for our purposes is in his story of the man born blind whose sight is restored. Jesus, confronting this man, who has just been excommunicated from the synagogue, asks him, "Do you believe in the Son of man?" (John 9:1–37). When the man asks, "Who is he, sir, that I may believe in him?" Jesus says, "You have seen him, and it is he who speaks to you." In this story the supernatural "Son of man," whose task is to judge the world and to inaugurate the kingdom of God, has been joined to the earlier, less apocalyptic messianic figure identified by Isaiah as the one who would bring peace and wholeness to life, making the blind see, the deaf hear, the lame walk and the mute sing as signs of the coming kingdom.

Jesus thus got interpreted in both roles of messiah. He was perceived as the supernatural "Son of man," the ultimate judge, as well as the source of wholeness here and now. His first coming was accompanied by a series of healing miracles that marked the in-breaking of the kingdom, but he would also come as the ultimate judge at the end of history to establish the kingdom of God. In both instances an attempt was being made to find language expansive enough to describe the experience people believed they had had with Jesus.

The life of Jesus was a life in which love was perceived to transform the unloved, acceptance to heal the pain of rejection, wholeness to overcome brokenness and life to expand until it transcended every limit. That was why stories were attached to him that told of people who found themselves resurrected by their contact with him. That is why the healing signs of the kingdom were attached to his memory as if they were events of history. That was the way people said, we have met the one in whom we now see the kingdom of God dawning. It was a human Jesus, so whole, so open, so free, so at one with himself that people became convinced that the holy God had come through his life into their lives. God was in Christ, and that God was the love that created wholeness. When they experienced Jesus' life, his disciples began to say of him that Jesus was the "first fruits" of the kingdom. Paul used that phrase twice (1 Cor. 15:20, 23; Rom. 8:23). James used it once (1:18). The book of Revelation also used it (14:4). The gospels were far more narrative in form, but they still proclaimed this perception of Jesus when they told stories of great healings, wrote parables of the final judgment and painted the portrait of Jesus as the "Son of man" who restored life with new sight, new hearing, new mobility and a new ability to speak.

No, these are not magical tales of a deity masquerading as a human being. No one ever heard the Jesus of history say that he was the judge who invited the saved to enter the kingdom of God on the last day. Yet the early Christians came to associate all of these things with the human Jesus. Powerful experiences drive expanded language into new forms. Jesus' followers sought to capture his meaning in the language of ecstasy and apocalyptic symbols, seeking words big enough to convey the meaning they had experienced. That is what it means to be the "Son of man" and that is how that title got attached to Jesus' memory.

In the life of the synagogue during those years between 30 and 70 CE, the powerful life-giving experience of Jesus was transposed into Jewish concepts and celebrated inside Jewish liturgy. Jesus was the

"Son of man"; Jesus was the inaugurator of the kingdom of God. When that experience was reduced to writing between the years 70 and 100, it took on narrative form as these images coalesced around him.

We must not forget that in the first gospel Jesus is not miraculously born. He even goes to be baptized for the forgiveness of sins—he whom we traditionally think of as sinless. At that baptism the heavens open and the Holy Spirit is poured out upon him. The voice of God acknowledges him as the "divine Son." Jesus wrestles with this dual identity; so do his disciples. How can the holy God be met in the human Jesus? That is the question the gospels seek to answer. It is also the question we must answer if we are to enter the Jesus experience.

Son of man? Yes, the whole one, the *ben adam* in its completeness, the mortal one who opens the door on immortality. That is who Jesus is: a human life so whole that God's life breaks through in him.

17

MINORITY IMAGES: THE SERVANT, THE SHEPHERD

He was despised, rejected, a man of sorrows and acquainted with grief.

A contralto solo from Handel's *Messiah*

Before the gospels were written, the expectations by which the disciples of Jesus lived during his lifetime had been turned upside down by the reality of his death. Jesus did not accomplish his purpose through the use of power. Rather, he lived his life laying down all claims to power and embracing powerlessness. He seemed to operate on the principle that in order to save one's life, one had to be willing to lose it. He seemed to believe that in order to conquer death, he had to accept it and even to enter it. In order to be who he was, he had to be willing to give himself away. These ideas were not the norms of the world in which Jesus' disciples lived. They were not natural to the humanity they knew. Yet their experience with Jesus seemed to authenticate his way.

This conflict led these disciples, caught between the Jesus experience and human reality, to search for a way to understand the meaning of life in light of the Jesus experience. Once again they searched inside their sacred tradition as it was celebrated and recalled in the synagogue. Out of that tradition they found two stories about weakness and powerlessness that ultimately led to strength and meaning. Then they wrapped these traditions around him so deeply that Jesus seemed to live out both patterns. Neither of these images was popular. Yet when the disciples processed their Jesus experience through them, these patterns changed the very heart of their own religion. Each deeply shaped the Jesus experience and finally set the stage for a new understanding of Jesus as the fully human one, which I now believe is the only way anyone today can ever understand what we mean when we use the word "divinity."

The first of these images is called the "servant," sometimes the "suffering servant." It was drawn by an unknown prophet, probably in the sixth century before the Common Era, and attached to the scroll of the prophet Isaiah. Today we call him Second Isaiah and we attribute chapters 40 through 55 of the book of Isaiah to him.

The second image is called the "shepherd," sometimes the "shepherd king." It was also drawn by an unknown prophet, probably in the late fifth or early fourth century before the Common Era, though dating this work is more difficult than dating Second Isaiah. It was attached to the scroll of the prophet Zechariah. If we were being proper, we would refer to this person as Second Zechariah. Since most people do not even know who First Zechariah is, the use of the term Second Zechariah is not common. Second Zechariah, however, constitutes chapters 9 through 14. Far more than most Christians realize, Second Isaiah and Second Zechariah shaped the way the Jesus experience was understood, coloring the details of the story recorded in the gospels. These images served as voices out of the Jewish past to provide the words the gospel writers put on Jesus' lips. We turn first to the "suffering servant."

The Suffering Servant of Second Isaiah

The Jewish nation had been defeated at the hands of the Babylonians first in 598 BCE and then, in a more debilitating and ultimate way, in 586 BCE. Only the aged, the lame, the deaf and the blind among the Jews had been left in Judea, which had been repopulated with other people—foreigners, Gentiles—who had "false gods" and strange customs. All others were marched to Babylon as prisoners to be turned into an underclass of laborers. The land the Jews left behind was defiled, they believed, by the presence of the many strangers. Even worse, while the Jews were in captivity miscegenation occurred in their former homeland and the people known later as the Samaritans were the result. These Samaritans were believed to have compromised Jewish racial purity, Jewish religion and Jewish integrity.

When Second Isaiah wrote his text, the Babylonian exile was nearing its end. Hope for release was rising. It was the second and third generation of the exile. Judea, their beloved homeland, with its capital city of Jerusalem that housed the temple, was vividly alive, but only in memories. When the first generation of exiles had died, those memories had turned into dreams and fantasies, which the next generation treasured as their links with a reality they had never seen and which they feared they might never see. Dreams and fantasies always seem to grow when not bounded by either knowledge or experience. So the Jerusalem that lived only in the eyes of their minds grew more golden, more beautiful, more mysterious and more desirable. These exiled people dreamed at first of a restoration that would bring renewed glory, of the day in the unknown future when they might reclaim the place implanted in their hearts so indelibly by their parents, their grandparents and even their great-grandparents. In the writings of Second Isaiah one cannot help but notice these fantasies and the yearning behind them, typical of conquered people who live for the day they can reverse their defeat and become once again a dominant nation on the face of the earth. In their weakness they yearned to possess power and in their poverty they dreamed of wealth and prestige. Second Isaiah spoke of the shame and disgrace that the Jews hoped someday would come upon their enemies, dooming them to perish (41:11–12). He dreamed of restored power when God would make of the Jews a "threshing sledge, new, sharp, and having teeth" that would "crush" the mountains and "make the hills like chaff" (41:15). In the dream of restoration this writer was still at this point looking for vengeance. "The wealth of Egypt and the merchandise of Ethiopia ... shall come to [the Jews]." Their enemies "shall come over in chains and bow down to [them]" (45:14ff.). His text was full of the not very noble but nonetheless human hope that their present subjugation would someday be turned into their own dominance over their captors and enemies.

The rise to world power of Cyrus, the king of the Persians, in the last half of the sixth century BCE fanned this hope. Here, under the leadership of Cyrus, was a military power that could confront Babylon. Furthermore, Cyrus followed a policy of religious toleration and of setting free captive peoples to return to their ancestral lands. The hopes of the Jews became concrete when Babylon fell to Cyrus in 539 BCE. The captive peoples sang for joy and began to celebrate their impending freedom.

The transition of the exiled people back to their ancestral home in Judea took both time and organization, so it did not happen at once. The promised day came, however, when the first exploratory expedition was ready to return. The person who became known as Second Isaiah was surely a part of this group. Travel was hard and dangerous in those days. The returning exiles went by foot with only the possessions they could carry. They were, for all practical purposes, an unarmed people. It was probably their weakness and their poverty that did most to keep them safe, for they were not lucrative targets for bandits and thieves. What gave them the courage to leave the known for the unknown was the pictorial dream planted in their minds by their forebears—a dream about the beauties and wonders of their God-promised homeland. This, combined with their yearning to be free, caused them to sing of the strength that God had given them. Second Isaiah's words capture this spirit of expectation. The words are best remembered in the King James Version of the text, because these are the words that Handel set to music in his exquisite Christmas oratorio entitled *Messiah:*

> Comfort ye, comfort ye my people,
>   saith your God.
> Speak ye comfortably to Jerusalem,
>   and cry unto her, that her
>   warfare is accomplished, that her
>   iniquity is pardoned:
> For she hath received of the Lord's hand
>   double for all her sins. (Isa. 40:1–2, KJV)

The unknown prophet went on to describe what it meant to return to one's homeland. It was not unlike the coming of the kingdom of God:

Every valley shall be exalted,
    and every mountain and hill shall be made low:
And the crooked shall be made straight,
    and the rough places plain:
And the glory of the Lord shall be revealed. (40:4–5, KJV)

In Cyrus Second Isaiah saw God's redeemer. He even called him the "anointed one," or *maschiach,* the Jewish word for "messiah" for which our word "Christ" is an English equivalent (Isa. 45:1). When Second Isaiah wrote, "How beautiful upon the mountains are the feet of him that bringeth good tidings, that publisheth peace; that bringeth good tidings of good,... that saith unto Zion, Thy God reigneth!" (Isa. 52:7, KJV), he probably had Cyrus in mind.

His emotions were unrestrained. "Break forth into joy," he wrote; "sing together, ye waste places of Jerusalem: for the Lord hath comforted his people, he hath redeemed Jerusalem ... ; and all the ends of the earth shall see the salvation of our God" (Isa. 52:9–10, KJV).

Fantasy and hope, however, are not the same as reality; and reality was destined to be the experience of this unknown prophet. Perhaps his words reflected the high anticipation of the exiles' return to the place about which he knew only through tribal memory. He thought of Jerusalem as God's shining city on a hill, the golden city, the place in which "your God reigns" (Isa. 50:1). The moment came, however, when this exploratory expedition arrived and the reality they saw was such that all their hopes perished and all their dreams disappeared as they do when one awakens out of sleep. I suspect those weary travelers wished they had never come. This is the Promised Land? This is the place our ancestors vowed never to forget? It was almost more than they could embrace. Judea was a wasteland. The city of Jerusalem was a pile of rubble. The temple was a field of weeds and broken stones. There was nothing anywhere that spoke of beauty. Every illusion of future grandeur died in that cold sober assessment.

Second Isaiah began to realize that the Jewish nation would never rise again. Power was not to be in their future. How could the Jews ever again presume to live out their vocation as the people chosen to bring God's blessing to all the nations of the world? No one would ever look to these pitiful Jews who lived in this poverty-stricken place for anything. They saw themselves as destined now to be weak, broken, powerless, defenseless, hopeless, the violated people of the world. When this reality collided with the fantasy of their hopes, reality won. Second Isaiah sank into a depression in which he looked again at his nation, his heritage, their God and their vocation as the chosen people. At that moment the destiny of his nation to return to grandeur as God's instrument died. This prophet's relationship with God also seemed to die. He despaired of the possibility of finding any destiny for his nation at all, any mission for the people of God in this new place. The land called Judea and this hopeless remnant of the people of God had now become so insignificant, so impotent, as not to matter much to anyone. Into the dark night of the soul Second Isaiah sank. How long he stayed there no one knows.

When he emerged, however, he was a startlingly different person. In that reformed persona, he sketched a portrait of one he called "the servant of the Lord," who was, I suspect, simply a symbol of the Jewish nation facing its future realistically. The servant was to live out the vocation that this unknown prophet was driven to see as the only possible vocation for those he thought of as God's chosen people.

Israel's role was no longer to seek power, but to accept powerlessness as a way of life. The "servant" was to go beyond Jewish boundaries to bring justice to the Gentiles, light and salvation to the world (49:6). The "servant" was to live out the tenderness of God for all people (55:5), to guide the thirsty to water (55:1), to set life free (42:7), to make people whole (42:7). He would accomplish this task not with power but through weakness and self-effacement. He would not resist hostility or pull back from maltreatment (50:5–6). His face would be set like a flint toward his purpose (50:7). Though afflicted, the "servant" would live in the expectation of a final vindication that would probably come not in history, but beyond history. This figure would finally be overwhelmed, meet a shameful death, even be slain as a criminal. That was all part of accepting the vocation of powerlessness.

Others would see the servant as the bearer of our sicknesses, the carrier of our sorrows, as one "wounded for our transgressions" and "bruised for our iniquities"; as one by whose "stripes we are healed" (53:5, KJV). His was to be a vicarious suffering. By his willingness to accept abuse, he would drain the world of anger and thus through him people would be brought to wholeness (53:3–5). In this way God would restore not the Jewish nation, but creation itself to its glory.

Second Isaiah's servant stood on the side of God and against evil. The "spoil" that would accrue to this servant was not honor and power, the tools of survival that are eagerly sought in the world of our insecurity; his reward, if that is the proper word to use at all, was a life set free, made whole, called to a new consciousness. It was a startling image, but certainly not a popular one. It seemed to appeal only to those who enjoyed suffering. So it was that the Jewish people corporately ignored the writings of Second Isaiah and followed the more appealing road to glory penned later by other leaders of the postexilic Jewish world—prophets like Ezra and Nehemiah. The victorious "Son of man" imagery captured their imagination far more than did the defeated and abused "servant" of the Lord; and so the image of the suffering servant languished for centuries. It was, however, incorporated in the scriptures of the Jews—primarily, I suspect, because it was attached to the scroll of Isaiah.

Some five hundred years later a first-century Jewish teacher who was clearly in the prophetic tradition emerged out of Galilee. He fit none of the popular images. He dared to walk outside and beyond all of the human protective boundaries. Ultimately, he was killed by the Romans in the first century of the Common Era. His disciples now found in the portrait of this discarded and neglected "servant" figure composed by Second Isaiah one whose weakness and powerlessness helped them to make sense out of the life of Jesus. Inevitably, long before the gospels were written, the image of the "servant" was wrapped about the memory of Jesus of Nazareth. No part of Jesus' life escaped the influence of the "servant." This was especially true for Luke. When Simeon the priest was said to take the baby Jesus into his arms to bless him on the fortieth day of his life, in a story that only Luke tells, he said that Jesus would be "a light to lighten the Gentiles, and the glory of [God's] people Israel" (Luke 2:32), words that clearly echo the role of the "servant" (Isa. 42:6). When the gospels tell the story of Jesus' baptism, they portray John the Baptist as preparing the way of the Lord with words that come directly out of the story of

Second Isaiah's "servant" (Isa. 40:3). The words spoken supposedly from heaven at the time of Jesus' baptism and repeated in the heavenly words spoken on the Mount of Transfiguration are also taken directly from the "servant" (42:1). The "servant" could not accomplish his purpose without undergoing abuse, rejection, persecution and death. Jesus was portrayed as walking the "servant's" path. The death of Jesus came to be understood through the image of the "servant." We have already noted how the content of the crucifixion story is drawn in large measure from the work of Second Isaiah, but now we see how easy it was to do that, since the memory of Jesus had already been organized around the vocation of living out the "servant" role. There are many other points of contact. After the story of the transfiguration, Jesus was said to have "set his face" (Luke 9:51) toward his destiny just as the "servant" did in Isaiah (50:7). The "servant" went to kindle fire (50:11), while Jesus, as portrayed in Luke, came to baptize "with the Holy Spirit and with fire" (3:16). When Luke had Jesus say, "Behold, we are going up to Jerusalem and everything that is written of the Son of man by the prophets will be accomplished" (18:31), there is little doubt that Second Isaiah was the prophet he had in mind.

In the resurrection narrative of Luke, we are told in the Emmaus road story that Jesus, not yet recognized, "interpreted to them the things about himself in all the scriptures" (24:27, NRSV). Later, when Jesus appeared to the disciples, Luke says that Jesus "opened their minds to understand the scriptures and he said to them, 'Thus it is written, that the Christ [the messiah] is to suffer'" (24:45–46). Only in Second Isaiah is a portrait drawn of one who through suffering and death sets people free.

This is a striking picture, not of an incarnate deity or a divine visitor, but of a human life that found a way to act out a meaning of humanity that transformed the world and created a new humanity in the midst of their old humanity. Second Isaiah thus became just one more in a series of Jewish images that pointed to a new way to look at Jesus. Now he had become the servant of the Lord, the human one who walked the way of powerlessness. Perhaps the most profound of all the images we find in the gospels, it needs to be raised to our consciousness, because through the lens of Second Isaiah the followers of Jesus began to draw a picture of a whole new Jesus.

The Shepherd King of Second Zechariah

There is some sense in which the prophet we call Second Zechariah leaned on the "servant" of Second Isaiah to create his image of the "shepherd king," for there are some strong similarities. Both were incorporated into the scriptures by being attached to earlier writings; and once there, both tended to be ignored. In time Christian scholarship began to discover Second Isaiah which emerged as a popular interpretive tool. Second Zechariah, on the other hand, remains obscure, its influence generally muted. Yet I believe a case can be made for the fact that not only Second Isaiah but also Second Zechariah shaped the memory of Jesus more dramatically than any other part of the Hebrew tradition.

The first thing to notice is that Second Zechariah is both overtly and covertly present in the background of each of the canonical gospels. The most obvious place, already referred to, is the story of Jesus' entry into Jerusalem. These verses are frequently read as the lesson from the Hebrew scriptures on Palm Sunday:

Rejoice greatly, O daughter of Zion!
Shout aloud, O daughter of Jerusalem!
Lo, your King comes to you;
triumphant and victorious is he,
humble and riding on an ass,
on a colt, the foal of an ass. (Zech. 9:9–11)

That connection raises in my mind a question about the historicity of the story of Palm Sunday. It looks like one more effort to portray Jesus in terms of traditional messianic expectations. That question becomes more intense as the work of Second Zechariah unfolds. The argument of the traditionalists that Jesus must have deliberately and overtly acted out this image as a way of making a messianic statement is, in my mind, the last gasp of a literalist mentality that is in perpetual retreat from reality.

As Second Zechariah's story develops, the enemies of the shepherd king are the sheep traders in the temple. In chapter 14 the prophet states that on the day of the Lord "there shall no longer be traders in the house of the Lord" (Zech. 14:21, NRSV). It begins to appear that the very dramatic telling of Jesus' act of cleansing the temple of those who bought and sold animals was also little more than the development of a messianic symbol. This means that even these stories are in the same category with the Bethlehem birthplace and the disciples being twelve in number.

A careful reading of Second Zechariah brings forth more echoes. The sheep merchants pay the "shepherd king" thirty pieces of silver, to be rid of him (11:12). He declines this payment, however, for he is no longer willing to be their shepherd. The "shepherd king" then hurls the silver back into the temple treasury. Then all of Jerusalem, says Zechariah, looks on him whom they have pierced and weep as for a firstborn son (12:10).

There is no doubt that when these passages were read in the synagogues among the early disciples of Jesus, the disciples came to believe that they were actually written about Jesus. With the hindsight of Easter, the storyline of Second Zechariah seems to go from the Palm Sunday procession, to the betrayal, to the crucifixion. The last chapter, chapter 14, which was regularly read in the synagogues as part of the celebration of Sukkoth, describes an anticipated experience that later will find echoes in the Christian story of Pentecost (Acts 2). In that passage Second Zechariah talks about the coming day of the Lord, when an apocalyptic battle at the end of time will take place. All the nations of the world will be gathered against Jerusalem in a version of Armageddon. The city will be taken, the houses looted, the women raped. Half of the citizens will go into exile; the others will be cut off from the city. When the darkest moment comes and no hope remains, "The Lord will go forth and fight against those nations. . . . On that day his feet shall stand on the Mount of Olives which lies before Jerusalem" (14:3–4). We remember that the triumphal procession of Jesus is said to have begun on the Mount of Olives. Second Zechariah then says that the Mount of Olives shall be split in two by an earthquake and only then will God come (14:4ff.). Recall that the gospels say that when Jesus died, a kind of spiritual earthquake occurred. Matthew makes it literal (Matt. 27:51), but instead of splitting the Mount of Olives, the earthquake splits the curtain of the temple that separates the Holy Place where the people can gather from the Holy of Holies,

God's dwelling place. The earthquake in Matthew is also said to have raised the dead (27:52). All of that is but a prelude to the arrival of the "day of the Lord."

Then Second Zechariah begins to list the signs of the "day of the Lord." Living water, a symbol of the Holy Spirit, will flow out of Jerusalem to the east and the west to embrace all the nations of the world. In the Pentecost story in the book of Acts, Luke offers a parallel: he says that when the Spirit fell upon the disciples they were able to speak in whatever language the people understood so that all the nations could be gathered together. Next, Second Zechariah says the Lord will become king over all the earth; on that day God will be one and God's name one. Presumably, God's people will also become one and peace will prevail. The land will bloom, the wine presses will be filled and Jerusalem will abide in security. Nations that once went up to Jerusalem to wage war will now go up only to worship the Lord of hosts, to keep the festival of Sukkoth, the celebration of the final harvest.

Can anyone imagine that this little work was not used to shape the Jesus story into the chronicle that we read in the gospels? Clearly the "shepherd king" became just one more image that the disciples of Jesus used to make sense out of the Jesus experience; in the oral period, they built on the messianic expectations found again and again in the Jewish scriptures and in the Jewish consciousness to shape the Jesus story. The Jesus of history, the real human being, becomes dim as we awaken to the possibility that so many of the gospel portraits are interpretations far more than they are eyewitness memories of a person of history. Yet that Jesus, a person of history, somehow was thought to have made each of these biblical images seem appropriate.

While the Jesus of history fades, however, the experience that he produced grows larger and larger. We begin to be aware, perhaps painfully so, that we can never really recapture the Jesus of history. That Jesus once seemed certain and secure. He was concrete, we thought. Now he is seen as a composite of mythological interpretations masquerading as history. In the findings of the Jesus Seminar 84 percent of the sayings of Jesus and a similar percentage of the acts of Jesus were deemed not to be authentic as historical words and deeds.[1] They are instead the products of the community that then attributed them to

Jesus. To lose the Jesus of history is not a tragedy, however, since we probably never possessed him except in an illusory way.

The issue that this analysis has raised over and over again is that there must have been something about this Jesus that was so powerful that it seemed appropriate for his disciples to wrap around him the sacred symbols of their worship, the myths of their messianic expectations, the most sacred heroes of their tradition, magnified to supernatural proportions. There was something about him that caused them to conclude that the God in whom they believed was present in and somehow with the Jesus they had known. That is what we must recover.

18

JESUS: A MAN FOR ALL JEWISH SEASONS

It is the very essence of the Christian claim that in the human
Jesus the reality, perhaps even the fullness of what we think
God is, has been met and engaged. Can that reality be
separated from creeds, doctrines and dogmas?

It surprises readers of the gospels even today to realize how
deeply shaped the gospel narratives are by Old Testament
images. When the fact that the gospels are interpretive pieces of litera-
ture, not literal records of what actually happened, is grasped, readers'
confidence in traditional biblical claims begins to waver. That is one
of the reasons why resistance to scholarly insights into the scriptures is
so high. It is hard to imagine or to recognize, given two thousand years
of literalism, just how little the gospel writers were concerned about
historical accuracy. They passionately wanted to interpret the experience they had had with Jesus and so, without apology or qualms of
conscience, they told their stories with references out of the Hebrew
scriptures and heightened the tales of heroic figures from the Jewish
past when they applied them to Jesus.

On almost every page of the gospels we find overt and oblique references to Jewish heroes. Indeed, the gospels simply cannot be read with
any intelligence until we embrace how totally the life of Jesus was
shaped by the reading of the Hebrew scriptures. I trust I have demonstrated that only in the synagogue could that kind of interpretive process have taken place. We started there and then went into the

messianic images that were present in synagogue worship. In the process of seeing Jesus through these Jewish images, we began to recognize the connection that the early Christians had made between Jesus and the liturgical life of the synagogue. I conclude this section of this book by laying out what is now to me an obvious pattern that opens still another door into the primitive memory of Jesus and that carries us as close to that primary Jesus experience as we perhaps can come.

Most Christians are familiar with what is called the church year. It is anchored in the two major events in Jesus' life, his birth celebration at Christmas and his resurrection celebration at Easter. The year is then fleshed out by a season that anticipates his birth, called Advent, and one that extends the celebration of his birth, called Epiphany. Easter is then expanded with the penitential season of the forty days of Lent on one side and with the seasons of Ascension and Pentecost, which marks the coming of the Holy Spirit, on the other. The church year thus enables Christians to recall annually the major moments in the life of Jesus and to appropriate these moments into their own spiritual patterns.

The synagogue also had a liturgical year, in which the great moments in Jewish history were relived and thus made timeless. Most Christians are not familiar with the celebrations of this Jewish year; so let me simply place them before my readers in the order that seems to be followed in the book of Leviticus (23):

- Passover: the fourteenth and fifteenth days of the month of Nisan (late March, early April). A celebration of the birth of the Jewish nation in the exodus.

- Shavuot or Pentecost: fifty days after Passover, on the sixth day of Sivan (late May or early June). A commemoration of the giving of the law to Moses at Mount Sinai.

- Rosh Hashanah: the first day of the month of Tishri (roughly late September or early October). An annual gathering of the people to pray for the coming of the kingdom of God.

- Yom Kippur: the tenth day of Tishri (late September or early October). A day of penitence and reflection on the ability of God to overcome the sin of human life and alienation from God.

- Sukkoth or Tabernacles: starting the fifteenth day of Tishri (normally our October). An eight-day celebration of the harvest.

- Dedication or Hanukkah: starting the twenty-fifth day of the month of Kislev (typically in mid-December). An eight-day celebration of the return of the "light of God" to the temple during the time of the Maccabees.

In those years before the gospels were written Jesus was remembered and recalled week by week in the context of the sabbath readings of the scriptures. What I want us now to engage is the reality that the liturgical year of the Jews also shaped the memory of Jesus very significantly. Indeed, I would go so far as to argue that Mark, the first gospel, was organized around this liturgical year, and that the gospels of Matthew and Luke, both of which followed Mark's general outline and copied great chunks of Mark's work, reflect quite significantly this same organizing principle. I approach this subject by raising two questions rarely asked: Have you ever wondered why Mark's gospel is so much shorter than the other synoptics? Have you ever wondered what the deficiency was that both Matthew and Luke found in Mark that caused them to want to rewrite it in an expanded version? Because that is exactly what these later two gospel writers did. Matthew expanded Mark in a specifically Jewish direction, while Luke rewrote Mark for his more cosmopolitan audience of dispersed Jews and Gentile proselytes who had begun to be attracted to the Jesus message. By looking at these gospels through the lens of the liturgical year of the Jews, I believe we can answer these questions and the insight that will inevitably flow from this discovery can be deeply illumining. It is now time to see how connections with the liturgical year of the Jews became the organizing principle in Mark first, and then in Matthew and Luke also.

The first building block of this interpretive theory came when I suggested that the placement of the crucifixion inside the context of the observance of Passover was a liturgical connection far more than a historical one. Let me assume that the case for this insight is made. Then, attaching the crucifixion story to the Passover, I will stretch the gospel of Mark backward against the remainder of the Jewish liturgical year. Mark 14 and 15 would be the Christian story of Jesus' passion read at the time of the Passover. Earlier, I sought to demonstrate that Mark's passion narrative is composed in eight segments designed to accommodate a twenty-four-hour vigil liturgy—segments that are visible within the Marcan text. That would leave Mark's Easter story (16:1–8) to be read on the sabbath after the Passover.

Moving backward from chapters 14 and 15, we see that the next major Jewish liturgical celebration is the Festival of Dedication. This festival, which is today called Hanukkah, comes in the month of Kislev, roughly corresponding to our month of December. This would be about three months before Passover. Working backward by assigning a single coherent passage of Mark's gospel to each sabbath, we discover that between these two celebrations, Passover and Dedication, there is enough material in the text to reach the beginning of the journey to Jerusalem, which starts in Mark at 9:30. This section contains all of the teaching by Jesus of the disciples along the route to Jerusalem, the entry into Jerusalem (beginning in chapter 11), the story of the cleansing of the temple and the teaching by Jesus in Jerusalem; it culminates in the apocalyptic chapter 13, set in the temple in Jerusalem, but discussing the end of the world.

Not coincidentally, I now believe, that brings us to the Festival of Dedication, which commemorates the moment during the period of the Maccabees when the light of God was restored to the temple. In that exact place in Mark's gospel (9:2–8) we have the story of Jesus' transfiguration, which proclaims Jesus as the new temple on whom the light of God now rests. Moses and Elijah, who appear with him (representing the twin pillars of Judaism), are made to be subservient to Jesus. This is not a place to build three tabernacles of equal rank, says the heavenly voice from out of the clouds, who pronounces Jesus "my beloved Son" and gives the divine order to "listen to him." The transfiguration of Jesus is the perfect story to incorporate the Feast of Dedication into the story of Jesus and it fits the liturgical calendar with remarkable accuracy. The temple, the meeting place between God and human life, has by this time, I am convinced, been destroyed by the Romans. In response to that calamity the followers of Jesus are projecting him as the next temple, the new meeting place between God and human life. Dedication celebrates the light of God being restored to the temple. Transfiguration celebrates the light of God resting on Jesus. The two stories are deeply correlated, suggesting that the story of Jesus is tracking the liturgical year of the synagogue. From this early story in Mark, John writing some thirty years later, would borrow the theme of identifying Jesus with the temple. "Destroy this temple and in three days I will raise it up," John's Jesus is made to say. To this incredible statement Jesus has the religious authorities say, "It has taken forty-six years to build this temple and will you raise it up in three days?" Then the author explains: "But he spoke of the temple of his body" (John 3:19–21).

Between Dedication in mid-December and the next earlier liturgical celebration of the Jews, which was called Sukkoth—the harvest festival—there is a period of approximately seven to nine sabbaths, depending on where Hanukkah falls.[1] Once again, continuing to roll Mark backward, we pass through many of the narratives describing events in the Galilean phase of Jesus' public ministry. There are healing stories such as the account of the demon-possessed man whose demons, which were legion, were expelled from him and entered a herd of swine, animals considered by the Jews to be unclean (5:1–20); the raising of Jairus' daughter, which was wrapped around the story of the woman with the chronic menstrual discharge (5:21–43); a story revealing Jesus' alienation in his home area both from his own family and the people in the synagogue (6:1–6); the commissioning of the twelve, with the ensuing debate that their mission created, including the story of John the Baptist's death (6:7–29); the feeding of the five thousand and Jesus' journey across the lake where he walked on water (6:31–56); his teaching on unclean things (7:1–23); his journey to Gentile territory on the border of Tyre and Sidon and Gentile healings of the Syrophoenician woman's daughter and the deaf man with an impediment in his speech (7:24–37); the feeding of the four thousand on the Gentile side of the lake and its interpretation (8:1–21), and finally the story of the blind man of Bethsaida and its unique placement next to Peter's confession that Jesus is the Christ at Caesarea Philippi, which we noted has connections with that blind man who was healed, but by degrees (8:22–38). Those are nine episodes, one for each sabbath between Sukkoth and Dedication, with a couple of these episodes being brief enough to be squeezed into seven or eight sabbaths should there be a need to do so.

This would mean that chapter 4 of Mark's gospel would be the passage that would come on Sukkoth, an eight-day festival that begins on the fifteenth day of Tishri. Sukkoth, a harvest festival, was the Jewish Thanksgiving Day. It was observed from mid to late October. (You may remember that we looked at some of the details of Sukkoth when we were discussing the story of Jesus' entry into Jerusalem prior to the Passover.) What is the narrative that Mark has in his gospel at exactly the time of year when Sukkoth is being celebrated? It is the harvest story of the sower who sowed his seed on four different kinds of soil, each of which yielded a different harvest. It is a long parable that the disciples ask to have explained, leading to further commentary on the parable. That parable is followed by additional harvest-related nature stories, like the parable of the man who planted his seed in the ground and waited for the earth to bring forth its fruit at the harvest, the parable of the mustard seed and finally the account of Jesus demonstrating his mastery over the forces of nature by stilling the storm. There is sufficient material in this long fourth chapter to provide readings for the eight days of Sukkoth. Once again we see an uncanny, close connection between the gospel's interpretation of Jesus and the themes of this great fall celebration of the Jews. The pattern begins to be clear.

Still spreading Mark's gospel backward from the original connection of the crucifixion with the Passover, we find that there would normally be only one sabbath between Sukkoth and the next great holy day in the Jewish liturgical calendar, which is Yom Kippur, the Day of Atonement, on the tenth day of Tishri. We have already looked in detail at how the symbols of this event were related to the life of Jesus of Nazareth. Now our task is to follow the backward track of the gospel to see if there are appropriate Jesus stories to be read at the observance of this solemn day of penitence. If half of chapter 3 of Mark served as the Jesus story on the sabbath between Sukkoth and Yom Kippur, then the Yom Kippur passages of Mark would be chapter 2 and the first half of chapter 3. Here we have a series of healing, cleansing stories: the man with palsy who is let down through the roof and then is healed by Jesus' pronouncing his sins to be forgiven (2:1–13); the calling of Levi from the receipt of custom into discipleship and Jesus' eating with publicans and sinners (2:14–17); teaching on the penitential act of fasting (2:18–22); the debate on the observance of the sabbath and whether or not the sabbath was designed to control human evil or to be a resource for the expansion of human life (2:23–28); the healing of the man with the withered hand in the synagogue on the sabbath, along with a series depicting the healings of sicknesses and the banishing of unclean spirits (3:1–12), and finally, the story of Jesus' calling the twelve and empowering them to be healers and to cast out devils (3:13–20). This final episode culminates in the charge that Jesus is "beside himself"—that is, is out of his mind or possessed by a demon (3:21–34). The unique thing about all of these episodes is that they portray Jesus as entering that which is unclean and restoring the victim of uncleanness to wholeness. That is exactly the message of Yom Kippur, the Day of Atonement! In that day, before there was any knowledge of germs and viruses as the physical cause of disease, sickness was regarded as punishment for evil. Mental sickness was defined as demon possession. For a Jew like Levi to work for unclean Gentiles was to make himself ceremonially unclean. In all of these accounts, then, Jesus is portrayed as walking into the realm of evil, cleansing, purging, redeeming the victims who were trapped in that realm. The Yom Kippur message is the theme of these stories and it is appropriate to the theme of that day in the liturgical year.

As we roll still further backward over the liturgical year of the Jews, we go past Yom Kippur and discover that just ten days prior to it, on Tishri 1, Leviticus mandates the celebration of Rosh Hashanah, or the Jewish New Year (Lev. 23:23–25). There would need to be readings in Mark's gospel for the one or two sabbaths that might fall in that ten-day period. Continuing to stretch Mark's gospel backward, we have sufficient material in verses 16 through 45 of chapter 1 to cover that. These verses cover the calling of the first disciples; Jesus' being identified by demons; hometown healing stories, including the healing of Peter's mother-in-law, and Jesus' rising public notoriety.

That leaves us with Mark's opening story (1:1–15), which, if our theory is to work, needs to be appropriate to the celebration of Rosh Hashanah, the Jewish New Year. Rosh Hashanah was celebrated by the blowing of the shofar, the gathering of the people, the proclamation that the kingdom of God is drawing near and a call to the people to repent as a way of preparing for the kingdom. What do we have in Mark's opening verses? It is the story of John the Baptist being the human shofar, crying in the wilderness to gather the people, to urge them to prepare for the way of the Lord and announcing the coming of the one who will inaugurate the kingdom of God. John gathers the people who come to him to be baptized in the Jordan River as a sign of that penitence and an act of their preparation for the coming kingdom. He is described as hailing the one who is to come later. Just to make sure that Mark's readers know who it is about whom John is speaking, Mark introduces Jesus for the first time in that setting. He is the one who will baptize not with water but with the Holy Spirit. Jesus is baptized, the spirit descends upon him like a dove and the heavenly voice identifies him as messiah, *maschiach*, God's son. It is a perfect Rosh Hashanah message.

Clearly, the organizing principle behind the gospel of Mark is neither memory nor history. It is the telling of Jesus stories appropriate to the liturgical year of the Jews—the same liturgical year through which the disciples of Jesus were living as worshippers in the synagogue. When one thinks about it, the fit is so complete and the order is so obvious. The first gospel was composed so that disciples of Jesus, the followers of the way, could have stories of Jesus to be read on the sabbaths of the year even as they still worshipped in a synagogue.

Why is Mark so much shorter than Matthew and Luke? Mark provides the disciples with Jesus stories that cover the sabbaths between Rosh Hashanah and Passover—that is, for six and a half months of the calendar year. Why did both Matthew and Luke feel a need to expand Mark, which each certainly did? It was to provide the disciples of Jesus with readings for the rest of the year. If that supposition is accurate, then we ought to find supporting evidence for that in the later two gospels. I believe we can do just that.

First notice that Matthew front-loads his gospel. A comparison of Matthew against Mark, the basis of Matthew's gospel, shows that from chapter 13 on, Matthew tracks Mark very closely. If Matthew's challenge is to fill the sabbaths between the sabbath after Passover, on which the resurrection story was read, and Rosh Hashanah in late September, he needs sufficient Jesus material to cover about five and a half months. Look at how he fills it. Mark starts with Jesus' baptism. Matthew starts with a long genealogy, which is part of his two-chapter birth narrative. Matthew gets to Jesus' baptism by John in chapter 3.

Then he expands Mark's one-verse story of the temptation in the wilderness to a full drama, with each of the temptations spelled out in chapter 4. In Matthew 5, 6 and 7, he gives us an expanded section on Jesus' teaching in the Sermon on the Mount. By the time he arrives at chapter 11, he has come to Rosh Hashanah, but he has already used Mark's Rosh Hashanah story featuring John the Baptist. He could not have saved the story of Jesus' baptism for Rosh Hashanah, since it had to come at the beginning of Jesus' public ministry. So what does Matthew do? In a Cecil B. DeMille–type flashback, he reintroduces John the Baptist by expanding a Marcan story about Herod imprisoning John. This is where, in Matthew and Luke only, John in prison sends a message to Jesus inquiring as to whether he is the one that should come, the expected messiah. Jesus responds with the words from Isaiah 35 that we explored in the chapter on healing miracles. He lists the signs of the kingdom that he claims are all around him: the blind see, the deaf hear, the lame walk and the mute sing. It is the Rosh Hashanah message. People see the signs and know that the kingdom of God is at hand. The timing on the liturgical calendar is exquisite.

There is one other clear sign in Matthew's gospel that links it powerfully with the Jewish liturgical year and offers compelling evidence that Matthew has also used this as the organizing principle of his work. Since Mark provided readings only from Rosh Hashanah to Passover, he left out a major Jewish festival called Shavuot, or Pentecost, which comes fifty days after Passover. On that day the Jews recalled the giving of the law to Moses on Mount Sinai. It was celebrated as a twenty-four-hour vigil. The longest psalm of the psalter, Psalm 119, was composed as a hymn to the beauty and wonder of the law for use during that twenty-four-hour service. Psalm 119 has an opening stanza of eight verses, the first two verses of which begin with the word "blessed." That is followed by eight segments of twenty-four verses, each divided into three stanzas. This means that there is a part of this psalm assigned to each of the eight three-hour segments of the twenty-four-hour vigil. When Matthew comes to the time of Shavuot, what is the content with which he fills his gospel? It is the Sermon on the Mount, which takes up three chapters and which is patterned quite obviously on Psalm 119. The Sermon on the Mount opens with an introductory stanza of eight verses, all of which begin with the word "blessed." We call those verses the beatitudes. Then Matthew follows with eight segments, a mini-commentary on each of the beatitudes in reverse order. Throughout the entire Sermon on the Mount Matthew presents Jesus as a new Moses, on a new mountain, giving a new interpretation of the Torah. It could not be a more perfect fit.

When one turns to Luke looking for corroborating data, it is not as obvious, because the community for whom Luke writes, made up of dispersed Jews and Gentile proselytes, is not nearly so rigid in following the Jewish liturgical year as Matthew's more traditional community. They are not into twenty-four-hour vigils or eight-day celebrations that are the hallmark of old-line Jewish communities, but the pattern is nonetheless present.

Examining Luke in detail, we discover that he also front-loads Mark with an even longer birth narrative and an even longer genealogy. He expands the baptism of Jesus story with much of the content of the Baptist's preaching. When Luke arrives at Shavuot, or Pentecost, he develops an episode in which John the Baptist says, "I baptize you with water; but [one comes after me who] … will baptize you with the Holy Spirit and with fire" (Luke 3:16). Remember, Luke is going to give a full account of the Christian understanding of Pentecost in chapter 2 of the book of Acts. The greatest gift of God to the Jews was the gift of the Torah at Sinai. That is what the Jewish day of Pentecost marked. Luke, under Paul's influence, will say that the greatest gift of God to the Christians is the gift of the Holy Spirit. In Acts he recasts the Jewish Pentecost with Holy Spirit content. In his gospel, at exactly the right place, he has John the Baptist point to the Pentecost story. When Luke reaches Rosh Hashanah he, like Matthew, reintroduces John the Baptist from prison and repeats the signs of the in-breaking kingdom from Isaiah 35. The theory that the organization of these gospels is based on the liturgical year of the synagogue fits time after time.

There is one other place in which Luke reveals that his order is determined by the liturgical year of the Jews. In Luke alone, following his flashback episode to provide a John the Baptist story for Rosh Hashanah, this gospel writer tells the story of the woman who washes Jesus' feet (Luke 7:36–50). There are some noteworthy things about this story. First, its placement is strange. In both Mark and Matthew this story comes in the last week of Jesus' life (Mark 14:3–9, Matt. 26:6–

13). In those accounts it occurs in Jerusalem in the home of Simon the leper. The woman is not named, her deed is not thought of as scandalous and her motive to anoint Jesus' body for burial is extolled. In Luke's narrative, however, this episode takes place in the home of Simon the Pharisee, setting up a more moralistic environment. It occurs not near the time of the crucifixion, but early in the Galilean phase of Jesus' ministry. The woman's behavior, unlike in Mark and Matthew, is portrayed as sinful. She is described as a "woman of the street," a synonym for a prostitute. She fondles Jesus' feet. Only in this version of the story, at least among the synoptic gospels, does this woman wash his feet with her tears and wipe them with her hair. Her immoral status is noted by the people at the table. Jesus is criticized: "If this man were a prophet, he would have known ... what sort of woman this is" (7:39). For Jesus to allow this unclean woman to touch him meant that he was made unclean. So what is Luke trying to communicate with the placement of his story and the heightening of this woman's sinfulness?

When the liturgical year of the Jews is placed against Luke's gospel, this episode comes at exactly the time when Yom Kippur, the Day of Atonement, would be observed. Luke needed a Jesus story for his Yom Kippur observance. Having Jesus touched by an unclean woman and having the woman made whole and clean while Jesus remains uncorrupted, served his purposes well. He heightened the woman's sinfulness in order to allow for the fact that when Jesus enters the world of sin to transform it, this account can then become a perfect narrative for Yom Kippur. It fits! As we have seen, time and again the pattern of the liturgical year of the Jews determined the order in which the stories were organized. This is the pattern in Mark and in the two gospels that are dependent on Mark, Matthew and Luke.

John is not part of this pattern. Rather, the Fourth Gospel appears to have been organized around a series of signs that demonstrate Jesus' divine power over nature, infirmities and even death. It is beyond the scope of this book to attempt an analysis of the organizing principle of John. Suffice it to say that, despite many in-depth commentaries on this gospel, I do not believe that the definitive interpretation of John's gospel has yet been written. I am confident that it too follows a liturgical outline.

One final note. People have long noted that Mark, Matthew and Luke all treat the public ministry of Jesus as being of one year in duration, while John says it lasted three years. We now see that this one year was not the length of Jesus' public career, but the length of the Jewish liturgical year to which the stories of the life of Jesus have now been attached.

Once again we are driven back to a new starting place. By the time we get to the writing of the gospels, Jesus has already been interpreted by and understood through the Jewish scriptures. Jewish messianic images have been applied to him and his life has been made to conform to those images. The story of his life is told, organized by the liturgical year that was followed in the synagogue. This liturgical year is now recognized as the organizing principle through which the words and deeds of Jesus are remembered, at least in the first three gospels.[2]

We have examined how the Jesus experience was originally interpreted. Now our task is to see what that timeless God experience was originally, what it is today and how we can enter it now. It is to that reality that this book has relentlessly driven. It remains only to spell it out as clearly as we can. For it is the very essence of the Christian claim that in the human Jesus the reality, perhaps even the fullness of what we think God is, has been met and engaged. Can that reality be separated from creeds, doctrines and dogmas? Is the Jesus who emerges from this analysis still in touch with the deepest claims that historically have been made for him? I believe he is and because I do, I enter the final phase of this book with great expectations and a lively faith.

Part 3

JESUS FOR
THE NON-RELIGIOUS

INTRODUCTION: JESUS REALLY LIVED

"Sir, we wish to see Jesus" (John 12:21). Indeed, he is a figure of history capable of being seen.

We have tried in these pages to separate the man Jesus from the myth. We have traced the dimensions of the interpretive process that was attached to him by Jewish disciples during the oral period of Christian history. Now I want to make a new case for Jesus for the non-religious; to introduce Jesus again to those who can no longer live comfortably inside the language and within the traditions of the religious system that historically has claimed to own him.

I begin in a humble, but an essential place, if I am to cover all the bases. Jesus was, first of all, a human being who actually lived at a particular time in a particular place. The man Jesus was not a myth, but a figure of history from whom enormous energy flowed—energy that still in our day cries out to be adequately explained. Nazareth in Galilee was his home, and his time on this earth began in the last years before what is now called the Common Era and ended within the first third of the first century of that era.

I start with these assertions because once the interpretive layers surrounding Jesus begin to be peeled away, as they have been in the earlier parts of this book, there will always be those who, following a special agenda, begin to assert that Jesus himself was a legendary creation.[1] I find their arguments unconvincing for a number of reasons.

First, a person setting out to create a mythical character would never suggest that he hailed from the village of Nazareth. Yet he was known as Jesus of Nazareth and, because that village was in Galilee, he was called a Galilean. Neither label claims the sort of dignity that might commend itself to mythology. Nazareth was a small, dirty, insignificant town of no notable distinction. Even people in the rest of Galilee looked down upon it. Hints of the negativity toward Nazareth are found in the gospels themselves. "Can anything good come out of Nazareth?" Nathanael is quoted as saying to Philip, when Philip informed him that "we have found him of whom Moses in the law and also the prophets wrote, Jesus of Nazareth, the son of Joseph" (John 1:45). Yet, despite the negative image attached to Nazareth, there is no effort in the gospels to hide Jesus' humble origins. Mark and Matthew each refer to Nazareth on four different occasions. Luke has eight references to Nazareth in his gospel and he mentions it seven more times in the book of Acts. John adds five Nazareth references to his story, three of which are in the crucifixion narrative, where it is clear that his Nazareth origins are undoubted. Jesus surely hailed from the town of Nazareth.

The very fact that a Bethlehem birth tradition grew up around Jesus is additional testimony to the embarrassment that his roots in Nazareth caused to the early Christians. If Jesus were only a mythological character, why would the mythmakers create a myth that would embarrass them? This minor detail would have been changed, I submit, if it could have been changed. It was not changed, however, because it was too indelibly a part of the Jesus memory. Nazareth was the place from which Jesus emerged. Jesus was a Galilean. Both facts vibrate with counterintuitive historicity.

My second reason for asserting the historicity of the man Jesus of Nazareth is that he clearly began his life as a disciple of John the Baptist; indeed, he was baptized by John "for the forgiveness of sins" (Mark 1:4). The negativity toward this idea was powerful enough that by the time the Fourth Gospel was written, John the Baptist did not actually baptize Jesus (John 1:19–34). Once again my reasons lie in the constant attempt on the part of the early Christians to prove Jesus' superiority to John, which was clearly a response to the historically verifiable fact that Jesus began his public career as a disciple of John the Baptist.

That is why this John was interpreted as the forerunner and portrayed as the new Elijah. That is also why his death was described in such a way as to make it fulfill a vow spoken by Jezebel against Elijah (1 Kings 19:1–2).[2] This is why John the Baptist is constantly made to utter all of the self-deprecating things that we have previously mentioned. I repeat them here for emphasis: "After me comes he who is mightier than I, the thong of whose sandals I am not worthy to stoop down and untie.[3] I have baptized you with water; but he will baptize you with the Holy Spirit" (Mark 1:7–8). Mark goes on to note that it was only when John was arrested that Jesus came into Galilee, "preaching the gospel of God, and saying,...'The kingdom of God is at hand'" (1:14). Matthew has John the Baptist protest his baptizing of Jesus, claiming that John needed instead to be baptized by Jesus, not the other way around (Matt. 3:14). Luke takes the most extreme position, saying that even the fetus of John recognized the superiority of the fetus of Jesus before either was born (Luke 1:41). John completes this apologetic agenda by having the Baptist say, "[The reason I] came baptizing with water [was] that he might be revealed to Israel" (John 1:31).

I submit that the memory of Jesus as a follower of John, and therefore as secondary to him, was still so powerfully abroad by the time the gospels were written that the fact could not be expunged from the record. The way the gospel writers dealt with it, therefore, was to make John himself speak of Jesus' superiority in every way possible. Once again, if the Jesus story were a myth, embarrassing details like his having been a disciple of John the Baptist would never have been included. Yet they are not omitted in any of our biblical records. The attempt is made rather to explain them away, because those details are real, just as Jesus was real.

The third reason I am convinced of the historicity of the person of Jesus is that he was executed. It took enormous energy on the part of the early Christians to turn the account of his crucifixion into a victory. We have examined already some of the ways they did this. It took researching the Hebrew scriptures and enfolding Jesus into those scriptures so deeply that his death could be transformed. Once again, that is the stuff of which history is made. Apologetic explanations do not develop unless there is a reality that has to be explained and defended. Jesus was undeniably a figure of history.

Beyond these three reasons, it is also possible to establish objectively and to defend the proposition that Paul was in touch with those who knew the Jesus of history. That is accomplished by leaning on the first-hand evidence we find in one of the undoubtedly authentic early works of Paul, the epistle to the Galatians. By accepting Paul's personally recalled time line in that epistle, we conclude that Paul was in fact in contact with some of Jesus' disciples very soon after the crucifixion and that they shared with him their firsthand memories of the Jesus of history. That is such powerful evidence that Jesus lived that I need to sketch that storyline briefly.

If we accept the consensus of New Testament scholars that the death of Jesus occurred in or near the year 30 CE and that the epistle to the Galatians was written no later than the year 53 CE (and it could be as early as 51), both of which dates are well established in scholarly circles, then we have boundaries of twenty-one to twenty-three years within which to work. We add to that the study of Adolph Harnack, a brilliant nineteenth-century church historian whose work on the timing of Paul's conversion has never been disputed. Dr. Harnack has argued that the date of Paul's conversion could have been no earlier than one year and no later than six years after the crucifixion.[4] That means that 31 to 36 CE becomes the time frame in which Paul's conversion took place.

Now we go to the epistle to the Galatians, where Paul explains what he did immediately following his conversion. We notice, first, that Paul tells us almost nothing about that conversion experience. Those details are supplied only in the book of Acts, written by Luke some thirty to forty years after Paul's death. The historicity of the Acts story is clearly suspect. All Paul himself says in Galatians is that he persecuted the church of Jesus and tried to destroy it. He adds that when God called him—or, in Paul's words, when God "revealed his Son to me" (Gal. 1:15)—he did not go to Jerusalem but rather went into Arabia, where he remained for three years. That pushes our time line forward to the years 34 to 39 CE.

Then Paul says he went to Jerusalem and conferred with Cephas (Simon Peter) for fifteen days, but saw no one else except James, the Lord's brother (Gal. 1:18–20). Next Paul says that he went to Syria and Cilicia and spent fourteen years there (Gal. 1:21, 2:1). That brings us to the years 48–53 CE, which puts us well into the range of the date for the writing of the epistle to the Galatians. After that fourteen-year hiatus, Paul says he then returned to Jerusalem with Barnabas and Titus and laid before the apostles the gospel he preached among the Gentiles (Gal. 2:2–5). Paul describes in detail the accommodation reached at that gathering (Gal. 2:6–10). What we learn from this first-hand source in Galatians is that within three years of his conversion, Paul had conferred with Peter and had seen James, the brother of Jesus. This would have been no fewer than four and no more than nine years after the crucifixion. Peter and James, the Lord's brother, were people who knew the Jesus of history. A wider consultation took place with others eighteen to twenty-three years later, certainly within the range of an average memory. While urging my readers not to claim too much for this time reconstruction, I think we can be clear that full-blown myths are not created in so short a time. The historical fact of Jesus' historicity thus becomes the starting place for a new analysis of Jesus. It is not yet a very big claim, but we are dealing with a life actually lived. Jesus' real humanity is not in question.

That is where we begin. As demanded in the words of some Greek visitors to the disciples recorded in the gospel of John, "Sir, we wish to see Jesus" (12:21). Indeed, he is a figure of history capable of being seen.

WHO IS THE GOD MET IN JESUS?

The Lord is my light; ... whom then should I fear?
Ps. 27:1

With the Lord on my side I do not fear.... The Lord is on my side to help me.
Ps. 118:6–7

So Jesus was a real human being of the first century. That designation alone would characterize millions of people. The unique thing about this Jesus was that his real humanity came to be viewed as the vehicle through which God entered the life of this world. The word "God," however, is a human word and it conveys a particular meaning. Human words do not describe reality outside human experience. The word "God" does not exist outside the human use of that word. So the second step into a new understanding of Jesus must be found in bringing what we mean by the word "God" into our consciousness. I begin with a true story.

Several years ago, I was being interviewed by an English religion writer named Andrew Brown for a feature in the magazine section of the *Sunday Independent,* one of the quality papers in the United Kingdom. Andrew was a clever, personable and iconoclastic young man whose company I enjoyed enormously. After providing him with a tour of the diocese that I was serving at that time as its bishop, so that he could observe the way our churches were engaging the issues of urban

America, Andrew began to ask me about my concept of God. I responded by saying that the intellectual revolution of the last five to six hundred years had rendered the traditional God concept unbelievable. This meant that I could no longer think of this God as a being "up there" or "out there" who could and would intervene, answer prayers and reward and punish according to the divine will. Andrew became both wide-eyed and incredulous as the discussion continued. In his story, published a couple of weeks later, he praised some of our diocesan initiatives, but went on to say that no matter how creative or innovative this bishop might be, in the last analysis he really no longer believed in God and had in fact become an "atheist bishop." It was a clever phrase, bound to be quoted and repeated; the words "atheist" and "bishop," when juxtaposed, set all sorts of negative forces into motion. It was also, in my opinion, a profoundly ignorant conclusion, revealing both the limits of human vocabulary and the egotism of a human being who imagines that the human mind can actually describe either the realm or the being that we have come to call God. The fact is that, with rare exceptions,[1] most of the religion writers in the newspapers of the world today are theologically unlearned persons. Andrew Brown certainly was.

The word "atheist," for starters, does not mean, as people commonly assume, one who asserts that there is no such thing as God. It means, rather, that one rejects the theistic definition of God. It is quite possible, therefore, to reject theism without rejecting God. Andrew Brown could not and did not make that distinction. Most people are locked inside a similar mindset. Let me say it in a slightly different way. I am a God-intoxicated human being, but I can no longer define my God experience inside the boundaries of a theistic definition of God. Therefore, when I say that God was in Christ or when I assert that I meet God in the person of Jesus, I mean something quite different from the theological definitions of the past that forged doctrines like the incarnation and the trinity, both of which depend on a theistic definition of God. So in order to get to the essence of who Jesus was and even who Jesus is, I must get beyond the traditional theistic definition of God that I now regard as both simplistic and naïve, to say nothing of being wrong.

This quest will carry me back to the dawn of human self-consciousness, where I believe theism was born. It will also help us understand why theism has such a powerful hold on human minds and highlight the needs within the human psyche that theism meets. It will account for the strange fact that while the theistic definition of God has been all but destroyed by the advances in knowledge that created the modern world, religious people continue to cling to it with an irrational tenacity. Modern people today function as atheists, yet they still struggle in the religious dimension of their lives to grasp tightly an artificially respirated theism. What people need to hear and to embrace is that the theistic definition of God was never about God; it was always about human beings desperately in need of a coping system that would enable them to live with the anxieties of what it means to be human. So theism can die without God dying. That is the conclusion to which I have come. Now I turn to share the steps I took to reach that conclusion. It has been a long journey, but I hope a successful one. It begins, quite literally, at the beginning of planetary history.

This planet earth, according to the best estimates of our cosmologists and physicists, is far older than Ireland's Bishop James Ussher proposed in the seventeenth century with his suggestion that the earth was born on October 23, 4004 BCE! This planet was born as an extension of the explosion that scientists today call the big bang, which is believed to have brought the whole universe into being. It is called the big bang because everything that is today appears once to have been part of a mass of indescribable density, the explosion of which resulted in the hurling of enormous particles and cosmic dust into the vastness of space. This dust and those particles ultimately coalesced over eons of time into galaxies and planetary systems with bodies rotating around stars and tied to their orbits by various forces like gravity. The universe itself may be as much as 12 to 16 billion years old, with the particular solar system of which the earth is a part being a relative youngster at approximately 4.6 to 4.7 billion years of age. There was no life in our solar system at its inception, at least none on the planet earth, for the conditions necessary to support life did not yet exist. The surface of the earth was little more than a red-hot, boiling sea of molten rock, constantly being bombarded by comets, asteroids and debris from outer space. It would be up to a billion years or so before life, which is defined by the ability to reproduce itself, was to arrive or emerge.

How life first developed on this planet and even when it developed is still a subject of some debate, but appear it did. Its first form was that of a single cell that could subdivide. That was as far as life advanced for perhaps two billion years! The next step in the life process occurred when single cells began to cluster around one another, a process that allowed for cell differentiation to develop and for multicellular organisms to become part of this world. Still microscopic in size and still at home primarily in the sea, this entity called life experienced its next major advance after countless millions of years: the division into two distinct parts that we today identify by the words "plant" and "animal." Plant life and animal life even at that moment of their separation were deeply interconnected and were always mutually interdependent. Over the next period, again lasting millions of years, these life forms began to expand and to proliferate, filling the seas with living things. When millions and millions of years later the land on this planet earth finally became hospitable for life, both plant and animal forms began to gravitate toward this new environment by entering riverbeds and estuaries, finally climbing out of the sea and onto dry land. As recently as 2006 scientists discovered in the Canadian Arctic a tetrapod that represents a transitional phase between sea creatures and land creatures. It was dated about 375 million years ago.[2]

The developing and ongoing dialogue between living things and this new land environment created more adaptations in the relentless struggle of life forms to survive. Thus great varieties of life evolved in this churning world, as again millions of years flowed by. As yet there was no sense, or perhaps at best only a most rudimentary sense, of consciousness in any of these life forms. Every day millions of life forms were consumed to keep other life forms alive, but no one was conscious of this fact. The fragile quality of life on the planet earth went through several experiences of near extinction, but life's grasp on this planet was not ultimately destroyed and made comebacks after each disaster. The first glimmers of consciousness appeared as a kind of chemical response to the stimuli of the environment, but as different forms of life developed, this embryonic consciousness developed with them.

Many millions of years later, life evolved into reptilian forms and eventually those reptiles established their dominance over the life of the world. The brains of these creatures had become sufficiently developed to allow a conscious response to fear and threat, known as the "flight-or-fight response," to enter the cycles of life. At this early time the response was only instinctual, for this dawning consciousness had as yet no sense of time, no memory of a past and no anxiety connected with a future.

Perhaps no more than sixty-five million years ago, something happened to alter dramatically the earth's climate. Many scientists postulate that it was a collision with a giant comet sufficient to throw the earth out of its orbit. Whatever it was, the dominant reptiles, the giant dinosaurs, became extinct and with their demise the rule of the reptiles over the life of this planet ended. That catastrophe opened the door, as always seems to happen in the world of nature, for a different form of life to arise, and so the mammals, with all of the new potential that these warm-blooded creatures offered, came into dominance. Our earliest mammalian ancestors appear to have been mouselike little creatures that populated the grasslands of what is now eastern Africa. With the reptilian competitive advantage gone, the mammals proved capable of moving into a wide variety of new environments that allowed them to proliferate into numerous new forms and species as they wandered across the face of the earth.

The survival battle and the struggle for dominance tilted first toward one group and then another among these mammals until a particular line of apes, who possessed the potential of new intellectual skills, came into prominence. Intelligence proved to be the superior gift as the power of mind over the power of body won out. The great cats with their strength and speed and the large mammoths and elephants with their size and power made these creatures relatively secure in their own environment, earning for themselves later titles like "king of the jungle," but they lacked the capacity to continue to expand in brainpower. The increased brain size and the heightened levels of consciousness that were present among the less physically powerful apelike mammals began to propel their rise toward dominance. These creatures organized their communal life in interesting ways, forming clearly visible pecking orders. They developed the ability to hunt for food in cooperative packs instead of simply as individual predators. Their intellectual achievements increasingly offset their unformidable size and lack of speed. As their brains continued to develop in ever more complex ways, elements of advanced planning came to be part of the life of these creatures and they played this advantage in the battle for survival. Sometimes the hunt in packs required, as the price of success, the sacrifice of one or more of them. Because the survival of the species had apparently become a higher value than the survival of a single member, these creatures accepted that price. Here was the rudimentary development of tribal identity, later called patriotism, which would honor the one who was sacrificed so that the pack could survive.

In time, certainly no more than one to two million years ago (and possibly even later than that), a creature, humanlike if not yet fully human, emerged out of this apelike background in the ever-evolving process called life. None of this happened in a straight line, but came rather in fits and starts and some of the developing species reached only dead ends. These humanlike creatures began to be skilled in the making of both tools and weapons. This activity of tool-making or weapon-making meant that these creatures had developed a capacity to anticipate the potential use of those tools or weapons. At least in a preliminary way, the ability to think abstractly and the capacity to deal with and to plan for things that would occur in the medium called time began to mark this evolving form of life. Human beings were getting close, but they had not quite yet arrived.

That moment would not come until somewhere between fifty thousand and one hundred thousand years ago, a mere nanosecond on the clock of the earth's existence, when three things entered life that announced the arrival of human beings, as we now define them. The first was that consciousness grew into self-consciousness and awareness into self-awareness. The second was that the medium of time was expanded so that these human creatures could, in a conscious way, remember the past and recall it, and anticipate the future and plan for it. The third was that these creatures began to identify human sounds with both objects and actions, and in this way language, which is the essence of abstract thinking, came into being. At some specific moment, perhaps not at the same time, or in the same place, and certainly not in one solitary individual who might be called the mythological Adam/Eve, the first of the species that we identify as *Homo sapiens* came into being. This planet earth now possessed an inhabitant who was self-conscious, was time-aware and had the ability to communicate with words. Something new and wondrous had emerged out of the evolutionary soup—something that was destined to transform natural history into human history.

I try to imagine that mythical moment in which consciousness became self-consciousness and awareness became self-awareness. What was it like in the creatures in whom this new reality was dawning over whatever number of years it took to become the norm? All we know is that these human creatures evolved to the place where they saw themselves not as part of nature, but as separate from nature, even as standing over against the natural world. These human creatures had evolved to the place where they could look out on the world from a new center as separate, self-aware and self-conscious beings. It was probably both a startling wonder and a traumatic moment of fear and enormous anxiety. What does it mean to see yourself suddenly as one who is alone, fragile, self-consciously living in fear in the midst of powerful natural forces that you can identify, but over which you have no control? I suspect these first of our human ancestors shook in their skins at the new vision of what life had become and all that it now entailed. While they could experience these powerful changes, they could not possibly understand them except in the most primitive of ways.

Accompanying this self-awareness was the sense that their lives were lived inside an ever-flowing dimension called time. These human creatures recognized that there was a time before they existed as conscious creatures and there would be a time after that conscious existence ended. That is, they came to see themselves as bounded on each end by a sense of being transitory. Embracing their own finiteness, they began the inevitable contemplation of their own mortality. Finally these creatures developed the ability to articulate in symbolic sounds their fears and at the same time to embrace their limitations, their powerlessness and their sense of meaninglessness with the power of words.

Look at what this meant. It is one thing to die; life in many forms does that in vast numbers daily. It is quite another to know that you are going to die, to plan for it and to accept its inevitability. That was the human situation. It is one thing to be unaware that your existence has no meaning, as is the case for the billions of insects that are devoured each day as food for other living things; it is quite another to deal with that reality consciously and to battle against it. It is one thing to be part of the routines of life and death in the world of nature; it is quite another to be aware and self-conscious of the fact that you are a link in the food chain.

Human beings, as the centers of consciousness, now know that they will die and are aware that they will disappear. This is the knowledge that raised (and still raises) the questions of meaning and meaninglessness in them. Because that knowledge is now inherent, every human being is forced to inquire as to whether or not humanity's self-conscious life has any ultimate significance. To be human is, therefore, to endure the trauma of self-consciousness. It is to be aware of the existential shock of the threat of nonbeing. No other living thing before us has ever been required to embrace this level of anxiety. Part of what it means to be human is to know ourselves to be chronically anxious creatures. It means seeing ourselves as those who must embrace our own mortality. It means that if life has no ultimate meaning, we alone of all other creatures embrace the threat of meaninglessness. In response to that threat, human life is driven to create meaning. It was and is the human experience to tremble before these realizations. It is, however, also the acknowledged human destiny not to win the struggle for meaning, for survival or for life. The fate of all living creatures is to lose, but only the human life knows this self-consciously. It is thus not easy to be human. We will be felled, destroyed and eaten by natural enemies—that is what germs and viruses are, after all—and our flesh and bones will in our turn feed other forms of life.

If the anxiety initially arising out of this knowledge had not been banked by our ancient forebears, I don't think that self-consciousness could have survived. It would have been a step in the evolutionary process that could not be sustained, because what was required to sustain it was more than our human coping mechanisms could manage. That is the moment in which I believe this emerging human being asked the question for which the concept of God, understood theistically, was the answer. Theism is, I believe, a direct result of the trauma of self-consciousness. Theism is not God; it is rather a human coping mechanism.

Human beings began to ask questions like these: Is there someone or some presence in the universe like me, self-conscious and aware, but possessing more power than I possess, and able thereby to cope with the anxieties of existence that I now face? Where does this presence abide? Will this being or this presence be my ally or my enemy in the struggle to survive? Will this being or this presence use the power I imagine it must have to come to my aid? How can I win the favor of this being? How can I accommodate this "other's" presence? How can I secure the blessing of this power?

At first this thinking process took a very basic form. The lonely self-conscious human beings observed that there were living things, plants and animals, that existed quite independently of human life and so our ancient ancestors wondered where these living things came from, just as they wondered about their own origin. They observed vital natural forces in the world, like the flowing of a river, the tides of the ocean, the power of the wind, the warmth of the sun and the light of the moon. Some power must animate these things and make them able to do the things they do, they reasoned. Could that power protect and defend them also? To these things human beings began to assign a force that they called spirit. Spirit was unseen, mysterious, yet its power could be readily observed. Could they relate to this world of spirit, win its favor and enjoy its protection? the human creatures wondered. Out of the sky, they observed, came thunder, lightning, wind, rain, warmth, cold. Was there a spirit beyond the sky who controlled these forces? Was that spirit benevolent or malevolent? Could they do anything to make that spirit more friendly? What was it that might please the source of these apparently living things?

In time these individual spirits, thought to inhabit both creatures and vital forces in the natural world, provided the content for human beings' earliest religion, called animism—that is, the belief that something called spirit animated all that lived. The religious task was not to anger these spirits, but to please them so that they would serve our needs. God as something external to our life, supernatural in power, was born. Theism had appeared.

As life evolved and changed, so did theism, but it never transcended its original definition. When the human shift from hunters and gatherers toward more settled agricultural activities occurred, theism took on the form of the earth mother who brought life out of her womb to sustain the human struggle for survival. In that transition, theism began to display feminine characteristics. Later these supernatural spirits came to be thought of as something like a family of gods or spirits living in a polytheistic universe. Still later these divine powers, sometimes called gods, seemed to organize according to earthly standards of tribal life, with varieties of powers and functions, but with a supreme deity ruling over lesser spirits. This was when the human imagination conceived of a heavenly court under the leadership of a Jupiter and Juno or a Zeus and Hera. Still later, patriarchy drove the feminine out and theism moved from the world of many spirits to the form of one solitary deity who, like a tribal chief, ran the world as a kind of expanded tribal god who watched over and protected only the tribe that served this particular deity as its chosen people, and later who, as the universal God, ruled over all of life as a kind of king of the universe.

Yet in each of these images the theistic definition of God remained steadfast, ever saluted, and always intact. God was, as I see that definition emerging, "a being, supernatural in power, dwelling outside this world and able to invade the world in miraculous ways to bless, to punish, to accomplish the divine will, to answer prayers and to come to the aid of frail, powerless human beings." As soon as this theistic idea of a deity was established, anxiety lessened, since anxiety was the primary reason for the human creation of this theistic deity in the first place. Now, these human beings reasoned, there is a being beyond us, more powerful than we and capable of defending and protecting us, the self-conscious ones. All that was needed to turn this theistic coping device into a religious system was to discern what it was that pleased this deity. What would it take to gain divine favor or to avoid divine wrath in order to enlist the help of this supernatural being in the struggle to survive? The moment that question was asked, religious systems, all of which are consciously devised to accomplish exactly those goals, came into being. Human life was now generically defined as "religious human life." Analyze any religious system and you will discover that it contains two specific divisions. The first is: What is the proper way to worship so that God's favor will be gained? The second is: What is the proper way to behave or to live in order to gain God's approval? Later, in more formal religious settings, this would be called our duty toward God and our duty toward our neighbor and would be enshrined in the Hebrew tradition on two tablets of stone as the Ten Commandments.

Security, however, is not finally achieved until the religious system successfully claims to possess ultimate truth by some form of divine revelation. This claim of authority normally comes in one of two forms. Either this truth has been revealed to some human entity who stands near to God—a high priest, for example—or the absolute will of God has been spelled out in some inspired writing which God's representative alone can interpret properly. It is this claim to possess absolute truth that keeps anxiety in check. Relativity in religious claims must be repressed, because it always allows our original debilitating anxiety to return. Under this system the idea that we have genuine security requires that we do not doubt the meaning of our own created security system. So the idea of God as the Almighty One, who watches over us and protects us, came into being. We win this God's favor with proper divine worship. We please this God with lives marked by proper behavior. When in trouble, sorrow, need, sickness or any other adversity, we pray to this God for intervening help and we expect answers. When tragedies strike, we wonder what we have done to incur the divine wrath. This is the meaning and the legacy of theism and it became the dominant content of all religion that is theistic in its self-understanding. What we need to embrace from this insight is that human religious systems have never been primarily a search for truth; they have always been first and foremost a search for security.

Because theism was the primary way human beings conceptualized God, it was inevitable that when a group of first-century people believed that they had encountered God in the story of Jesus, they saw theism as the content of Jesus. The Jesus story was thus turned into an account of a theistic God coming to our rescue, invading the human world from above. Theism was the fully operative definition of the God we claimed we had met in Jesus. A literalized concept of incarnation was and is the theological language used to convey this idea. The doctrine of the trinity, which purports to define the reality of God, brings Jesus and the theistic concept of God into oneness.

The invading God from above needed a way to get into the human arena to engage the human situation, so a landing field was created capable of receiving the deity. Christians identified that landing field as the virgin birth. Through this miracle the theistic God put on human flesh and came among us. While he was on this earth, this Jesus (as he was described) could do all the things that people assumed God could do, for he was God in human form. So stories were told in which Jesus stilled the storm, walked on water, expanded the food supply, healed the sick and even raised the dead. If people pleased the God that they claimed to have met in Jesus, this God, still theistic in nature, would bless them by answering their prayers, intervening in their history and finally by accepting them into eternal life at the moment of their death, overcoming once and for all the human anxiety about our finitude.

The ancient human anxiety met by the development of the theistic understanding of God is still today operative in most of the traditional forms of Christianity. Religious systems are very slow to change. Theism still seeks to give meaning to life, to answer our questions about our self-conscious existence with authority and to calm our anxiety about mortality with promises of eternal life. The fires of anxiety, born in self-consciousness, are thus banked by religion and we are content, if not grateful, to live inside the theistic definition of God that we created. Theism, therefore, is not who God is. Theism is a human definition of who God is. There is a vast difference.

So our questions about Jesus must shift in a revolutionary new direction. What was the experience that his disciples were trying to articulate when they declared in a thousand different ways that in the human Jesus, the theistic God had been revealed? Is a dying theism the only way to make sense out of the God experience? Can we remove the theistic concept of God from our understanding of God and still be worshippers? Can we lift the theistic God overlay from the life of Jesus and still be Christians? I believe we can. Indeed, I believe there is no other alternative if we want to live as Christians in this twenty-first century. That is why we had to go through the exercise, in earlier chapters, of separating the myth of Jesus from the Jesus of history. That is why we needed to examine the primitive images by which he was understood. That is why we now must separate God understood theistically from the experience of God that we claim for Jesus. That is the insight I want to pursue.

The next step in discovering who Jesus is, is to allow the irrelevant theistic language with which we have surrounded him to be shattered until it lies in a million pieces at his feet. Then, as we look again, Jesus for the non-religious begins to come into view. So does a new sense of what it means to be human. That is when we ask whether or not theism was ever an asset to humanity. Is survival the same thing as living? We look at that question next as the journey goes on.

RECOGNIZING THE SOURCES OF RELIGIOUS ANGER

Once an idea of God begins to die it is like Humpty Dumpty: "All the king's horses and all the king's men could not put Humpty Dumpty back together again!"

The traditional way we tell the Christ story makes an ogre out of God, a victim out of Jesus and angry people who must be eternally grateful and thus hopelessly dependent out of us.

The signs of the death of a theistic understanding of God are all around us. Many of us will not allow ourselves to see them, because we have no alternative and would rather live with an illusion than try to embrace reality. It will not work, however, because once an idea of God begins to die, it is like Humpty Dumpty: "All the king's horses and all the king's men could not put Humpty Dumpty back together again."

One has only to look at the data. We no longer ascribe tsunamis, hurricanes, or heat waves to the desire of the supernatural God to punish evildoers. We do not interpret human sickness as punishment imposed on a victim by an angry deity. We no longer have confidence in the idea that God will punish our enemies or vindicate our cause in warfare. All of these are things we once attributed to the theistic God, but we now explain them with no reference to a supernatural deity whatsoever. In the words of English biblical scholar Michael Goulder, the theistic God in our time has become "unemployed." This God "no longer has any real work to do."[1]

Theistic images, however, continue to be employed in liturgy, sermons and hymns, although they make less and less sense to those who hear them. Attempts to look at Jesus outside the familiar theistic patterns are resisted vigorously in ecclesiastical circles. Perhaps the unstated source of this strange and irrational response is that we know of no other way to talk about God. We fear that if theism is dismissed, only a bottomless pit remains. Human life appears to be no more capable of living with this all-consuming intuitive anxiety and fear than were our first and most primitive forbears. Many forms of religion are little more than cultural manifestations of the fear of nothingness. That is why people become hysterical when theism is challenged.

There are growing numbers of people in the Christian church today who know that they cannot continue to pretend that these images have credibility without encountering problems of integrity. They no longer want their religious life to be like a game of charades. I must confess that I am in that category. I know that I must either find a way to move beyond the theistic patterns of the past in search of a new way to speak of and to engage the ultimate reality that I call God, or be honest about living in a godless world. There is no other alternative. Thus the next step in my search for a Jesus for the non-religious requires the radical decoupling of Jesus and theism.

Change does not come easily in the realm of religious ideas. Before one can move out of a traditional and comfortable place, more is required than simply the statement that the old place is no longer a viable position to occupy. People do not move out of their religious security zones until something powerful forces them to do so. In fact, it must first be demonstrated that actual harm will occur if a move is not made.

I now want to make the case that the harm of continuing to live with an unbelievable theism is clearly seen in two places. First, theism as a way of understanding God has, I believe, actually served to diminish our humanity. Second, theism seems to give rise to inordinate and destructive religious anger. By putting flesh on both of these contentions, I hope to create in my readers a yearning to move beyond the traditional theistic understanding of Christianity into a bold, new and as yet undescribed place.

It is my conviction that the essence of the Christian gospel can be summed up in words attributed to Jesus in the Fourth Gospel: "I have come that they might have life and have it abundantly" (10:10). If abundant life is the ultimate value to which Christianity is dedicated, as I believe it is, then we must judge all contemporary expressions of Christianity by the standard of their ability to enhance life and where there are failures we must seek to understand why.

I observe first the fact that for some nineteen hundred years institutional Christianity lived comfortably with prejudices based on gender, race and sexual orientation. With the emergence of the twentieth century, however, Christianity started to fade precipitously, beginning in Europe and spreading to the United States. Power shifted dramatically from institutional Christianity to a rising, vigorous, secular humanism. It was this secular spirit that proceeded to rout the prejudices with which Christianity had accommodated itself for so long. This enabled the twentieth century to become the most dramatic century in human history for the rise of human rights.

Women first broke open the social order and demanded equality in the voting booth, before the law, in education, jobs, professions and even the military. Next the back of racism was broken as segregation fell and doors opened through which black Americans could and did walk until they reached the highest pinnacles in the world of social, political and business life in America. Finally, in the second half of the twentieth century, gay and lesbian people abandoned their closets and demanded and won equality and acceptance. I do not mean to suggest that following the twentieth century there was no more sexism, racism, or homophobia, but I do mean to say that all of these prejudices were routed in that century and began their long and inevitable marches into oblivion. No prejudice in human history has ever been debated publicly, as each of these has been, that it did not proceed to die. Debated prejudices are always dying prejudices. The debate is actually part of the death process.

My question is: Why did these enormous transformations of consciousness take place only when Christianity receded and secularism rose to replace it? Why was institutional Christianity unwilling to challenge these dehumanizing practices when they had the power to do so? If there is no connection and these occurrences are just coincidental, then why did so many parts of organized Christianity resist these changes so vigorously? Why is it still true that the largest expressions of institutional Christianity continue their relentless battle against the full equality of women in both church and society? Why do Christian leaders in the highest places still today seek to wrest from these newly emancipated women the power to make decisions about their own bodies? Why is the most segregated hour in America today still the hour of worship? Why is the strongest bastion of homophobia in the developed world today still the Christian church? What is there about Christianity, organized as it is today around the concept of a theistic God, that seems to require a perpetual victim? Does not removing prejudice, enhancing the humanity of those that the stereotypical definitions of our religious past cast into the role of victims, actually serve well the stated purpose of Jesus to bring abundant life to all? Has the theistic way in which we have traditionally conceptualized God and through which we have defined Jesus been a factor in our blindness? I think it has; but before drawing this conclusion, let me look at our Christian and religious history from a different perspective from which additional data can be drawn.

A cursory look at Christian history will provide ample evidence to support the conclusion that there is a very high correlation between theistic religion and killing anger. Religious people are loath to face this fact, but it is painfully and obviously true. One has only to listen to conversations about religion among people holding competing views to see how quickly anger surges. These conversations rapidly escalate into high levels of noncivility. Voices rise, emotions flow, interruptions occur, threats are made and insults are exchanged. Religious discussions become war zones that not infrequently make street brawls look civilized.

In the conflicts that I have engaged in my life as a bishop, the levels of hostility that I have been forced to absorb have been all but inconceivable. Vitriol has come by way of hate mail, abusive telephone calls and threats against the well-being of the members of my family. It has included sixteen genuine death threats that could not be dismissed as insignificant. When I was walking in procession in full academic regalia prior to being given an honorary degree from a major university some years ago, the dean of the medical school at that university used that opportunity to berate me for removing his comfort level in church. Does disagreement in any other area of life result in that kind of public rudeness among strangers? The fascinating thing about this kind of abusive behavior is that the hostility typically comes from fellow Christians—in my case, some of them well known in evangelical and catholic circles. None of my death threats came from an atheist, a Buddhist, or a Muslim. They were most often delivered by Bible-quoting Christians who defined themselves as true believers, men and women who said they were acting in the defense of or on the instructions of God. God, indeed, appeared to justify their killing rage, their overt anger. The connection between religion and anger is real.

Sociological studies pointing to the same conclusion indicate that almost all of the cultural prejudices that have been faced by our society in the past century are far stronger among religious people than among non-religious or secular people. A case in point is seen in that region of the United States that calls itself the Bible Belt, the region in which I was born and where I lived for the first forty-four years of my life. America's Bible Belt is generally coterminous with the states that formed the Confederacy in the American Civil War. Every statistic reveals that churchgoing is higher in that region than in any other part of our country. The Bible is read and taught more thoroughly there than anywhere else in the nation. Religion is more overtly practiced there. This religion, however, manifests itself in behavior that is historically both angry and violent. Slavery is a cruel suppression of the humanity of the one who is held in bondage, but the people of the Bible Belt defended that evil institution with all their might, even quoting scripture to support its presence and practice. Slaves were not only beaten and executed without fear of reprisal from the Bible-reading population, but they were also refused education and their families were broken up on the slave blocks. This behavior surely reveals both anger and violence, yet the vast majority of the oppressors of slaves were devoutly religious Christians.

When slavery was ended by defeat on the battlefield at the conclusion of the American Civil War, it was quite self-consciously replaced in the Bible Belt by its bastard stepchild, segregation. A political deal was struck in 1876 that handed the presidency of the United States to Republican Rutherford B. Hayes in exchange for his willingness to allow the suppression of black people in the South in the form of a legal system of segregation. This dehumanizing social pattern was not an accident of history. So this cruel anger against fellow human beings continued in the most religious part of the United States.

Attempts to bring segregation to an end through the civil rights movement some seventy-five to one hundred years later resulted in even more violence and suffering, including the deaths of many innocent people. Representative John Lewis, who serves today as a Democratic Congressman from Georgia, in the decade of the sixties was beaten with lead pipes wielded by the "law-abiding" police when he sought to end discrimination through quite legal means.[2] Fire hoses and police dogs were turned on demonstrators throughout the South. Children in churches were murdered by bombs. Civil rights workers were kidnapped and executed. States in which the churchgoing percentage was the highest closed their public schools to prevent admitting black children, preferring the encouragement of total ignorance to the destruction of their patterns of discrimination. No one can deny the anger that gripped this section of the country as segregation was forced to die. Nor can anyone deny that the Christianity of that region justified and encouraged that anger.

I lived through those years in a small town of seventy-five hundred people in eastern North Carolina. Anger literally seethed in people's personal conversations and in their emotional defense of the practice of segregation. When Martin Luther King, Jr. was assassinated in Memphis, in the heart of the Bible Belt in 1968, some Southern editorial writers rejoiced and proclaimed that he got what he deserved.[3] These very editorial writers were in most cases the voices of the social and religious establishment in their communities and, as such, were quite official spokespersons of the religious South. They, together with the judges, the members of the various juries and other elected officials continued to cooperate in this violence, while never ceasing to be Bible-reading, church-attending Christians. The conviction of the last man to be accused of murdering civil rights workers occurred as recently as 2005. His name was Edgar Ray Killen, and his crime was the murder of James Chaney, Andrew Goodman and Michael Schwerner—

a crime that occurred in 1964 in Philadelphia, Mississippi. Every effort to bring this man to justice earlier had been thwarted by the people of that state on many levels. Previous trials had resulted in hung juries. When Killen was finally convicted, it was interesting to note that he was identified in press accounts not simply as a member of the Ku Klux Klan, which was well known, but even more significantly as a Christian preacher in the Baptist Church.[4] Yes indeed, there is a very real connection between religion and anger.

More evidence of this connection becomes apparent when one listens to the content of much Protestant preaching, in which the preacher describes with some enthusiasm, not to say glee, what God has in store for those who do not heed the preacher's message. Is that anything less than religious anger projected onto a punishing deity? Not to be outdone by this aspect of revivalistic Protestant Christianity, Roman Catholic leaders portray in no uncertain terms both their attitude toward and the presumed destiny of those they call schismatics. Anger time after time receives divine sanction.

The church's official participation in religious persecution throughout Christian history is well documented. Those who have disagreed with official church positions have been excommunicated, tortured and burned at the stake. I have seen in a San Diego museum a touring display of instruments of torture used during parts of Christian history by Christian leaders on those they called heretics. It included an iron collar with a spike aimed at the throat of the victim, which would be tightened until it produced either "conversion" or death. There were also devices used to impale the deviant thinker that left the victim's intestines shredded. Can anyone really deny that these are the manifestations of religious anger?

Religious wars have been among history's cruelest. The "Crusades" were little more than ecclesiastically sanctioned acts of torture and terrorism. Their primary purpose was quite simply to kill infidels, which was somehow thought to be justified by the God they served. Anger thereby received the scent of religious perfume.

Christianity has encouraged centuries of anti-Semitism, stretching from the "church fathers,"[5] through the leaders of the Reformation,[6] down to and including popes such as Pius XII. It is still voiced today by many Protestant leaders. It was no less than the elected head of the

234 Jesus for the Non-Religious

Southern Baptist Convention who proclaimed on national television, "God Almighty does not hear the prayers of a Jew."[7]

As a result of this destructive rhetoric Jews have been at one time or another banished from almost every nation in Christian Europe. Those not banished were ghettoized. The anti-Semitism that blamed the Jews for the bubonic plague in the fourteenth century reached its crescendo in the twentieth-century horror of the Holocaust in Nazi Germany. The Christian nations of Europe and North America did little or nothing to mitigate this suffering. Can anyone argue that this does not represent a killing anger that has lived historically at the heart of Christianity and that is still present there today?

Scrape away from traditional Christian teaching the piety and the stained-glass attitudes, and one finds cesspools of anger, boiling cauldrons that have ignited religious violence in every generation. Christians need to own this part of their history.

The question that this analysis raises for me is: What is there about Christianity itself or the way in which Christianity has been traditionally understood that both encourages and actually produces anger inside those who claim to be disciples of Jesus? That anger is far too real and omnipresent to be regarded as accidental or coincidental.

It has not just been the perceived enemies of the Christian church who have felt the sting of this religious anger. The fact is that this anger has also been turned inward on believers when they gather for worship. One can easily document in the words of both Christian liturgies and hymns the presence of incredible levels of self-negativity and self-rejection. That is nothing more than debilitating hostility in the name of God. Yet this behavior is today still viewed in some circles as a positive sign of true religion. Is it not revealing that worship is frequently the arena for experiencing self-hatred?

God's grace is "amazing," we sing in a well-known hymn. Why? Because it saved a "wretch" like me! Why, we must ask, is the grace of God thought to be best seen in the denigration of our humanity? Another hymn, "How Great Thou Art," associated with the crusades of evangelist Billy Graham, tells us that God's greatness is best illustrated in Jesus' willingness to take upon himself the burden of our evil. In the same vein, "He died for my sins" is the mantra most frequently heard on Sunday morning in Christian worship. That powerful guilt message says that the evil within human life made the death of Jesus necessary. Are we not in this act of liturgy reduced to being villains in the drama of salvation? One of our hymns says this quite overtly:

Who was the guilty? Who brought this upon you?
Alas, my treason, Jesus, hath undone thee.
'Twas I, Lord Jesus, I it was denied thee:
I crucified thee.[8]

What does it say about our definition of human life when the perennial plea of Christian worship is for mercy? "Lord, have mercy on us; Christ have mercy on us; Lord have mercy on us," we chant. What kind of human being constantly begs for mercy? Can anger that has been turned inward ever be a source of life? Are we human beings ever helped by being told how hopeless, wretched and evil we are? Does that ever make us whole? Does it ever make us more loving?

I submit that this constant onslaught of ecclesiastical negativity comes directly from our theistic portrait of God, who has been traditionally understood as a punishing parent figure. The majority Christian interpretation of Jesus suggests that he took our punishment for us on the cross of Calvary. In the shedding of the divine blood of the totally innocent one, the wrath of God has been turned away from us. Our evil is not removed; it is covered over. So we fill our worship life with theistic themes: "I am not worthy to gather up the crumbs" from the divine table. "I have been washed in the blood of the lamb."

If Christians ever stop to think about these words, then surely we must realize that they are not benign. Does not the constant message of guilt and degradation guarantee that Christianity, as traditionally understood, will be marked by anger projected onto someone else? Does it not make guilt the essential ingredient in Christian life? Is not guilt the primary ecclesiastical weapon that the church has employed for centuries to control human life? The basic modus operandi of the Christian church throughout history has been to make its people constantly aware of their failures, their inadequacies and their weaknesses. Does this activity not also define Christian people as chronically dependent, ever-rebellious children who deserve the wrath of the judgmental God? Is not the gospel of Jesus regularly proclaimed as the story of God's divine and ever-gracious rescue of a hopelessly sinful people from the fate they have truly earned? The message of salvation, stemming from a theistic understanding of God, is laden with a sense of the guilt of human ineptitude and of the intrinsic evil that marks human life. God alone can erase it and so we beg and we grovel and we never grow up spiritually.

The traditional way we tell the Christ story makes an ogre out of God, a victim out of Jesus and angry people who must be eternally grateful and thus helplessly dependent out of us. That cannot ever be the "good news" of the gospel, nor can it be an expression of the love of God. This mentality will never provide human life with the power needed to set us free to be the persons we are meant to be. It will always be crippling and wounding. It will never lead to abundant life. Gratitude at being rescued never turns into wholeness. All of these things have been built into the traditional definition of what it means to be human and the church confronts worshippers with this attitude quite regularly. It cannot help but be a major source of the anger that is so deeply a part of the Christian life. Denigrated people always denigrate. Hated people always hate. Abused people always abuse. Punished people always punish. That is the peculiar law of humanity. Our way of understanding God and Jesus has played a major role in the creation of our religious anger. It has justified our prejudices, taught us to hate ourselves, abused us emotionally and told us of our need to be punished, perhaps through all eternity. In so doing, it has fed the violence that has been so regularly exhibited by Christian people throughout Christian history.

This was made indelibly clear to me by one of my students, Katie Ford, at Harvard Divinity School in 2000. In a sermon in her homiletics class, she articulated her experience of traditional Christianity in these words: "Christianity has given us a God who caused the death of his son, the damnation of disbelievers, the subordination of women, the bloody massacre of the Crusades, the terror of judgment, the wrath toward homosexuals and the justification of slavery. The Father God embodied in the creeds is a deity who chooses some of the world's children while rejecting others. He is the father of wrath, the father of male ordination and female submission, the father of literal and spiritual slavery."

We Christians have historically rooted our faith story not in the beauty and wonder of God's creation, but in the presumed depravity of human corruption. We have made "original sin" the lens through which we have viewed Jesus, rather than what Matthew Fox has called "original blessing."[9]

The reason religion has become so fierce in our day is that we know on both conscious and subconscious levels that this very super-natural concept of God has died and that the religion of fear and control is not holding. Our inability to face the death of this God serves only to heighten our anxiety and to cause us to build our de-fenses to ever-higher levels. It also gives rise to religious rage that verges on hysteria. The fact remains, however, that the theistic God is dying—perhaps has already died—and nothing we do can finally suppress that reality.

We know there is no theistic god just above the sky, keeping record books and standing ready to reward or punish us on the basis of our deserving. We know we live in an ordered world in which mathemati-cally precise natural laws govern a clockwork universe. The interven-tion of the theistic god from above to accomplish the divine will or to respond to the fervent prayers of the faithful, whether they be for mercy or for healing, is no longer credible. Miracle and magic both have faded from our world.

We know that natural selection in evolution and the Darwinian concept of the survival of the fittest, together with DNA evidence,[10] make it quite clear that human life is not just a little lower than the angels as we once taught, but is just a little higher than the apes as we now understand. Religious objections to evolution are very telling. Evolution forces us to entertain a new definition of what it means to be human. Human beings are in fact part of an unfolding unity called life. We are deeply connected with all living things, from the apes to the cabbages. The unique thing about human beings is that in us this reality called life has entered into full self-consciousness.

Christian people can no longer live in denial. Theism is not mor-ally neutral. The death of theism is greatly to be desired. That truth is finally dawning on us. We are beginning to suspect that the riddance of theism just might be the doorway through which we have to walk to reach both a new humanity and a new maturity. It also might serve to lower the decibels of religious anger by tempering the negative image of human depravity that theism has fostered. Who needs a God who would require the death of the divine Son before being willing to forgive a fallen humanity? That is a portrait of God as a divine child abuser. We should rejoice in the death of such a deity. A parent who would act toward his or her child in the way we suggest God has acted would be called immoral. I think it is high time we proclaim the theistic God to be immoral also. Moving beyond theism, separating our understanding of Jesus from our theistic understanding of God, is not only a moral imperative; it is also the only pathway into the future of a loving Christianity. Viewing Jesus as the incarnation of a theistic deity is thus doomed. We need to move on to new possibilities. Once we walk away from theism I think we can.

I have no concern for what is happening in institutional Christianity today. It is, in my opinion, little more than the final dance of rigor mortis. Today's church spends its energy in losing battles about such things as authority, scripture, women, sexuality and homosexuality, about which its history reveals it knows very little. It is the anger that is both overt and covert inside institutional Christianity that is most revelatory of its current status. When an institution spends its time defending the indefensible, when it abdicates its responsibility to seek new forms in which to proclaim its essential truth, when it offers its world either a Jesus enshrouded in a mythology that violates everything we know about our world or no Jesus at all, when it extols unity over truth, then it is clearly time for either the death of that institution or a bold new direction. Surely there must be another way.

I now turn to propose such a way. I seek to sketch the outlines of a new Christology that is true to the Jesus experience while walking away from the traditional Jesus explanations. What emerges is a portrait of a life in which the human opens to the divine, in which the sacred is not isolated from the real, but is an expression of it. It is a portrait that I call "Jesus for the Non-Religious."

JESUS: THE BREAKER OF TRIBAL BOUNDARIES

To the degree that theistic religious systems are expressions of tribal mentalities, and all of them are, then religion will finally prove not to be an asset to humanity.

When I was a child growing up in North Carolina, a state which nestles between Virginia to its north and South Carolina to its south, I joined willingly in building my state's reputation and thus my own, by referring to North Carolina as either "the mountain of hope between two valleys of despair" or "the valley of humility between two mountains of conceit." It did not occur to me to think that these ego-expanding exercises in state pride were nothing other than one more manifestation of the human survival technique that we call tribalism. Human beings are by definition tribal people. At the dawn of self-consciousness, tribalism was the pathway to survival. We embraced that option and defined our humanity within it. The theistic God became the God of the tribe.

Tribal thinking exists on almost every level of human life, from the international to the local. The United States is today a multiracial, multicultural nation made up of many different tribes. Yet on September 11, 2001, when this nation was attacked by terrorists from another country and culture, the people of this nation came together as if we were one people and responded in a traditionally tribal way. Flags were flown from homes and businesses where they had never flown before. They fluttered from automobiles and bicycles on the campuses of the same universities where, just a generation ago during the Vietnam War, flags were being burned and anti-Americanism was the rule not the exception. "God Bless America" was sung on every public occasion. I was never sure whether it was intended as a prayer or a command. The corporate purpose of this nation was expressed in a unified willingness to punish, even to destroy, our attackers.

In international athletic competitions like the World Cup, the tribal mentality of the various participating nations is quite apparent in the stands. National colors are worn; faces and bodies are painted; passions run deep. Wars have actually been declared in Central America after a defeat in a soccer match! While tribalism may be obvious on the level of nation-states, it also exists on lower levels. State loyalties and regional rivalries are filled with tribal fervor. One has only to witness a New York Yankees vs. Boston Red Sox baseball game to see how intense tribal emotions can become. University rivalries on far more local levels feast on these feelings—feelings that not only fill stadiums, but also keep alumni giving at high levels, since very few old graduates quite escape the tribal allegiances of their younger days. Traditional university rivalries like Cambridge vs. Oxford, Harvard vs. Yale, University of Virginia vs. Virginia Tech, North Carolina vs. Duke, or Texas vs. Texas A&M, to mention some of the world's most famous ones, are filled with tribal rhetoric. A University of Virginia student explaining why Virginia Tech had artificial turf in its outdoor stadium said, "Their homecoming queen ate all the grass!"

Tribalism is seen in the way we portray our enemies. A New Zealand athletic shirt proclaims, "I root for two teams, New Zealand and whoever is playing Australia." When tribal feeling is exacerbated in times of war, tribal propaganda always dehumanizes our enemies to make it easier to hate or to kill without qualms of conscience. One does not kill human beings in a war; our victims are not someone's child, spouse, or parent. No, one kills rather the Huns, the Krauts, the Japs, the Nips, the VC, the insurgents, the fanatics, or the terrorists. One could never understand the Rape of Nanking during World War II, My Lai during Vietnam, or Abu Ghraib during the second Iraq war without understanding this insight into the tribal nature of humanity. Tribal mentalities are deeply embedded in every human being. Westerners in their lingering prejudice act as if tribal warfare in Africa were something not quite modern or civilized. They do not seem to realize that Western Europe has always been divided on tribal lines—England is dominated by the Anglo-Saxon tribes; France is the country of the Franks; Germany is the land built on a coalition of Germanic tribes, especially the Prussians; Hungary is the land of the Huns—and that almost every human dispute the world over arises out of tribal history. There is within us all a basic, dominant, intrinsic fear of those tribes different from our own, a predisposition to be on guard against them, to reject them, to attack and even to kill them. This tribal tradition arises out of our deep-seated survival mentality and it feeds something at the heart of our insecure humanity. We are tribal people to our core. Far more than we will consciously admit, the religions of the world, including Christianity, rise out of and undergird our tribal thinking. They are all very deep expressions of a tribal mentality that worships a theistic tribal protector.

The reality is, however, that the more we sink into tribal attitudes, the more our lives are consumed with hatred; and as a direct result, the less human we become. In times of tribal conflict the natural survival instincts within us take over and are hurled at our enemies. When there is a common enemy, our hostilities always go outward. Political coalitions have been built by exacerbating tribal fears and identifying the enemy to be hated. Hitler rode to power by galvanizing the latent German hostility toward the Jews into the policy of the Nazi movement. In America political victories have been won by exciting racial or sexual fears in order to unite against a visible, common enemy. The defeat of one's enemy is believed to be the pathway to survival; in a similar manner, losing to one's enemy is the pathway to annihilation. Tribal divisions always raise our levels of hatred, prejudice and defensiveness. This tribal mentality may well have been an asset in the human struggle to survive during the evolutionary process, but unless it is transcended, a deeper humanity ceases to be a possibility.

One cannot be fully human so long as one is consumed with hatred against those who threaten one's survival. In recent years the presence of suicide bombers has made this mentality abundantly and fearfully clear. The fullness of humanity always falls victim to the need to survive as a tribe and to the mind-set of tribalism that, since the dawn of self-consciousness, has been part of the human makeup. If the purpose of Jesus, however, was and is to bring life abundantly, then we need to realize that this goal will never be possible until both our tribal mentalities and our tribal fears have been addressed. The view of Jesus as the incarnation of the theistic deity, who was originally the God of the tribe, is not likely to address that issue. There is far too much in every religious system of every nation and in the portrayal of their tribal God that validates the hatreds of the tribal people.

Tribal hatreds diminish the humanity of the victims. That is the purpose. Tribal hatreds, however, also diminish the humanity of those who are the haters. That is not so well understood. To the degree that theistic religious systems are expressions of tribal mentalities, and all of them are, then religion will finally prove not to be an asset to humanity. That is as true for the Jesus who has been wrapped in the power of theistic religion as it is for anyone else.

This tribal God of Israel was still alive and well in the first-century Jewish world in which Jesus of Nazareth lived. It was inevitable, therefore, that the fully human Jesus confronted this tribal mentality. Our first task in seeking to understand what it was in the Jesus experience that convinced his disciples that they met a transforming God-presence in him is, therefore, to watch how he dealt with the tribal mentality and how he empowered his disciples to step beyond all tribal boundaries into the fullness of humanity that his life so clearly exhibited.

The tribal boundary which Jesus confronted was seen in the ultimate human fault line that formed the Jewish worldview. Jews divided the world into the members of their own small nation, who were "us," and the Gentiles, who were "them." Every Jewish person lived inside that division. The Jews were God's "chosen ones"; the Gentiles, God's "unchosen ones." The Jews were confident that they knew the will of God, for God had given them the Torah on Mount Sinai, teaching them how to live and how to worship. Pleasing the theistic deity was the way to make God favor, protect and defend them, which is what tribal gods were designed to do. The Gentiles, on the other hand, had no Torah, no revelation of God's will and no law. They were, therefore, defined as the unclean, the uncircumcised and the nonkoshered people. Jews did not eat with Gentiles. Jews did not intermarry with Gentiles. Jews did not even *interact* with Gentiles. The humanity of the Jews was, in Jesus' day, marked by this tribal boundary. The question that needs to be addressed is, How could one be fully human if one was busy rejecting all those who were not Jews? That was the tribal dilemma in the first-century Jewish world and into that dilemma the fully human Jesus walked.

Our task, then, is to trace in the gospel tradition the echoes of the transforming power that Jesus made visible and public. Those echoes, we will discover, paint a consistent portrait that points to the power present in Jesus' life, a power that people began to identify with God.

Even though the earthly life of Jesus came to an end around the year 30 CE, the power of this Jesus was such that Paul, writing in the early fifties, could still make a claim that was so astonishing in that time that it must have hit his readers like a message from outer space. To the Galatians Paul wrote that inside the Christ experience people had with Jesus, all of their tribal barriers melted away! In Christ there is "neither Jew nor Greek," neither Jew nor Gentile (3:28). To the Romans, a few years later, Paul still had this sense of the Jesus experience when he wrote that salvation has come from God in the person of Jesus and is available "to the Jew first and also to the Greek" (1:16). Paul says a few verses later, "God shows no partiality" (2:11). Later Paul asserts, "For there is no distinction between Jew and Greek; the same Lord is Lord of all and is generous to all who call on him. For 'Everyone who calls on the name of the Lord shall be saved'" (10:12–13, NRSV). These were astonishing claims. The power of Jesus had expanded Paul's tribal boundaries and, through him, had enabled the followers of Jesus to embrace the world.

In the epistle to the Colossians Paul or one of Paul's disciples continues to state the same transcending message that shrinks tribal identity to nothingness: "If you have been raised with Christ," he writes, "there cannot be Greek and Jew, circumcised and uncircumcised, barbarian, Scythian, slave, free …, but Christ is all and in all" (3:1, 11). Those claims, when fully understood, are still powerful, even incomprehensible descriptions of the Christ experience. Something about this Jesus has been sufficiently unique and life-changing to enable us to set aside the million-year-old human survival characteristic of tribal identity and to feel his call to a new level of humanity. That is not the portrait of an invading deity who is rescuing the fallen. That is, rather, the story of one who empowers others to be so deeply and fully human that they can actually escape the security lines built to serve their primitive survival needs. It is nothing less than a breakthrough in human consciousness.

That theme, once it has been recognized, can then be seen in almost every page of the New Testament. A whole transforming sense of a new humanity was the very essence of what people found in Jesus. It was deep in the memory that people had about the Jesus experience. In the first gospel to be written, Mark tells us of a man named Levi, a Jewish tax collector who had compromised his faith and his tribal identity by becoming an employee of the hated Gentile conquerors. By every then-current Jewish standard he was unclean, but Jesus called him to step across that barrier and become his disciple (Mark 2:13–15). Levi responded and did so. It became a transforming Jesus memory.

Later Mark is quite specific in saying that when Jesus departed from Jewish territory by crossing the Sea of Galilee, a great crowd followed him. Mark identifies the members of that crowd as being "from Judea and Jerusalem and Idumea and from beyond the Jordan and from about Tyre and Sidon" (3:7–8). Many of these areas, especially those regions beyond the Jordan and near Tyre and Sidon, were inhabited by Gentiles. Jesus proclaimed his message of reconciliation to "unclean" Gentiles and in so doing called his followers to step beyond their tribal boundaries and taste the meaning of a new and enhanced humanity, a humanity that did not hate, fear or denigrate members of another tribe. It was not an accident that, in a story to which I have previously referred, Mark closes his gospel with a Gentile soldier standing beneath the cross as the first interpreter of the meaning of Jesus' death. God was seen in the life of Jesus as a power that one could give to others, even *different* others, not hiding in fear behind tribal hatreds. This picture of human life far transcended the sacrifice mentality that would later overwhelm both the Jesus portrait and the Jesus memory.

Matthew is by every measure the most Jewish of the gospel writers, and therefore the one most likely to be sensitive to tribal boundaries. It is Matthew, however, who wraps his story of Jesus inside an interpretive envelope calculated to break open the tribal mentality and to move beyond the tribal boundary. Matthew celebrates this persistent theme that he found in the life of Jesus from his birth through his death and resurrection by showing how it was that tribal boundaries were transformed by Jesus from being ultimate in people's lives to being trivial. He goes on to proclaim that anything which places limits on our humanity and keeps us bound in a primitive survival mentality cannot and will not survive inside the Jesus experience.

Matthew opens his gospel with the story of a star shining in the heavens to announce Jesus' birth. The light of that star is not limited to the sight of those who live inside the national boundary of the Jewish world. Visible to people in every nation, stars are universal symbols for all human beings to see. It is this announcement star, Matthew says, that draws the Gentile magi across their tribal barriers of fear and insecurity in a journey to the place where, he asserts, Jesus was born. That is the meaning of his opening story. We should not miss its meaning by literalizing this story of the wise men. This is not a story about real people who once followed a real wandering star. If we do not read accurately this opening narrative, recognizing that the wise men were symbolic Gentiles who were drawn to Jesus, then it is inevitable that we will miss Matthew's great conclusion. For the final story in this gospel is equally powerful and inclusive. In that account Matthew portrays the risen Christ on a mountaintop in Galilee where Matthew has him say to his band of disciples the only words Matthew attributes to the post-Easter Jesus. Surely such a final word must have been, in the mind of this author, of great significance. What was that word? It was the reverse message of the star, which drew the Gentiles to the Jewish Jesus. Matthew proclaims that Jesus' final word was designed to propel his Jewish disciples to go into the lands of the Gentiles: "Go therefore and make disciples of all nations,... teaching them to obey everything that I have commanded you [such as, Love others as I have loved you]. And remember, I am with you always, to the end of the age" (Matt. 28:19–20, NRSV). Go to the Gentiles; go beyond the boundaries of your fears, he was saying. Go to those who are different, whom you have defined as unclean, and proclaim to them the limitless love of God.

The missionary imperative at the heart not only of these verses but of Christianity itself is not something designed to convert the heathen, as imperial Christianity has asserted through the ages. It is not a command to make the thoughts of others conform to your thoughts about God. It is rather an invitation to enter the experience of a new humanity—a humanity expanded beyond tribal limits and thus beyond the quest for survival. It is a call to share with all people the life-giving power of love that always enhances human life and that frees us to cross constricting security barriers. That is what the Jesus experience was and is all about.

When we turn to Luke this theme of inclusiveness and the need to lay aside our security blankets of tribal thinking in order to become fully human is laid out once again, and quite dramatically. Luke, the author of both the gospel that bears his name and the book of Acts, has crafted a story that shows Jesus beginning his life and ministry on the outskirts of the Jewish world in the insignificant village of Nazareth, then journeying to the heart of the Jewish world in Jerusalem to reclaim that city and its zealously religious and tribal people for the power of love. Luke never has Jesus or his disciples turn back toward Galilee, but rather he pictures this dawning universalism as something that moves inexorably into the heart of the Gentile universe, into what was the capital of the non-Jewish world, the city of Rome, where Luke's story concludes.

Luke closes his gospel by reminding his readers that the disciples of Jesus have been witnesses to the meaning of the life of Jesus, which has moved through suffering and death to resurrection for the sole purpose of calling "all nations, beginning from Jerusalem" (24:47). You now must move beyond tribe to humanity, he says. Luke has Jesus repeat those marching orders at the beginning of the book of Acts: "You shall be my witnesses in Jerusalem and in all Judea and Samaria and to the end of the earth" (1:8). The ends of the earth, please recognize, would be those places where the Gentiles live. He says, in effect, You are to go beyond the survival mentality that thwarts your humanity. You are to go beyond tribal barriers to those who are different, those whom your need for security has taught you to hate or to regard as unclean. There is something about this Jesus that erases tribal boundaries, that calls people to step beyond security systems and that flows into a new humanity unbounded by the walls of protectionism. That is one huge dimension of what it means to say that God was experienced as present in this man Jesus.

Finally, when Luke tells us, again in the book of Acts, the story of the outpouring of the Holy Spirit on the gathered body of disciples who were hiding in fear in an upper room, the experiential meaning of Jesus is once again driven home quite dramatically. In this narrative the disciples of Jesus were commissioned to be the church, to be the body of Christ. In this Pentecost story, the manifestation of the Holy Spirit's presence enabled these disciples to cross every tribal boundary, symbolized by the varieties of language, by speaking in the language their hearers understood. Just to make sure that Luke's audience got the full power of that message, Luke adds that those hearers consisted of "Parthians, Medes, Elamites and residents of Mesopotamia, Judea and Cappadocia, Pontus and Asia, Phrygia and Pamphylia, Egypt and the parts of Libya belonging to Cyrene, and visitors from Rome, both Jews and proselytes, Cretans and Arabs" (Acts 2:9–11). For the level of geographical knowledge available in the first century, this was a very impressive worldview, stretching from Libya and Rome in the west through Greece to reach throughout the lands of the Arabs, Persians and Babylonians to Mesopotamia in the valley created by the Tigris and Euphrates rivers in the heart of modern-day Iraq.

All of these stories from the New Testament make it clear that the meaning of the Jesus experience was that he empowered others to lay down their survival barriers, to step beyond tribe, beyond language, beyond the fear-imposed levels of our security. We are, said this list of biblical witnesses, called to step into a humanity that opens to all people the meaning of life and thus the meaning of God. That was the gift that Jesus had to offer.

When we begin to penetrate this Christ meaning, as it is depicted in the gospels, we find that what the gospel writers were trying to convey was not the tribal message of rescuing the sinners, saving the lost or attempting to patch up our insecurities. It was rather a message designed to call those who had experienced the presence of Jesus to translate the full humanity they met in him into a new and inclusive kind of life for themselves. It called people to risk stepping outside defenses, beyond fears and insecurities, and to embrace in a way not known before what it means to be human.

It was the power of Jesus' full humanity that issued this call and invited his disciples into its meaning. When our humanity is thwarted by fear, when we hide behind self-erected security barriers, we inevitably set up conflict between survival-oriented people. When our humanity is called to risk all in loving those who are different in a quest for a fulfillment that expands life, then we have a very different image of what it means to be human. In the fully human one, Jesus, we see that the only way into the life of God is to walk into the meaning of our humanity, our complete humanity. Divinity does not make us more than human, as Christianity has so often taught. Rather, divinity is seen in the fullness of humanity when limits disappear and hatreds fade and a new creation emerges.

This is why the only way I can assert the presence of the divine Christ is by proclaiming the full humanity of the man Jesus, the unique and solitary life whose humanity, because it was whole and complete, was also open to the realm of spirit, which is to me the place where the human enters the very life of God. We need to recognize that even the word "divine" is a human word created to name a human experience.

When I look at this Jesus, I no longer see God in human form. That to me is now a very inadequate, theistic understanding of what divinity means. It was designed to meet tribal survival needs. I rather look at Jesus and see a humanity open to all that God is — open to life, open to love and open to being. It is a new way to think about Jesus, but as the bankruptcy of theism becomes obvious and as the supernatural God dies, it is a welcome alternative.

So the first barrier, which limits humanity with tribal identity, is broken open and in the process Jesus breaks out of the prison of tribal religion. It is the profoundly human Jesus that enables us to step beyond the tribal limits that so deeply impede our humanity. Jesus for the non-religious begins to take form.

JESUS: THE BREAKER OF PREJUDICES AND STEREOTYPES

Prejudice in all its forms is a disease that marks every human being. It is a survival technique.

Tribal identity, with all of its terrifying implications for human history, is not the only weapon that newly self-conscious people developed for the human survival kit. Self-consciousness made survival the primary goal around which we organized all of life and that affected the way our tribal religions developed. A self-centered survival mentality is a universal aspect of the self-centeredness that marks our species, but it is not, as religious people have been so quick to assert, the result of a fall or of some innate evil that lies at the heart of humanity. It is rather the reality of the evolutionary struggle: the battle for the survival of the fittest. It is the very nature of our humanity to spend our time trying, through whatever means are available, to win the upper hand against fellow human beings, to defeat our foes and to prove ourselves superior to all others. That is why prejudice is so deep within us all. Prejudice in all its forms is a disease that marks every human being. It is a survival technique. So to understand and to further the quest that leads to our becoming fully human, we must now bring the reality of human prejudice under our microscope. Like tribalism, prejudice is a distorting power that prevents us from becoming fully human.

Prejudice operates through an overt act of human projection, which involves three steps. First, we designate the victim. Next, onto that victim we project all our inadequacies, hurts and fears, whether they be real or imagined. Third, we reject the one onto whom these human feelings are now projected. We are thus not to be blamed for these things; the victim is. It was the fault of the Jews, Christians once argued, that the kingdom of God had not fully come; they deserved the wrath of Christians because, by rejecting the message of salvation, they kept the Christian church from succeeding in its goal of world domination. It was the fault of the blacks that the Civil War came to the southern part of the United States. It was the fault of the Communists that the Depression rocked the world in the 1930s. It is the fault of women—who want equal jobs, equal pay and equal power—that family values are in decline. It is the fault of homosexuals that marriage is today under pressure.

Prejudice is always a public announcement of the inadequacies, the hurts and the fears of the prejudiced ones. Prejudice is just one more way in which we seek to gain the survival advantage. If we can successfully project onto our victim our own inadequacies, place on him or her all of the self-hatred we seem to have for ourselves, then we are justified in rejecting our designated victim. That is how the emotional argument goes. Rejecting our designated victims actually makes us feel an inflated sense of self-worth, so necessary to people whose deepest problem rises from the fact that either their life's circumstances or their religion has proclaimed that they are helpless and rejectable.

In our society race, gender and sexual orientation are the major arenas of prejudice. I have lived through and participated in the revolution that rose to overthrow each one of them. Yet it is also now clear to me that my Christian faith, with its message of an external savior operating on a fallen, helpless humanity, was actually used to bless and justify my former attitude toward each of my designated victims. The experience of facing this fact drove me to a whole new understanding of who Jesus is. I now see him not as the invasive deity who in the act of coming to our rescue actually confirms the low estate of our humanity and thus drives us to make more victims on whom we can pretend to overcome our lack of a sense of self-worth, but as the one who calls us to a new humanity. Salvation is not confirmation of our sinfulness, but the empowerment to step into a new consciousness that transcends any sense of inadequacy.

I turn first to examine those prejudices based on race. We looked at racism's external presence in the earlier chapter on anger; now we need to look at how it was and is religiously justified. I can best do this autobiographically, because prejudice was a reality in the air we breathed in my childhood. I was raised in the segregated world of the American South, where the very existence of black people kept, as they were, in ignorance and poverty made it possible for uneducated white people, like those in my family, to avoid feeling inferior about themselves. Members of my family would say, "At least we're not Negroes." (That was the word we used in polite society.) Black people were defined in that world, on the one hand, as dependent, childlike, incompetent and dumb and, on the other, as potent, virile and full of sexual power. People never seemed to notice the contradictions present in these competing fears or to recognize the need in the prejudiced one on which both definitions played. All of those designations, rather, served to justify the cruel and inhumane way people of color were constantly treated. For example, if one became convinced that people of African descent were naturally dumb and uneducable, the next logical conclusion was that civil authorities did not need to waste time, effort or money trying to overcome so basic and inherent a flaw in their inferior humanity. Thus a segregated school system with quite inferior education for black children was right, proper and natural. There were many cultural expressions designed to enforce the image of ignorance as a factor in racial stereotyping. For example, I was once advised that to tell if a watermelon is ready to eat, you thump it, and "if it sounds empty, like a n__r's head, it is ripe." The person who gave me this tip spoke matter-of-factly, with no apparent sense that these words were reinforcing a killing prejudice.

As noted above, the charges were made in my segregated childhood that black people were by nature dependent and childlike. This, of course, justified our treating them as children so that whites could feel grown up. Black slaves in American history were regularly disciplined with corporal punishment, even in their adult years. They were never paid well enough to become economically independent, so they had to grovel before the presumably superior whites in order to procure enough of the world's goods to survive. In later generations black activists would cast scorn on those they called "Uncle Toms," profoundly unaware that the "Uncle Tom" syndrome was a technique that black people used as a necessary means of survival. Servile, flattering obedience, which was the mark of the "Uncle Tom," got black slaves out of the fields and into the homes of their oppressors, where better food was present and where they could regularly ingratiate themselves with their masters and mistresses.

The suggestion that black people were, as a race, lazy and shiftless was particularly revealing. I heard those two adjectives placed together in racial epithets many times in my upbringing. I recognized these two words as a tool of projection when I realized that it was the white people of European descent who were calling those whom they had kidnapped from Africa lazy and shiftless—and yet they had brought them to America to do the hard manual labor that whites were either unable or unwilling to do in the fields. Who were the lazy, shiftless people in this scenario? How ably black slaves served to keep white inadequacies buried in the unconscious! Prejudice and its real meaning, however, always slips out in our language. In my childhood, when a white person, like my own mother and father, had to put in a rigorous and demanding day of hard physical labor, the common slang expression they would use was "I had to work like a n__r today!" Again, who is the lazy one? Who is the shiftless one? Prejudice says far more about the lack of self-worth of the perpetrator than it does about the reality of the victim.

The other great fear, the other source of anxiety in the heart of the white Southerner, was sexual in nature, and this brought the second half of the prejudiced definition into play. Black males were portrayed in Southern folklore as filled with animal-like passion and sexual potency. Shakespeare's tragedy *Othello*, written in a different land and time, played on that theme. The white Southerner's greatest articulated fear was expressed in a statement that was offered as the last word, the irrefutable conclusion, in almost every debate about segregation: "Would you want your daughter to marry a Negro?" I heard that phrase thousands of times in my Southern upbringing. Since we do not have arranged marriages in this country, the unconscious assumption being expressed here was that if our daughters could marry black men, they would, because of the presumed sexual prowess that white males feared that black men possessed. Perhaps that is why it was built into the Southern code of chivalry that white males had to protect white women from sexual violation by blacks. Most of the lynchings of black males in the South were related to real or imagined sexual violations of white women. A white woman who had become pregnant by a black lover could always protect herself by crying "rape" and accusing anyone she wished of being the father. The idea that the white woman had cooperated in this act was inconceivable to white males, so on to the named or suspected perpetrator of this crime against white female virtue the lynching posse would descend—despite the well-recognized fact that white men regularly (and with impunity) violated black women sexually!

No racial history can ignore how deeply interconnected sex and race were in Southern prejudice. The white fear of "miscegenation" and "mongrelization of the races," as Southern whites called it, actually occurred, of course—but with black women being the victims of white men. Black memories are filled with these episodes.[1] It is because of this almost universal practice during the days of both slavery and segregation that there are almost no people left in America in whose veins flows only the blood of their original African home. White males dealt with their feelings of sexual inadequacy by suppressing black men and violating black women. Some of these violators have now been named by newly discovered DNA evidence, including such well-known people of the past as Thomas Jefferson, America's third president, and such well-known people of more recent times as South Carolina's racist, segregation-defending governor and senator, J. Strom Thurmond.

If we accept that prejudice is part of the human survival syndrome, where does that take us? If we become the winner by making our victim the loser, does that victory overcome the sense of inadequacy that placed survival at the heart of self-conscious human life in the first place? Hardly. It is but one more manifestation of it. Nor does it address the survival issue for us to tell the Jesus story as God entering human life to rescue us from the self-deprecating aspect of our humanity. That story only confirms our chronic inferiority. We will never become whole by rejecting or hating others. That was something that

Jesus understood, but he understood it out of his humanity rather than out of some presumed identity with an external reality called divinity.

Step once more, quite consciously, away from the supernatural framework with which we have so distorted the Jesus of history and look again at his humanity. Look at the way Jesus dealt with the dehumanizing racial prejudices of his day. The unclean, rejectable scum of the first-century Jewish world were called Samaritans. They were half-breeds whose bloodlines had been corrupted by their Jewish ancestors' marrying Gentiles. They were also largely viewed by the religious establishment as heretics, since the true worship of God had been compromised by the Gentile (read "pagan") side of their ancestry. Jews so deeply loathed the Samaritans that, when traveling from Galilee to Jerusalem, they would normally cross the Jordan River in the east and journey through the desert, recrossing the Jordan River coming west to approach Jerusalem from the south. By going this route, they could avoid breathing the foul air of Samaria on their trip. A prejudice that actually inconveniences the life of the perpetrator, as the Jewish prejudice against Samaritans did, is powerful and deeply engrained.

How did Jesus deal with this prejudice? One has only to look at the gospels for a moment to see how the human Jesus behaved toward this and other dehumanizing forces of his day. Luke is the gospel writer who seems most to focus on Jesus' response to prejudice, though John also addresses it powerfully. Paul says that in Christ there was "neither slave nor free" (Gal. 3:28), but he never uses the word "Samaria" or "Samaritan"; neither does Mark or Matthew. Luke, however, is quite specific on this issue. He has Jesus say that the message of the gospel must be heard in Samaria (Acts 1:8); its light must be shined on that debilitating human condition called prejudice. Luke portrays Jesus dealing with Samaritans in two powerful accounts.

Luke's first account (10:29–37) contains a parable Jesus tells about a man whom we have come to call "the good Samaritan," an interesting title since it assumes that the adjective "good" is not normally used to modify the noun "Samaritan." This parable turns on the relationship between tribal exclusiveness and religious duty.[2] The Torah defines the ultimate religious duty to be that of showing compassion toward those who are in need. It also defines Gentiles (and Samaritans), as well as people who are or might be dead, as unclean. Jesus' parable places two religious representatives of Judaism, a priest and a Levite, into a situation in which ritual holiness collides with compassion. The point of this story is that, for those two men, compassion lost. It frequently does in tribal religion, where the humanity of others is denigrated. The half-breed, heretical and unclean Samaritan, on the other hand—who probably did not have the benefit of having studied the Torah—was not infected with tribal religious definitions. He was able to see only a human being in need, a need to which he gave his time, his concern and his means.

In this parable Jesus was telling his listeners that, because there are no lines drawn in the sand that can limit the love and compassion of God, so there must be no lines drawn in the love of one human being for another. This was a radical and challenging conclusion. You cannot be human, Jesus said, and be prejudiced. Prejudice always violates humanity. Prejudice may serve your need to survive, but it will never serve your need to be whole, to be fully human. If you cannot escape these debilitating aspects of your frightened humanity and move beyond the boundaries of fear that cause you to build yourself up by tearing another down, you can never be fully human. That was and is the Jesus message. Salvation comes in Jesus' call to you and in his empowering of you to lay down such security systems as tribe and prejudice in the quest for a new, non–survival-oriented, selfless humanity. That is a gift only a fully human person, not a masquerading deity pretending to be human, could ever accomplish. That was the insight into the wholeness of the humanity found in the life of Jesus that enabled people in his time to see God as present in him.

In Luke's second Samaritan story, the ultimate meaning is the same (Luke 17:11–19). Ten lepers, we are told, came to Jesus as he was going through a region between Galilee and Samaria, asking for mercy. Leprosy, a skin disease that literally causes the body to rot, was a scourge of the Middle East. Lepers were outcasts, unclean, untouchable, forced to live in leper colonies outside the population centers. Jesus saw these ten lepers, we are told, and responded to them by sending them to see the priests, as the Torah requires, to certify that they had become clean from their leprosy and thus could rejoin the social order. The lepers obeyed this command of Jesus and, according to the story, they experienced a miraculous healing. These people who had been the rejectables of the world were now physically whole people. Nine of them never looked back, rushing to claim their new status. One only, said Jesus, seeing that he was clean, turned back in gratitude to thank Jesus, the source and agent of his healing. While the other nine were presumably devout Jews, this man was an unclean half-breed, a heretic, a foreigner, a Samaritan. Jesus said, "Rise and go your way; your faith has made you well," words that imply, I believe, the essence of Jesus' message: "Go and be who you are!"

Jesus was about wholeness. As a result, he saw humanity from a new perspective. He believed that the humanity in one person could touch the humanity in another and empower that other to step out of the fears, tribal security systems, defining prejudices and other boundaries behind which human beings seek an illusive security. That wasn't something just *he* could do: the call of God seen in Jesus, the fully human one, made the meaning of humanity a gift available to *every* life. That is why people saw what they called God in the human Jesus. His humanity opened his life into all that God means. Those who experienced Jesus experienced this new quality of life. They saw it, felt it and claimed it. It is the Jesus experience we seek, not the first-century explanation of the Jesus experience. There is a great difference between the two.

When John wrote his gospel, he combined his understanding of what it meant to be a Samaritan with what it meant to be a woman, and in this manner brought gender issues and prejudices into focus as another symbol of the way self-centered, survival-oriented human beings deal with the trauma of being self-conscious and fearfully inadequate creatures. The common prejudice against Samaritans is clearly operative in John's gospel. He relates the story of a member of a Jewish crowd saying of Jesus, "Are we not right in saying that you are a Samaritan and have a demon?" (8:48). To combine being Samaritan with demon-possession was meant to diminish. Earlier in the narrative, however, John combined being a Samaritan with being a woman, and thus in this patriarchal society presented us with one who was the recipient of a double dose of the prevailing human definition of inadequacy. This is John's story (4:7–42, quotes paraphrased):

A Samaritan woman went to draw water from the well. Jesus, alone at the well when she arrived, asked her for a drink. She responded that he had broken the custom, since he—a Jew—was asking a Samaritan woman for water. John interrupted his storyline at this point to make sure that his readers knew how inappropriate that was. Jesus continued to violate this cultural taboo by quite deliberately keeping the conversation going. If the woman knew who Jesus was, he said, she would be asking him for the gift of "living water." In the Jewish world "living water" is always a synonym for the Holy Spirit, who is conceived of primarily as a life-giver.[3] The woman, caught in her literal pattern of thinking, responded that Jesus had no way to give her water. "You do not even have a bucket and this well is too deep to reach water without one," she asserted. She went on to compare him unfavorably to her ancestor Jacob, who gave the people this well.

Jesus then reverted back to the deeper meaning of water as spirit or life force. He noted that the water in the well satisfied only a momentary thirst that would have to be satisfied again and again. The quest for survival, like the drinking of water to satisfy thirst, was likewise an endless daily quest, he suggested; but no matter how hard one tries, the quest for survival can finally never be successful. Finitude and mortality are part of who we are. Yearning to be whole is like yearning for one's thirst to be forever satisfied. The water that Jesus had to give, he suggested, would break the cycle of this human quest for power, success, or whatever makes one feel momentarily victorious. He offered, he said, "a gushing spring within you that issues in eternal life."

The woman, recognizing her need for such a gift, but still seeing it on the most literal of levels, asked for this "living water." It would make her life easier, she said, since she would no longer have to come to the well to draw water. Jesus continued both the conversation and this woman's hope by saying, "Go get your husband and come back." The implication was that she would then receive what she was requesting.

At this point in the story the woman revealed the brokenness of her own quest for human fulfillment. "I have no husband," she said. Jesus then, as John tells it, opened up the fragile quality of her life: "You have had five husbands," he said, "and the one you have now is not your husband." Feeling vulnerable at the realization that he had stared deep into her soul, she sought to employ God in her defense. She asked whether she could worship God on that Samaritan mountain or would have to go to the temple in Jerusalem, where the Jews thought

God actually lived. Jesus transformed the conversation by stating that true worship has little to do with place or liturgy, but with life in the spirit, where wholeness is experienced and where truth is known. Then the woman shifted the theme of the conversation once more, this time to the idea of the coming messiah. It was a theistic image, since the messiah in her mind was a supernatural figure who would come from heaven to her rescue. Jesus then, in John's rendition, claimed the messianic title for himself, but he redefined "messiah" as the one who now invites her into wholeness. That is a very different concept from the one who rescues.

In this episode Jesus again addressed the meaning of prejudice, but he shifted his attention (and ours) to those people who are female. Women, representing fully 50 percent of the human race, were in Jesus' time treated by the male half of the population as little more than chattel. The Jewish religion supported that view: according to the book of Genesis, women were created by God solely for the purpose of serving the lordly male as helpmate (Gen. 2:18). Later, in the Ten Commandments, building on this sense of second-class citizenship, women were actually defined as property: "You shall not covet your neighbor's ... wife ... or his ox, or his ass, or anything that is your [male] neighbors" (Exod. 20:17). Polygamy made sense if a woman was defined as property, for a man could have as many wives, sheep, or cattle as he could afford.

Throughout human history there has been a perennial war between men and women. Males have sometimes even held over females the power of life and death. In Jesus' day a Jewish man could divorce his wife simply by saying, "I divorce you," in the presence of witnesses. The woman, on the other hand, could not escape a marriage no matter how cruel her husband might be, for she had few human rights. Some societies, reflecting the devaluing of the feminine, have actually encouraged widows to throw themselves on their husband's flaming funeral pyre, for in those societies a woman has had no value except as her husband's wife. Other societies have bound the feet of women so that their lack of mobility would make them easy to keep under constant surveillance. In still other cultures, girls have been forced to undergo genital mutilation in order to remove the possibility of sexual pleasure, and with it the desire to stray from the domination of the male to whom a woman's body would later be committed. Men have been free to beat their wives throughout most of Christian history, and women have been forced to promise obedience to their husbands as part of the marriage liturgies of Christian churches well into the twentieth and twenty-first centuries. What is the motivation for this inhumane behavior, which is still so deep a part of our cultural understanding of life?

Powerless women, as a means of survival, have been driven to use the allure of their bodies, their ability to provide pleasure in the meeting of male sexual needs, to secure the slightest bit of security. For most of Western history women have been relegated to second-class status, with the Christian church validating that definition as God-inspired and God-imposed. In many times and places they have not been educated, been allowed to own property in their own name or been given the power of citizenship expressed through voting. They have been victimized by these and many other patterns, all of which were designed to impose an inferior status. A woman's lack of size, speed and physical strength was used to relegate her to a state of child-like dependency that clearly met those eternal survival needs that are always operating in the male. In the most basic relationship in human society, the male met his survival needs by claiming that the female's lower status was God's plan in creation. That way if the woman objected, she had to fight against God also.

The trouble is that here, as in every other survival-oriented relationship, one cannot be human if one must achieve power by diminishing another. Sexism is one more humanity-robbing prejudice. It victimizes the woman by treating her as subhuman. We understand that when we take the time to consider it. Jesus understood something more, however; he understood that sexist prejudice also warps the man and diminishes his own humanity. Treating another human being as subhuman always makes the perpetrator subhuman. No one can finally be built up at someone else's expense. It simply does not work.

The Christian church, however, with its male Father God, seems to suggest that it does. In invoking the name of a supernatural invasive theistic deity, who is believed to regard human beings as fallen (and therefore as second-class), the church seems to validate male behavior. If the Christian Father God sees human beings as broken, fallen, sinful, inadequate, weak, dependent and childlike, obviously in need of God's protection and rescue, do Christians not validate a misogynous attitude on the part of those males who believe that they emulate God's very nature when they regard women as broken, fallen, sinful, inadequate, weak, dependent and childlike, and perhaps most important of all, obviously in need of male protection and rescue? Yet that kind of human behavior, so much a part of so many religious systems, never leads to wholeness for either men or women, and thus it violates the deepest understanding of God that was given us in Jesus of Nazareth.

Once again we need to scrape away the image of Jesus as a heaven-sent rescuing savior and look at those echoes of what he does that shout loudly about his real identity, the person he was and is. He engaged the Samaritan woman at the well in conversation about theology, the nature of God and liturgy and the proper way to worship God. He thus poured into that woman a respect, a dignity that called her into new dimensions of what it means to be human.

Other narratives in the gospels support this revolutionary yet deeply humanizing portrait. Luke's gospel, for example, gives us the story of Jesus visiting the home of two sisters, Martha and Mary (10:38–42). John's gospel tells us that these sisters lived in the village of Bethany, near Jerusalem (12:1). With Jesus as the guest of honor, Martha, apparently the older sister, accepted the role of the woman imposed on her by society and busily scurried around in the kitchen, preparing the meal. Mary, on the other hand, stepped outside the box of female expectations and positioned herself in the role of a pupil, perhaps even a rabbinic student, sitting at the feet of the gifted teacher and daring to assume that she was capable of learning. Martha, feeling the hostility that always seems to be present in those who are not free, entered the room and demanded of Jesus that Mary be forced to return to the realm of "woman's work" in the kitchen. Luke tells us that Jesus declined that request, consoled Martha (trapped as she was inside role expectations), and held up Mary's choice as "the better part that will not be taken away from her." It is a stunning story of the patterns of imposed definitions being broken open by the call to a new understanding of what it means to be both female and human.

The gospels tell us of another way in which Jesus ignored religious and societal definitions in favor of wholeness and humanity: he had female disciples. Mark, Matthew and Luke all record this truth. Such an understanding of a nonsexist Jesus has been very difficult for the male-dominated Christian church, which has historically had little sense of what the glorious liberty of the children of God is all about. The male leaders of this church throughout Western history have used their power to build themselves up by oppressing the female half of humanity. The reality of Jesus' commitment to having female disciples is, however, deeply written into the biblical story. The women disciples are by and large unnoticed until the gospels move to the final moments in Jesus' life—his death and resurrection. Then suddenly the women become not just visible but vital parts of the story, perhaps because, as Mark says, at the time of Jesus' arrest all the male disciples "deserted him and fled" (14:50, NRSV). Only at the cross does Mark inform his readers that these women had followed Jesus since the very beginning of his public life. From Galilee these women had come up with him to Jerusalem. Mark then names these women as Mary Magdalene and Mary the mother of James and Joses and Salome (15:40).

Matthew adds his witness to the presence of the women by writing, "There were also many women there [at the cross], looking on from afar, who had followed Jesus from Galilee, ministering to him." He, too, names them: Mary Magdalene, Mary the mother of James and Joseph, and the mother [unnamed] of the sons of Zebedee (27:55, 56). Luke describes the mourners at the cross in this way: "All his acquaintances, including the women who had followed him from Galilee, stood at a distance, watching these things" (23:49, NRSV). Luke alone referred to these women earlier, in the Galilean phase of Jesus' ministry. He described them there as people of means, "who provided for them [some texts say *him*] out of their resources" (Luke 8:3, NRSV). Luke also names them: Mary called Magdalene (please note, not from Magdala), Joanna, Susanna and many others.

These same women who helped Jesus during his ministry and cared for him at his death also star in the resurrection dramas painted by all four gospels. Furthermore, in every Easter account Magdalene is either listed first among the women as if she is of a higher status (Mark

16:1, Matt. 28:1 and Luke 24:10) or is said to be the only mourner at the tomb and the first witness to the resurrection (John 20:1). There is no doubt that Magdalene was the head of the women disciples just as surely as Peter was the head of the male disciples. Clearly, then, the traditional picture of Jesus wandering around Galilee with twelve male disciples is simply not biblically accurate. Throughout his entire public ministry he had male *and female* disciples who are known by name. That is a startling portrait for the first century, but it is quite consistent with the understanding of Jesus as the fully human one, who broke every barrier and crossed every boundary that impeded full humanity.

People have speculated through the ages about what the relationship between Jesus and Magdalene really was. Was she his partner, his wife, his lover? The data on any theory are not substantial enough for certainty. There is, however, a strong case that can be made, I believe, for the possibility that Jesus and Magdalene were husband and wife. I sought to make that case in a previous book[4] and will not repeat it here, for my point now is quite a different one: here I want to show that Jesus acted out of his whole and free humanity, revealing a life not bound by human survival needs, unwilling to participate in the security-building prejudices that enhance one by diminishing another. That is where divinity lies, not in a God who in Jesus enters the human arena from the realm of heaven as a divine visitor. Jesus' power is the power of human wholeness that ultimately opens, invites and enables human beings to step beyond defense lines where incomplete humanity always hides in order to experience full humanity. The divine presence of God in Jesus of Nazareth is not known through various theories of incarnation; those are but attempts to form human explanations for a reality for which we have no words. Divinity is met when humanity becomes so whole and so deep that one sees a defenseless, powerless one who is capable of giving himself away fully. That is the moment when the human Jesus opens our eyes to all that God means and enables us to see all that God is.

This Jesus must not be allowed to be captured by the later church image of the external theistic deity, who comes to rescue a fallen world of lost sinners. There is no salvation in divine rescue. Rather, salvation means being called to wholeness, celebrating oneness with who you

are and who God is. Rescue might produce gratitude, but not wholeness. For that reason, viewing Jesus as the incarnation of the external,
heavenly deity cannot be the final meaning of the Jesus experience.
There is salvation, I believe, in the fully human Jesus who reveals what
human life can be, an existence free of tribal boundaries, free of prejudice, free of sexism and free of fear. Such a life will inevitably empower others to step into that promise; and when they do, they will, I
believe, experience the reality of God.

This portrait of Jesus that I am seeking to describe is best seen
within the Bible in the writings of the Fourth Gospel. This divine Jesus
will be hidden from our eyes, however, if we read John as confirming
the traditional myth of Jesus as an invading deity, as God in human
form. That is how people tend to read this Johannine portrait—literally, not experientially. It is, however, not through the divine that we
experience the human; rather, it is from within the human that we experience the divine.

Before we can see Jesus as fully human, we must break the patterns
of antiquity. It is through the fully human one that our lives are open
to experience all that the word "God" means. That is surely the meaning that flows through John's gospel when he writes, "The Son gives
life to whomever he wishes" (5:21, NRSV). The same theme echoes
when John writes, "For as the Father has life in himself, so he has
granted the Son also to have life in himself" (5:26); "If you knew me,
you would know my Father also" (8:19); "Whoever sees me sees him
who sent me" (12:45, NRSV); "He who has seen me has seen the
Father" (14:9); and finally, "[Just as God] has loved me, so have I loved
you" (15:9). The claim is made in these passages that Jesus is what
God is, because in the fullness of Jesus' humanity we can experience
what it means to live beyond the barriers of our evolutionary past and
soar into a humanity that is spirit-filled, open to the source of life and
love and what Paul Tillich called, as his name for God, the "ground of
being."[5]

It is a powerful portrait—a vision of what it means to live fully,
love wastefully and be all that one is capable of being. Because these
are the gifts met in Jesus, he becomes for us the doorway into what
human beings mean by the word "divinity." This is what it means to
me to call Jesus Lord, and thus the Christian life becomes for me a

journey through Jesus into the life of God. It is the human life of Jesus that opens me to see God as the very depth of the meaning of Jesus' life. To live "in Christ" is to become what life was meant to be. This is what Paul called a "new creation," in which all things, including our sense of what it means to be human, are made new. In this way Jesus becomes the revelation of God and even the bearer of all that God means. That is the Jesus I want to serve, the Jesus I call Lord, the Jesus who both entices me and compels me.

JESUS: THE BREAKER OF RELIGIOUS BOUNDARIES

Being a Christian is not to be a religious human being; it is to
be a whole human being. Jesus is a portrait of that wholeness;
and that is why he is for me, in his complete humanity, the
ultimate expression of God.

Another device that our species used to cope with the awakening of self-consciousness and anxiety was the development of religion. People have great difficulty getting outside their
survival needs sufficiently to see religion in this light, but even the
most cursory glance makes it clear that religion at its core represents
compensatory, human activity.

Powerless people deal with their immobilizing fears in interesting
ways. They convince themselves that they are protected in their weakness by the power of an omnipotent God who stands as their defender.
Then they project an ultimate meaning and purpose onto this external,
divine being of their own creation as the means of escaping the dread of
life's apparent meaninglessness. Finally, they create the hope that the
mortality which they now know marks their life will not be ultimate,
since they find in that same eternal God a quality of infinity that over-
comes the transitory character of their lives. Out of these three modali-
ties most of the religious systems that we know came into being, offering
very soothing answers to the very real anxieties produced by the trauma

of awakening to the fact of self-consciousness, which is the reality of human life.

Only when we recognize that this is the nature of all religion do we finally understand the irrational claims that regularly emanate from religious institutions. It is comforting to convince yourself that you are in possession of the ultimate truth. That is why it is the habit of religious systems to pretend that they speak with God's authority and cannot, therefore, be challenged. That is why there is a driving need inside religious systems to purge or to kill alternative or deviating voices.

As I noted in chapter 20 and repeat here for emphasis, religious systems are not primarily about the human search for truth; they are rather about the human search for security. Religion must, therefore, be understood as one more human coping device deliberately designed to create security in a radically insecure world.

It is an act of enormous courage to embrace what it means to be a self-conscious human being. It is not easy to live with the awareness of the unrelieved anxiety that is the mark of human life. That is why human beings are almost inevitably religious creatures. Religion meets a desperate and chronic need in the human psyche and has, therefore, a tenacious hold on human life itself. Self-created security is, however, never real. The fact is that religion as it has been traditionally practiced has never provided genuine security, but only its illusion. Most religion has in fact served as an opiate for the people.[1] That is why the proposal of a Jesus for the non-religious has the possibility of becoming an alternative pathway into the holy.

It is a fascinating study to examine Jesus' attitude toward religion and the faith system in which his own life was nurtured. He broke religious boundaries again and again in his attempt to call people into a new humanity and even to introduce them to a God presence that manifested itself in the fullness of his own humanity. Anything that puts limits on humanity, anything that teaches one to hate, reject or violate another, cannot be of God. That is what Jesus said in a thousand ways. That is why he so deeply threatened the religious leaders of his own time.

The earliest gospel portrait of Jesus was that of a God-infused but fully human life. The Jesus of that portrait lived loosely attached to the security-producing religious rules. God was not part of his security system; God was connected with what it meant to be human. God was viewed as that which enabled him to set aside the rules of religion wherever they impinged upon the quest for human wholeness. Jesus was life-oriented, his followers tell us. So much of his teaching was celebratory. He frequented parties and banquets. He lived with zest. I turn now to examine the gospel portrait of his relationship with religion itself. It is a fascinating study.

His religion taught Jesus that moral rules are ultimate and that if one violates these rules one must endure the prescribed punishment, lest the wrath of God fall on the whole community. That is a mentality that inevitably produces a sense of external righteousness and fierce judgment. It is a mentality that creates community enforcers of the rules of God. It never, however, creates love. It never expands life. So what does Jesus do with this mentality? One has only to read the gospels to see that he pushes its boundaries, steps beyond its religious barriers, and calls others to follow.

I begin with the story of the woman caught in the act of adultery, found in John (8:1–11).[2] She was hauled by the scribes and Pharisees from her lover's bed and taken before the moral gendarmes of that day. They knew the rules. They knew what Moses taught. They believed that the moral laws had to be obeyed, lest the whole community fall into moral anarchy and incur the wrath of God. They knew the stories in the Bible that told of just that consequence happening.[3] They were infected with that image of the vindictive theistic God for whom judgment and reward or punishment were the primary markers. This woman was clearly guilty; they had caught her in an unmistakable position of moral compromise. If they did not react in judgment, the theistic God would, they believed, write down in the record book, alongside their names: "He [or she] failed to uphold the rules by not dispensing the obviously deserved punishment that this adulterous woman required."

Perhaps there was also hidden away in their controlled hearts a sense of envy: if *she* got away with it, then why were *they* not likewise free to roam? Why were they forced to conform? They wanted to see a payoff for their righteousness. They might well have suffered what Paul Tillich has called "the vengeance of the denied possibility."[4] The sense of freedom that was present in Jesus was always frightening to established religious folk. "If we must obey the moral rules, then, by God, so must she!" they said. So the guilty woman was brought to Jesus. Stoning was to be the method of execution. It was so convenient. Stones were plentiful throughout that tiny region of the world, requiring little effort to pick up and hurl, and no special place of execution was needed.

John portrays Jesus, however, as responding quite differently than the religious leaders had expected. Understanding that moralism and judgment are not weapons that achieve wholeness, Jesus stood between that woman and her accusers. He raised the moral standard by questioning how deserving any of her accusers were to be her judges. It is ever the same today. Which one of us can walk in another person's boots? Which one of us understands what motivates a particular act done by another? What are the needs, conscious and unconscious, that are being met in accusatory thoughts and actions? From what inner source have those needs arisen? "Let him who is without sin cast the first stone," Jesus says. Are apparently righteous people righteous because they have broken no moral laws? Or are those people righteous because they have suppressed their ability to love, or perhaps simply because they have never been caught? Had this public stoning been carried out, would this woman's accusers, or Jesus himself, have become more deeply and fully human, or would they have become less human, more violent, and thus more prone to hate, to reject and to do inhumane things? Moralism and righteousness finally never issue in love or new life; they issue only in law and religious control. The quest for humanity is not the same as the quest to be religious.

Jesus seems always to set humanity ahead of religious law, thus subverting that law, in all its embodiments, to a higher goal. In another example, Jesus challenges the imposition of religious rules involved with the worship of the theistic deity who handed down decrees from on high. It was the sabbath, says Mark, and the disciples were going through grain fields (2:23–28). Being hungry, they plucked heads of grain. The champions of the theistic religion of control immediately invoked the law of God to condemn this violation. The disciples were doing what it is not lawful for people to do on the sabbath, the moralists said.[5] Jesus responded by citing a case in which King David ate the ceremonial bread of the presence, which the law stated was reserved only for the priests. This bread was to be used only in extreme cases — that is, when it was necessary for them to alleviate a killing hunger. Then in one of his profound reversals of all religious law, Jesus inverted the priorities of his religion by declaring that religious rules, even those rules pertaining to the tribal-defining observance of the sabbath day, cease to be moral unless they serve the purpose of enhancing human life. That is the only purpose, he asserted, for all religious rules. Human life was not created to fit into the sabbath laws, he proclaimed. The opposite is true; the sabbath laws were designed as an aid in the enhancement of human life. If religious rules do not enhance life, then they must be set aside in the name of humanity. That was a startling religious shift of authority, tradition and law! Contrary to thousands of years of religious teaching and practice, the ultimate purpose of religion is not to please the presumed external supernatural deity, Jesus was saying; it is rather to enhance humanity. When the two are in conflict, enhanced humanity always trumps the rules. This was a powerful moment of insight, a transforming symbol of a new consciousness, an indicator of the fact that Jesus saw human life as the place where God is met. At that moment God seemed to come out of the sky as an external authoritarian parent figure and began to be experienced as a presence dwelling in the heart of human life.

Mark drives this insight home in his next Jesus story (3:1–6), which once again shows Jesus on the sabbath in the synagogue — this time confronted by a man with a withered, perhaps a paralyzed hand. That condition was clearly a chronic, non-life-threatening malady and, therefore, one that must not be allowed to diminish the holiness of the sabbath. Jesus responded by asking, in effect, If on the sabbath one can do good and prevent harm from continuing for a single day longer, should that act of goodness be postponed? In other words, is justice or goodness that is postponed ever either just or good? Since life is finite, an act of kindness postponed means a day lost in that person's life. Mark says that Jesus, angry at how religion was used to distort life and to increase suffering, healed the man in that sabbath moment and the religious authorities reacted on cue with great hostility. What else should we expect, since their power was threatened by one who did not abide by their religious rules designed to control behavior? Their authority was relativized by one who seemed to be saying that religious rules used to ensure the winning of the divine favor of the external God might not be valid. Anarchy would be the result, they claimed, because those rules were necessary to keep life under religious domination. If Jesus were allowed to sustain that kind of challenge, their religious authority would be destroyed.

It was no wonder that these validators of a controlling deity would conspire with the political authorities to remove this threat to law, order and, above all, their religious power. Church and state both always seek the ability to impose order on an unruly and fallen world. Jesus, on the other hand, seemed to believe that the eternal need to control life through the use of religious rules is nothing more than the perpetuation of the incomplete human situation. Authoritarian religion engages only in damage control. Its goal is to keep dangerous human propensities in check. Jesus saw the human situation quite differently. He saw humanity as a journey out from under control and rules toward wholeness. He called people to step beyond rules, defenses, tribal boundaries, prejudices and even religion to embrace abundant life. That is a unique approach to life and to religion. That is why Jesus was so startlingly different, why he seemed to be of another human dimension and why his followers came to see God as part of his identity.

Another mark of almost every religious system is that it seems to have definitions of what constitutes ritual purity and what it is that makes some people clean and others unclean. There are many references in the Torah to a prohibition against touching a woman during the period of her menstrual flow (see Lev. 12:1–8 and 15:19–30). In many ancient religious systems, and the religion of the Jews was no exception, a woman was defined as unclean during her menstrual cycles. She was seen as possessing negative power, making it necessary for her to be ostracized as a potential danger to tribal well-being during that time. For those few days each month she was covered with a sense of culturally imposed shame. Religion does that to people on many levels.

Against this background we read the story in Mark's gospel of a woman whose menstrual flow was constant, not periodic. This would mean in the value system of that culture, that she was perpetually unclean. We are told that she had sought medical help for her problem, but to no avail. Her sense of self-worth had plummeted; she saw herself as cursed and with that judgment inevitably came a diminution of her humanity. She was an object of fear and scorn. With what must have been, therefore, enormous strength of character, she decided to break out of her religiously imposed prison. She would seek out Jesus, about whom she had heard, and she would physically touch him. She must have had some sense that he would receive her touch without condemnation and thus would break through the barriers that repressed and compromised her humanity. She hoped to be made well in this action. As Mark tells this story, that touch brought her healing and Jesus is said to have experienced power flowing out of him.

Mark adds to the drama by depicting Jesus as turning to inquire, "Who touched me?" The disciples ridiculed his question, since, they said, he was constantly being jostled by the crowd. This, however, said Jesus, had been a purposeful touch. The woman, sensing what had happened to her and recognizing that she had received healing, approached Jesus in fear and trembling, confessing that she had deliberately touched him. The laws of the Torah said that this touch made Jesus unclean and the purity laws required that he engage in cleansing acts within a prescribed number of days. As this woman knelt before Jesus, knowing that she had contaminated him, her fear was that once more religious rules and purity laws would be used to reject her.

She, however, told Jesus her story anyway and he received it with love and grace. I suspect that he even touched her again to lift her up and he said to her, "Daughter," a term of a human relationship of great significance, "your faith has made you well." Did faith mean that she believed the right things? Of course not. It was her faith that her life could be more than she had heretofore known. It was her faith in the love that could and did set her free to be something dramatically different. It was her faith in the divine power that flows out from one human being to another to heal. Jesus, says Mark, sent her away in the peace of a new sense of wholeness.

In this narrative we catch yet another insight into Jesus' conviction that one must step beyond security-giving religion in order to be fully human. He lived this out in every set of circumstances. That was, I submit, why people came to believe that in Jesus something more than humanity was present. They had never confronted this kind of humanity. That is why they identified him with God. Humanity that was free and whole was of a different dimension. Because they located God above the sky, they thought Jesus must likewise have come from above. In reality divinity always comes from below, from earth. God did not come down from some heavenly sphere above the sky to enter human life. Human life emerged into a wholeness that was seen as a manifestation of God and was then called divinity. That is what the Jesus experience was all about.

The religion of an external, supernatural God always achieves and maintains power by identifying the outcast and guarding against allowing that outcast's polluting presence to live inside the citadels of holiness. The outcast is generally defined as one who is different. Fear adds other adjectives: loathsome, scary, contagious, bearing the signs of God's rejection. Such judgments are usually grounded in ignorance. In the culture in which Jesus lived, that role was filled by those called lepers. The law in Leviticus called for all lepers to be immediately identifiable, lest the polluting presence of that disease corrupt others. The lepers' clothes had to be torn, their hair disheveled, so that people would recognize them as those to be avoided. The lepers had to keep their upper lip covered and cry out constantly, "Unclean, unclean" (Lev. 13:45). Lepers were quite literally excommunicated from the society and forced to live outside the camp or the city walls. The law also prescribed rituals that lepers had to go through in order to be certified as clean; only after fulfilling those rituals were lepers allowed back into the social order (Lev. 14:2–3). It is, therefore, fascinating to see what the gospel writers say about Jesus confronting a leper.

Mark is the first to relate such an encounter (1:40–45). A leper comes to Jesus, drawn, the text suggests, by a sense that Jesus has the power to heal him. "If you choose, Jesus, you can make me clean," he says. Jesus responds, according to Mark, by touching the leper. That is an understated, simple description of what was surely a profound and personal act. That public and overt touch of one infected with leprosy would have sent shock waves through the crowd and it would have caused the walls of organized religion, whose power is based on its ability to distinguish the clean who are to be embraced from the unclean who are to be purged, to vibrate in fear. "I do choose," Mark records Jesus as saying, "be made clean." Jesus' action here is consistent with the portrait in other gospel texts of Jesus breaking the religious rules and voting for life and wholeness. Can you imagine what the touch of a human being means to one who is defined as literally untouchable? That touch carries with it the restoration of life and the enhancement of humanity. Ignorance is forced to retreat in the face of the humanity that recognizes no barriers which can exclude. That was the kind of humanity Jesus exhibited, and that humanity defined divinity in a whole new way.

Moral judgment is not life-giving; love that transcends the boundaries of judgment, as Jesus' love did, is. The fear of that which we do not understand always erects barriers against life. That is what religion, seeking to please an external deity and thus to gain divine favor, does over and over again. Successive generations of those who claim to be followers of Jesus, calling themselves "the body of Christ," still time after time violate all that Jesus was and is in order to serve the needs of both fearful people and authoritarian institutions.

Who are the lepers, the unclean people of Christian history? They have had many faces. First it was the Gentiles who, responding to the message of Jesus, sought membership in the Christian community while it was still primarily a Jewish movement. Paul championed Gentile inclusion. Peter championed a prerequisite religious tradition as the only doorway to Jesus. Peter, we are told, finally saw the light.

The story of Peter's conversion to this universal God experience is told in the book of Acts (10:1–48). While sleeping on a rooftop in the middle of the day, Peter dreamed of a great sheet let down from heaven on which were located all the animals that the Torah called unclean. A voice from heaven said to Peter: "Rise, Peter, kill and eat!" Peter responded by saying that he was a kosher-observing Jew and did not eat unclean food. The voice from heaven said, "Peter, what I have called clean you must not call unclean." Peter rose and went to the home of a Gentile named Cornelius and baptized him. Then, Luke says, Peter watched the Holy Spirit fall on Gentiles. It was a life-changing moment that Peter, we are told, interpreted by saying, "Now I know that with God there is no partiality." A barrier-breaking Jesus again and again moves people to new levels of consciousness, even through his disciples. A Jesus who steps beyond the security systems of fear to create new life is at the heart of the gospel portrait.

In an earlier story in the book of Acts (8:26–40), another barrier fell when Philip the deacon baptized an Ethiopian eunuch. This man was a double threat to the religious rules of the times: not only was he an unclean Gentile, but his physical situation of castration also made him unacceptable. Moses was quoted in the Torah as having said, "He whose testicles are crushed or whose penis is cut off shall not be admitted to the assembly of the Lord" (Deut. 23:1). Please note that this text is not plagued by either relativity or ambiguity. It is what Bible-quoters through the ages, in defense of their prejudices, have called "the clear teaching of the word of God." Its meaning was obvious to the disciples. Yet Philip set that rule aside overtly and baptized that castrated eunuch, once again challenging the religious rules in the name of a higher humanity. That was the action to which he felt the meaning of Jesus had driven him.

Other barriers erected in fear throughout history by the followers of Jesus were destined to be similarly dismantled. Jesus' disciples in every generation have struggled against their own survival mentality. Indeed, one can view Christian history as a constant battle between the religious rules of yesterday and the freedom that seems to stem relentlessly from Jesus of Nazareth. Throughout history, even though victims have differed, the barriers to celebrating their full humanity have been overcome again and again. We could tell the story of mentally ill people, African-American people, Jewish people, left-handed people, gay and lesbian people, all of whom have been made to feel the sting of religious rejection. In time, however, each of these exclusionary barriers has fallen before the same power that people experienced in Jesus. God is not a heavenly judge. God is a life force expanding inside humanity until that humanity becomes barrier-free. This was the God revealed in the fullness of Jesus' humanity. It was a new God definition that shifted our old view of an external force into something found at the center of life. The being of this God calls us to be; the life of this God calls us to live; the love of this God calls us to love. Jesus lived the life of God. That is why we proclaim that in his life the source of life was seen. In his love the source of love was seen. In his courage, which enabled him to be fully human, the ground of all being was seen. That is the experience that the word "incarnation" was created to communicate. It is not a doctrine to be believed so much as it is a presence to be experienced.

It was Dietrich Bonhoeffer who first coined the phrase "religionless Christianity."[6] Bonhoeffer said that when humanity "comes of age," by which he meant when human beings develop the ability to set aside the external supernatural parental God of theistic religion, a new day in human consciousness would dawn. For far too long that theistic God has blinded us to the God of life, love and being, who emerges at the heart of humanity and who is the ultimate depth and meaning of the Jesus experience.

The call of Christ for me has thus become a call to journey beyond every barrier that shackles and limits our humanity and its potential. Jesus was not divine because he was a human life into whom the external God had entered, as traditional Christology has claimed; he was and is divine because his humanity and his consciousness were so whole and so complete that the meaning of God could flow through him. He was thus able to open people to that transcendent dimension of life, love and being that we call God.

That is the basis for the Christology of the future. Being a Christian, again in Bonhoeffer's words, is not to be a religious human being; it is to be a whole human being. Jesus is the portrait of that wholeness; and that is why he is for me, in his complete humanity, the ultimate expression of God.

THE CROSS: A HUMAN PORTRAIT OF THE LOVE OF GOD

The world always seems to stand aside, the waters always seem to part for one who knows where he or she is going.

When you do an audacious thing, you do not then tremble at your own audacity.

Before I can conclude this new portrait of Jesus outside the boundaries of religion, at least as religion has been traditionally understood, I must return to that climactic moment at the center of the Christian story. What is the cross of Calvary all about? Why should it be something which, as our hymns say, we stand beneath or in which we glory?[1] What does the cross mean? How is it to be understood? Clearly the old pattern of seeing the cross as the place where the price of the fall was paid is totally inappropriate. Aside from encouraging guilt, justifying the need for divine punishment and causing an incipient sadomasochism that has endured with a relentless tenacity through the centuries, the traditional understanding of the cross of Christ has become inoperative on every level. As I have noted previously, a rescuing deity results in gratitude, never in expanded humanity. Constant gratitude, which the story of the cross seems to encourage, creates only weakness, childishness and dependency. It causes us to extol liturgically the greatness of God, while accepting the wretchedness of human life and the cost to God of saving one like me. Yet one can hardly read the story of Jesus without seeing the cross as the ultimate revelatory moment. So it becomes imperative to move beyond the explanations of antiquity and seek to isolate the experience that people had with the crucified one. It is that experience, I suggest, that both inspired the resurrection narratives and shaped the Christian Eucharist. This interpretive task requires us to remove the image of the theistic deity to whose will Jesus was said to have been obedient unto death, in order that we might discover the power to transform life that must have been present in the crucified one. That is now our final task.

The cross was presented in the gospels as the unavoidable destiny of Jesus. He was, said the gospels, crucified in accordance with the expectations of the prophets. The theme of the cross was said to be that of finding fulfillment through weakness. As we have seen, Jesus' crucifixion was interpreted through the lens of such Hebrew images as the Passover, the Day of Atonement, the "servant" of Second Isaiah who absorbed the world's abuse and returned it as love and the "shepherd king" of Second Zechariah who was betrayed into the hands of those who bought and sold animals in the temple as a prelude to the coming day of the Lord. Our task has been not to read these at face value as history, but to ask what the Jesus experience was that led to these interpretations of the violence of his crucifixion. Let me now try to reconstruct the totality of the drama that culminated in the cross.

I think we may be sure that between Jesus and his closest followers there was a particularly intense relationship. They interacted on many levels. Jesus' disciples listened to his teaching; they both felt its impact on themselves and saw its impact on others. People around Jesus questioned his right and his authority to do what he did, but in their very questions they bore eloquent testimony to the presence of something quite different and authentic in him. The gospels captured this reaction in such verses as, "Where did this man get all this? What is the wisdom given to him? ... Is not this the carpenter, the son of Mary?" (Mark 6:2–3). "They were astonished at his teaching, for he taught them as one who had authority, and not as the scribes" (Mark 1:22). "When the crowds saw it [the healing of the paralytic], ... they glorified God, who had given such authority to human beings" (Matt. 9–8). "One day, as he was teaching the people in the temple ..., the chief priests and the scribes with the elders came up and said to him: 'Tell us by what authority you do these things, or who it is who gave you this authority'" (Luke 20:1–2). The power that was in him, the effect he had on both his followers and others—these things were inevitably part of the Jesus presence that the disciples absorbed slowly and incrementally over the days, weeks, months, perhaps even the years of their association with him.

The disciples also had the opportunity to live inside the relationship that Jesus seemed to have with God. That, too, they had to process. He called God "Abba," a word of intimacy and communion. They watched him pray. Perhaps they even heard him reciting passages of the scriptures and wrestling with their meaning. There was a sense among the disciples that somehow Jesus had loved them into being loving. He had called them to step across the tribal barrier that separated Jew from Gentile, and had done so himself with a Syrophoenician woman (Mark 7:24–30) and with a Roman centurion (Luke 7:1–10). They knew that he was not bound by the prejudice that Jews had erected against Samaritans, against women, against children. All of these moments were stretching experiences for the disciples and their lives were clearly expanded by them, whether they were always happy with the result or not. Jesus appears to have talked constantly to them about something called the kingdom of God that was breaking into human history. That was, at least, the dominant theme in the way his teaching was remembered. Perhaps the disciples sensed that in some way his very life was a sign of this kingdom. They wondered what those words "the kingdom of God" meant; they also wondered how the life of Jesus might be related to that kingdom.

The disciples appear to have seen in Jesus a rare integrity. He had within himself, they tell us, the courage to be all that he was meant to be under every set of circumstances. Their memory of Jesus cast him as one free of the need to be defined either by his friends or by his enemies. That freedom was compelling. I suspect the disciples yearned to possess it.

Jesus also appears to have been deeply present to others. He lived, it seems, inside what Paul Tillich called "the eternal now."[2] He engaged people so totally that when anyone stood in a relationship with Jesus, it seemed as though time actually stood still. Whoever Jesus encountered, whether it was the rich young ruler or the woman by the well, he engaged that person, as the disciples tell it, inside what might be called "the intensity of eternity." In so doing his very presence challenged the hierarchy of human values that assigns varying levels of worth to people. Each person, for Jesus, seemed to have the potential to become whole, to be invested with infinite worth. People who met him seemed to be expanded by that meeting.

In the mindset of that day, when sickness and disease were believed to be signs of divine disfavor and punishment, Jesus was remembered as embracing the sick, laying his hands upon them, bathing the places on their bodies that were thought to bear the curse of divine wrath. He was also remembered as allowing the touch of the woman of the street who washed his feet with her tears and dried them with her hair (Luke 7:36–50). The immorality of this woman was judged by the religious leaders to be a sign of her rebellion against the ways of God. Jesus' actions seemed to challenge that definition of immorality again and again. He called into the inner circle of disciples a tax collector, unclean because of his association with the Gentile conquerors of the Jews (Mark 2:13–14). If even this man, who had used his compromised position to increase the misery of his own conquered people, was worthy, then clearly *no* life for Jesus was beyond transformation. Jesus welcomed into the embrace of his love powerless children whom the disciples wanted to reject. These and other generous actions were the things the disciples saw, the things they pondered, the things that fascinated them, attracted them and in some cases even repelled them about this Jesus. Always, however, they wondered about Jesus as each of his actions forced them to reconfigure their own values. Life with Jesus must have been like living inside an eternally changing kaleidoscope.

Whatever it was that Jesus actually assumed God to be, that reality was a powerful presence in his own life. God was likened by him in his teaching to a wide variety of rather common, even pedestrian symbols. God was like a father who welcomed home the prodigal son (Luke 15:11–32). God was like a shepherd who searched for a lost sheep (Luke 15:3–7), or like a woman who swept diligently until she found a lost coin (Luke 15:8–10). The God Jesus seemed to know was one in whom all were welcome to come just as each one was (Matt. 11:28). Those finding their way to God could be as noisy as the clamoring widow who would not stop knocking on the door until all her needs were met (Luke 18:1–8), or they could be like those who in the secret recesses of their hearts found a forgiveness so gracious and limitless that it reached into the meaning of eternity (John 8:1–11). His disciples must have participated in all of these experiences.

Jesus seemed to appear to those who knew him best to be larger than life, which caused them to attribute to him the power to control the forces before which most human beings feel helpless. It should, therefore, be no surprise that supernatural tales gathered around him in an age when the miraculous was thought to be commonplace. Perhaps it was that people near Jesus were so totally and constantly fed from the deep spiritual wells within him that they began to envision great hosts of people sharing in such a spiritual banquet at which there was always more food than could be consumed or digested, no matter how large the crowd (Mark 6:35–44, Matt. 14:13–21, Luke 9:10–17, John 6:1–14).

The disciples also perceived in Jesus a man on a mission. They were not sure what that mission was, but its reality was never in doubt. The world always seems to stand aside, the waters always seem to part for one who knows where he or she is going. The idea that "his hour" had not yet come or that it finally arrived at the time of the crucifixion is a note clearly present in the gospel narratives (Mark 14:41, Matt. 26:45, Luke 22:53, John 2:4). That special "hour" somehow got connected in the minds of his followers with what the ancient Hebrews had called the "day of the Lord." That connection only served to heighten the mystique in Jesus and this became the thing that in time attracted to him the messianic expectations found in many parts of the Jewish sacred scriptures. One thing that was clear is that Jerusalem drew Jesus like a magnet. His "hour" had to come in that holy city. In some way, the underlying themes in those who remembered him suggested that his "hour," the "day of the Lord," and Jerusalem itself were inextricably bound up in Jesus' mind. His was an enchanting, a mystifying presence.

All of these themes seem to come together in the story of Jesus' crucifixion in Jerusalem. That was obviously both a primary as well as a traumatic and devastating memory that challenged so much else that his followers had associated with him. His death seemed to them, in the intensity of their grief, to be nothing less than a profound divine *no* articulated by an external God in judgment on the meaning of his life. A messiah could not die. The Jews did not think in terms of a dead messiah. When Jesus died, therefore, it was assumed that any associations they had made between Jesus and the promised messiah were dashed, seemingly forever. The Jesus who had so deeply confronted the beliefs of the religious hierarchy was dead—and shamefully so; the Torah called one "accursed" who was hanged upon a tree (Deut. 21:23). The members of that hierarchy were clearly the victors. Jesus was the loser. The disciples of Jesus had to wrap their minds around what seemed like the inevitability of these conclusions. If Jesus was dead, apparently the heavenly parental God had not seen fit to spare him. The disciples had to assume that Jesus had been wrong, perhaps deluded; and if he had been wrong, then so had they. "Duped," "misled," "guilty"—these were words they were forced to entertain about themselves.

Yet this conclusion failed to satisfy, because the disciples' inner conflict did not go away. The reality of Jesus' death kept being challenged by the reality of their experience in life with him. How could God say no to the message of Jesus that was one of forgiveness and love? How could God be offended by one whose life reached across every divide to enhance the humanity of all that God had made? How could Jesus be so profoundly an agent of life and not also be an agent of God? How could one give life and love away so freely and still be guilty of a capital crime? Nothing added up and therefore nothing ever seemed to find resolution. The inner turmoil and tension that the crucifixion brought to the disciples of Jesus was palpable, excruciating and never-ending.

That unresolved tension is one reason I believe that there was a considerable period of time between the crucifixion, which was the experience that created the tension, and the resurrection, which was the experience in which the tension was ultimately resolved. "Three days" is the liturgical symbol that stands for that period of time. Parts of the gospel story, as previously noted, imply that the transformation of Easter was separated from the trauma of the crucifixion by a considerable amount of time (Luke 24, Acts 1, 2, John 21). For those who study the cycles of grief, there is evidence in these passages that causes them to date that state of the disciples' grief somewhere between six months and a year after the crucifixion.[3]

What we see in the gospels, written at least two and perhaps even three generations after the tragedy of the crucifixion, is the way these tensions were reconciled. Jesus' death was given purpose. It was, said Paul, "for our sins" and "in accordance with the scriptures." The words supposedly spoken by Jesus from the cross change from the cry of dereliction, "My God, my God, why hast thou forsaken me?" found only in Mark (15:34) and Matthew (27:46), to the sense of triumph and victory found in Luke's portrayal of the last words, "Father, into thy hands I commit my Spirit" (23:46), and in John's allusion to a new creation in which Jesus proclaims, "It is finished" (John 19:30), to play on the story from the book of Genesis in which the work of creation is completed and the eternal sabbath has begun (Gen. 2:1).

It was well after the crucifixion that the death of Jesus began to be likened to the death of the paschal lamb. It was also at this point that the death of Jesus began to be likened to the death of the sacrificial lamb of Yom Kippur, that later death being understood as a ransom required by God to overcome the brokenness of creation and as the blood sacrifice that paid the price of the fall. In the connection of Jesus with the paschal lamb the power of death was said to have been broken. In his connection with the lamb of Yom Kippur, the meaning of atonement was said to have been achieved. His death, finally understood inside these symbolic interpretations, now was said to have the power to split the veil in the temple that had always separated the Holy Place where the people could gather, from the Holy of Holies where God alone was thought to dwell (Mark 15:38, Matt. 27:51, Luke 23:45). These were some of the symbols that transformed the death of Jesus from an intolerable tragedy to a purposeful act of redemption.

All of this evolving understanding of Jesus took place within the commonly accepted theistic concept of God. This God of creation had been offended by human disobedience. This God, who lived above the sky, demanded punishment and restitution. When the punishment was more than a fallen human being could endure, then overcoming the sins of the world and achieving oneness with God became something that only God could accomplish. So in an infinite act of grace God entered history in the person of Jesus, through a miraculous birth. God demonstrated divine power in the life of Jesus, by Jesus' ability to do what only God could do: forgive sinners, heal sickness, overcome the distortions of a fallen world, manipulate the forces of nature as their creator, stand between life and death by raising the dead and by walking out of the tomb in which some had sought to bind him and finally by miraculously ascending into the sky to complete the round trip and to present to God a redeemed creation and a redeemed humanity. This became the way the Jesus story was told, hinted at first in the gospels, and later made both concrete and dogmatic in the creeds and still later in the doctrines and sacraments of the church. Explanations, however, always assume the reality of the worldview in which those explanations are formed. When that worldview dies, any explanations attached to it also die. If the experience of meeting God in Jesus is identified with an explanation that assumes a first-century view of God, heaven and miracles it also will inevitably die. That is where we are today and that is why it is necessary to free Jesus from the shackles of the religious view of yesterday, to propose a portrait of "Jesus for the Non-Religious."

Our question becomes a different one: What does the Jesus experience reveal about life, about God, about purpose, about the eternal search for oneness and about what it means to be at one with God? Only if we can answer this question can the cross become for us a usable symbol instead of a sign of the theistic deity's sadistic nature, which required the sacrifice of the son to pay the price of sin. When that theology enters our liturgies, it contributes to human degradation and feeds the fetishes that Christians have developed around the cleansing power of the shed blood of Jesus. It is this external framework—with its language of sacrifice, its abusive, punishing picture of God and its definition of human life as fallen, sinful and broken, capable only of begging for mercy—that has become bankrupt and that must now be dismantled. That is what our journey through the pages of this book has sought to do. The anxiety experienced by many is that when this structure is dismantled, nothing is left. If that is so, then let us be honest and face the fact that Christianity has died and the history of a post-Christian world has begun.

However, I, a twenty-first-century believing Christian, do not accept that conclusion. My task is not to respirate artificially the symbols of yesterday. They are, in my opinion, neither worthy nor capable of respiration. My task is to enter the experience that gave birth to these now dated and dying symbols and then to find words appropriate to my worldview to convey the power of the Jesus experience. I cannot do that for all time any more than the disciples could. I can do it only for my time.

I cannot tell anyone who God is or what God is. Neither can anyone else, though we have pretended to do just that for centuries through our creeds and doctrines. The reality of God can never be defined. It can only be experienced, and we need always to recognize that even that experience may be nothing more than an illusion. Theism is just one more inadequate human definition of God that needs to be surrendered.

When I seek to speak of my experience of God, I can do so only with human analogies. Insects cannot tell anyone what it is like to be a bird. Horses cannot tell anyone what it is like to be human. Human beings cannot tell anyone what it is like to be God. That seems so elementary. So let me speak of my experience in the language of human analogy, for that is the only language in which I can speak.

I experience life to be more than I can embrace. To live it fully calls me beyond the limits of my human consciousness. I can, however, taste its sweetness and contemplate its eternity. When I do, I commune with the Source of Life that I call God.

I experience love as something beyond me. I cannot create it, but I can receive it. Once I have received it, I can give it away. So love is a transcendent reality that I can engage and by which I can be transformed; I can grow into a deeper understanding of it and contemplate its source, which I call God.

I experience being as something in which I participate, but my being does not come close to exhausting the content of Being itself. I am grounded in something so much greater than I am. Being itself is inexhaustible, infinite and indestructible. When I touch the Ground of Being, I believe that I touch that which I call God.

It is through the expanded consciousness of these transcendent experiences that I look at Jesus of Nazareth and assert that in his life I see what the word "God" means. My view of God and even of the God I meet in Jesus is a subjective description of what I believe is an objective reality.

I have sought to understand Jesus as a boundary-breaker, as one who calls people to step outside the circles of their security systems. His was a life that recognized the reality that fear stifles humanity, builds protective walls, creates defining prejudices and erects religious systems designed to give security to chronically frightened people. To walk the Christ path is to be empowered to step outside and beyond these various human security systems. It is to walk beyond all religious forms that bind our humanity in order to enter the religionless world of a new humanity. It is to seek divinity not externally but as the deepest dimension of what it means to be human. It is to enter divinity only when we become free to give ourselves away. It is no longer to speculate about who or what God is but to act out what God means. It is to look at the fullness of Jesus' humanity and to see in that the presence of the divine. "God was in Christ" is not a doctrine that leads to theories of incarnation and trinity; it is an acclamation of a presence that leads to a wholeness, a new creation, a new humanity and a new manner of living.

Now we take this experience of God, an experience that issues in wholeness, and look once more at the story of the cross. Its brutality is not diminished, for crucifixion was a brutal form of execution in a brutal world, but the portrait painted by the gospel writers of Jesus becomes even more revealing than our piety has yet imagined.

It matters not to me whether any of the details of the cross story are accurate historically. I have long been convinced that they are not, since as I have already suggested, the gospels appear to be liturgically crafted documents based not on eyewitness accounts but on ancient Hebrew sources. They do, however, present a memory of Jesus of Nazareth, a portrait that I still find to be astounding.

Look first at the narrative of Jesus with which we still today open Holy Week. Jesus is riding triumphantly into Jerusalem. The air is festive. The crowd is large. The messianic symbol drawn from Zechariah is obvious (Zech. 9:9–10).

He comes as a king but without the symbols of power. Marcus Borg and John Dominic Crossan, in their book *The Last Week*,[4] contrast this procession with the procession of Pilate, who at the same time is coming from Caesarea to Jerusalem to put down any terrorist activity that might accompany the Passover. Power does not mount an ass! Power is not unarmed. The gospels tell us that many cast their garments before him on the road. Others spread leafy branches cut from the fields. All shout the words of the psalm of triumph: "Hosanna! Blessed is he who comes in the name of the Lord. Blessed is the kingdom of our father David that is coming! Hosanna in the highest" (Mark 11:1–10). There is no mistaking the messianic fervor that the gospel writers convey. The crowd wants to crown Jesus their king. That is high, head-turning rhetoric. Nothing is more seductive to insecure human beings than the sweet narcotic of human praise. Jesus, the whole person, is, however, not seducible. He knows who he is; he does not need human acclaim to be whole. His head is not turned. He rides on.

The Jesus parade moves inexorably through the week as the gospel writers portray those brief passing days. It winds through Bethany, back to Jerusalem, into the temple where confrontation is portrayed. The temple is reclaimed. It is not to be a den of thieves gathered to support institutional religion. It is to be a house of prayer for all the nations. There is to be no barrier that separates any people from the omnipresent God who permeates the universe and who cannot be limited in a holy place built by human hands, a place that somehow is said to contain all that God is.

During this week, the gospel portrait portrays the tension building. A parable is told in which the religious authorities want to kill the son of the owner of the vineyard. It is too close for comfort. Mark suggests that in the act of rejecting Jesus the religiously established voices, pretending that they speak for God, have succeeded only in making of Jesus a new cornerstone on which a new structure can be erected.

Then Jesus confronts the defining religious boundaries of his day and the religious rules of his tradition. He suggests that all of them bind our humanity and that none of them frees us to be. Who is married in heaven? Do the dead rise? What is the greatest commandment? Jesus parries all such questions. He is in touch with a different vision: Earthly rules do not apply to heaven. God is not a God of the dead but of the living. Love is the essence of the commandments. "Son of

David" is not a definition of the Christ life. Religion that is true does not lead to status. One's living is directly related to one's being. False Christs and false definitions of Christ will abound. Religious rules must be transcended. God is not found in power but in powerlessness. Always be prepared, for the Lord God comes unexpectedly in life. God is unfettered, boundless love. It is a powerful message lived and spoken by this man, Jesus of Nazareth, as people sought to recall him.

Then the drama, with a kind of divine inevitability, moves toward the death of Jesus. A woman anoints him for burial. The act of betrayal is done. The Passover is prepared and eaten. The symbols of broken bread and poured-out wine presage his broken body and his shed blood. The weakness of the disciples is portrayed. They brag, sleep, flee and finally deny. Jesus is arrested. He is alone. He is doomed. His life is near its end, but watch and observe the portrait the gospel writers painted of how he died: He was betrayed but he loved the betrayer. He was forsaken but he loved those who forsook him. His arrest was challenged but he demanded that his defenders put up their swords. He was falsely accused but he was silent in the face of his accusers. There was nothing defensive about him. Even when he was mocked and tormented, he loved his mockers and his tormentors. He was scourged and he loved his scourgers. He was denied and he loved his denier. He was crucified and he loved his killers. Hostility and rejection, abuse and death—these did not diminish his humanity.

That is a portrait of a fully human one who has no need to hate or to hurt. When a person is being killed unjustly, the human tendency is to cling to life, to opt for any tactic that gives one a chance to live another moment. Human dignity departs in the oldest of all human endeavors, the struggle to survive. Victims curse, fight, spit and struggle against their fate. When that does not work, they beg, plead, whine and pray. Whatever might give them a chance at life becomes an option they exercise in a desperate attempt to cling to existence. That is, however, not the portrait of Jesus' death that has been painted by the gospel writers, trying to capture the memory of the Jesus experience.

They remembered him, rather, as a whole person, one who possessed his life so fully that he could give it away. To those acting out the vengeance of the powerful against the powerless, Jesus, the powerless one, ministered to their broken humanity as expressed in violence.

"Father, forgive them" (Luke 23:34), Jesus was recorded as having said. A man probably regarded by the oppressors from Rome as little more than a filthy Jewish religious fanatic of no ultimate value nonetheless had the gift of *being*—a gift sufficient to ease the suppressed guilt that is always present in abusive people. So the dying victim spoke the word of forgiveness to their dulled souls. The crowd heaped scorn upon him, and he responded with compassion. A thief dying with him reached out to him in hope, and Jesus responded with a word of promise: "Today you will be with me in paradise" (Luke 23:43). One gospel, John, actually brings Jesus' mother to the foot of the cross and there Jesus is portrayed as commending her to the care of the beloved disciple, who will provide for her needs (John 19:26).

Please embrace this picture. I doubt that it is historically accurate, but it is certainly a portrait of the way the being of Jesus was remembered and it is therefore filled with insight into the character of Jesus and into the nature of the Jesus experience. This was a life so whole, so free, that he had no need to cling to it. This is the picture of one who has escaped the survival mentality that marks all self-conscious human beings. One cannot give away what one does not possess. Jesus possessed himself. Jesus gave his life away. The cross is not the place where the justice of God was satisfied in the suffering of the divine son. The cross is the place where the fully alive one could give all that he is to others, and in that act make all that we mean by the word "God" visible.

Humanity in its fullness becomes endowed with the marks and the meaning of God. Full humanity flows into the divine reality. Divinity becomes and is the ultimate depth of humanity. God is not some supernatural power over against the world or humanity. The meaning and the reality of God are found in the experience of human wholeness flowing in life-giving ways through all that we are. God is experienced when life is opened to transcendent otherness, when it is called beyond every barrier into an ever-expanding humanity. The first-century experience of Jesus was quite simply that people met God in him. "God was in Christ," they said—and we say with them—because life, love and being flowed through the fullness of his humanity.

Seen from that perspective, the cross is not a place of torture and death; it is the portrait of the love of God seen when one can give all that one is and all that one has away. The cross thus becomes the symbol of a God presence that calls us to live, to love and to be. It stands for a love that embraces the human diversity of race, tribe, nation, gender, sexual orientation, left-handedness, right-handedness and any other human variety found in life. The call of the God experienced in Christ is simply a call to be all that each of us is—a call to offer, through the being of our humanity, the gift of God to all people by building a world in which everyone can live more fully, love more wastefully and have the courage to be all that they can be. That is how we live out the presence of God. God is about living, about loving and about being. The call of Jesus is thus not a call to be religious. It is not a call to escape life's traumas, to find security, to possess peace of mind. All of those things are invitations to a life-contracting idolatry. The call of God through Jesus is a call to be fully human, to embrace insecurity without building protective fences, to accept the absence of peace of mind as a requirement of humanity. It is to see that God is the experience of life, love and being who is met at the edges of an expanded humanity. That is surely what the author of the Fourth Gospel meant when he quoted Jesus as proclaiming that his purpose was "that they might have life and have it abundantly" (10:10).

The religion called Christianity is dying, the casualty of an expanded worldview. The God experience in Jesus—that experience upon which Christianity was built—is newly dawning and will in time create new forms through which that new vision can live. Once Jesus is freed from the prison of religion, a renaissance and a reformation are possible. Jesus for the non-religious comes into view.

As my great mentor and friend John E. Hines once said to me: "When you do an audacious thing, you do not then tremble at your own audacity."

I anticipate and await Jesus' new explosion into the human consciousness.

CHRISTPOWER

Long ago, in the year 1974, I preached a sermon in St. Paul's Church, Richmond, Virginia, that I later recognized was a breakthrough in my own consciousness. St. Paul's was located in the heart of that old and great city that had once served as the capital of the Confederacy. Both Robert E. Lee and Jefferson Davis worshipped regularly in that church during the dark days of the American Civil War. I was, even then, seeking to find a new way to understand this Jesus, who was so clearly the central symbol in my faith tradition, but with whose image I wrestled constantly. My inner conflict and the tension it produced was familiar. I was drawn at that time, as I still am, to the person of Jesus in powerful and compelling ways. I was also bothered and ultimately repelled by the distorting myths that surrounded him and stifled by the controlling religion that appeared to have captured him. There were times when my frustration level was so high that I could barely perceive either his meaning or his power. I even wondered how I could with integrity continue to be identified with the institution called the church to which on so many other levels I was deeply committed. Those emotions found expression that Sunday in that sermon, which in the normal course of events would have been quickly forgotten by most of the people who heard it (and probably even by me). The "shelf life" of a sermon is brief indeed. Most do not linger in people's mind beyond the day they were heard, if they make it that long.

A gifted poet in Richmond, however, named Lucy Newton Boswell Negus, took that particular sermon and laid out its core message in free verse. She entitled it "Christpower." Her setting of this sermon was later published as the lead piece in a volume of poems that she created based on other sermons that I delivered at St. Paul's. That volume bore the title of this single poem,[1] and so the word "Christpower" entered my vocabulary and indeed my consciousness as few other words have ever done before or since.

In the writing of this present book, that poem has always been before me.

I therefore conclude this study of Jesus with the words that I articulated then and that Lucy Negus shaped in that now distant year of 1974. I do so because not only are the seeds that ultimately produced this book located in that poem, but in many ways it has been the focus of my study for over thirty years. I think it is fair to say that that study has shaped both my life and my career. There is a feeling of satisfaction within me now that I have finally put flesh on the bare bones of what was then but a sketchy outline of my understanding of who Jesus was and what his life meant. My direction has not changed, but the depth of my understanding has and so in this book a pilgrimage has been completed and a circle closed.

Christpower

Look at him!
Look not at his divinity,
   but look, rather, at his freedom.
Look not at the exaggerated tales of his power,
   but look, rather, at his infinite capacity to give himself away.
Look not at the first-century mythology that surrounds him,
   but look, rather, at his courage to be,
      his ability to live, and
         the contagious quality of his love.
Stop your frantic search!
Be still and *know* that this is God:

  this love,
     this freedom,
        this life,
           this being;
And
when you are accepted, accept yourself;
  when you are forgiven, forgive yourself;
    when you are loved, love yourself.
      Grasp that Christpower
       and dare to be
         yourself!

That is, I believe the pathway to God, the God whom I have encountered in the profoundly human Jesus.
Shalom!

                   John Shelby Spong

NOTES

PREFACE

1. Epigraphs that include no credit line are excerpted from the chapter they introduce.
2. See bibliography for details.
3. This is the motto of the Protestant Episcopal Theological Seminary of Virginia, founded in 1823. The phrase was coined by Dean William Sparrow.
4. This idea was first stated in a letter to Eberhard Bethge, Bonhoeffer's friend, and was later published by Bethge in a book entitled *Letters and Papers from Prison.* See bibliography for details.
5. Michael Goulder would not like being included in a list of Christians, since he resigned his ordination as an Anglican priest in the early 1980s and has proclaimed himself "a non-aggressive atheist." I do not draw that kind of line in the sand in making judgments. Michael has so deeply helped me to understand both my Christ and particularly the synoptic gospels that I could not fail to include him and to place him where, in my judgment not his, he belongs. By this footnote I take cognizance of his feelings.

CHAPTER 2: THERE WAS NO STAR OVER BETHLEHEM

1. In 1992, I published an entire volume on the birth narratives of Jesus, entitled *Born of a Woman: A Bishop Rethinks the Virgin Birth and the Place of Women in a Male-Dominated Church.* Though both the purpose and the thrust of that book are quite different from this one, there will be some overlap, particularly in the analysis of the texts contained in the scriptural birth accounts. For those who wish to pursue the biblical material of Jesus' nativity as it is presented in Matthew 1 and 2 and in Luke 1 and 2 far more deeply than I can do it in this volume, I refer them to that book. See bibliography for details.
2. In his book *Moses and Monotheism,* Sigmund Freud suggests that the kernel of truth behind this story was that Moses had been the son of an Egyptian princess by a Hebrew slave. Raised in privilege, Freud says, Moses made an adult choice to identify himself not with his royal background, but with his slave background. This, Freud argues, is the source of the strong Jewish sense that they were "chosen people." Those interested in following this argument fully might read Freud's book. See bibliography for details.

CHAPTER 3: THE PARENTS OF JESUS: FICTIONALIZED COMPOSITES

1. For those who want to examine the Q hypothesis and the debate about its date, I recommend the writings of John Kloppenberg, Burton Mack and Robert Funk and the Jesus

Seminar. I have not been convinced that Q is a first-century document, and therefore I do not look to it for pre-Marcan insights. Some scholars do, however, and they may be right. The debate goes on. A minority of scholars suggest that Q is nothing but Matthew's expansion of Mark and that Luke had both Mark and Matthew in front of him when he wrote. That would certainly account for the similarity. These scholars further assert that Luke preferred Mark, but occasionally incorporated Matthew's expansions and so created the second set of material common to both Matthew and Luke that gave rise to the Q hypothesis. The chief defender of this minority position is Professor Michael Donald Goulder of the University of Birmingham in the United Kingdom. I tend to be persuaded by Goulder's argument, but the great majority of American New Testament scholars are firmly in the Q camp. Goulder's critique of the Q hypothesis is found in his preface to his book *Luke: A New Paradigm*. See bibliography for details of this and other Goulder works.

2. The best book yet written on the Gospel of Thomas is entitled *Beyond Belief*, by Elaine Pagels, Princeton University's brilliant Department of Religion scholar and professor. Professor Bart Ehrman of the Department of Religion at the University of North Carolina has also explored this field significantly. Though I have not been convinced that the Gospel of Thomas is a first-century document, some scholars have, and I am not sufficiently versed in this debate to suggest that I am right and they are wrong. I say only that I tend to be skeptical of the early dating. Pagels and Ehrman are both included in the bibliography.

3. There is some suspicion that these words are a gloss added by an early copier, but they do not appear in the earliest documents of this gospel that we possess.

4. *Dialogue of Justin, Philosopher and Martyr, with Trypho the Jew*. See bibliography (under Justin) for details.

5. I include in the birth narrative the story of Jesus going to Jerusalem at age twelve, where Joseph and Mary are said to have accompanied him. This story, based I believe on a story about Samuel, forms the last part of Luke's birth material.

6. For a much fuller analysis of Matthew's creation of the character Joseph than space will allow me to develop here, I refer you to my chapter on Joseph in *Liberating the Gospels: Reading the Bible with Jewish Eyes*. See bibliography for details.

7. In Luke 8:19–20 the mother of Jesus is mentioned but not by name as Luke gives us a very condensed version of Mark's story when the mother of Jesus and his brothers come to take him away.

8. The story of the fetus of John the Baptist leaping in Elizabeth's womb to salute the fetus of Jesus in Mary's womb has many connections with Esau and Jacob leaping in Rebekah's womb in the book of Genesis (25:20–23).

9. When one reads the official Vatican proclamation from 1950 declaring Mary bodily assumed into heaven, one discovers that it is based in large measure on the fact that no grave for Mary has ever been found. That is hardly compelling evidence for anything.

CHAPTER 4: THE HISTORICITY OF THE TWELVE DISCIPLES

1. C. C. Torrey, a New Testament scholar of note in the early twentieth century, said that this word meant "sons of the thunderstorm." *The Journal of Theological Studies* 11, no. 1: 136ff. Others have rendered the word "constant noise" or "disturbance."

2. Jerome, *Treatises on St. Mark*, found in *Catholic Encyclopedia*.

3. Josephus, *The Jewish War*. See bibliography for details.

4. This can be found in chapter 16 of my book *Liberating the Gospels*. See bibliography for details.

5. Pagels discusses this point in her book *Beyond Belief*. See bibliography for details.

CHAPTER 5: MIRACLE STORIES IN THE GOSPELS: ARE THEY NECESSARY?

1. This is the oft-repeated chorus in Archibald MacLeish's play *J.B.* See bibliography for details.

CHAPTER 6: NATURE MIRACLES: INTERPRETIVE SIGNS, NOT HISTORICAL EVENTS

1. Paul Tillich, *The Courage to Be.* See bibliography for details.

CHAPTER 7: HEALING MIRACLES: A VISION OF THE KINGDOM OF GOD

1. Both of these comments were made in response to a mine disaster in West Virginia. President Bush obviously sought to cover all the bases.
2. Compare prayers for the sick in the 1928 Episcopal Prayer Book in its section entitled "The Visitation of the Sick" with those in the 1979 Prayer Book, found beginning on page 436.
3. There are many people who helped to bring the world to a new appreciation of the Jewish background to the Christian scriptures. On the Jewish side such authors as Martin Buber, Alexander Herschel, Geza Vermes and Samuel Sandmel come immediately to mind. On the Christian side Krister Stendahl, Paul Van Buren and Michael Goulder are standouts. I regard my own book on this subject, *Liberating the Gospels: Reading the Bible with Jewish Eyes,* to be still the best book of my writing career. Books of these aforementioned authors are present in the bibliography.
4. There is a suggestion that the child convulsed by an "evil spirit" in Mark was also "mute." This is isolated and treated by Matthew as a separate event (Matt. 9:32–33).

CHAPTER 9: THE CRUCIFIXION NARRATIVE: LITURGY MASQUERADING AS HISTORY

1. Even today, Jews always set a place at the Passover meal for Elijah.

CHAPTER 11: THE ETERNAL TRUTH INSIDE THE MYTHS OF RESURRECTION AND ASCENSION

1. *The Human Face of God* is the title that John A. T. Robinson gave to his book on Christology. See bibliography for details.

CHAPTER 12: INTRODUCTION: EXPLORING THE ORIGINAL IMAGES OF JESUS

1. John A. T. Robinson was both a hero and a mentor to me. This book and his book on Christology are both in the bibliography.
2. James Pike was America's most controversial, popular religious thinker in the post–World War II period. He served as chaplain at Columbia University, dean of the Cathedral of St. John the Divine in New York City and later Episcopal bishop of California. Among his books are *A Time for Christian Candor* and *If This Be Heresy.* See bibliography for details.
3. Each of these has helped to shape what many call the post-Christian world. See bibliography for details of their representative books.
4. "The way" was a movement in the synagogue based on the book of Deuteronomy, which posed a way of life and a way of death. The Jesus movement was a new approach to the way of life.

CHAPTER 13: THE ORAL TRADITION: WHERE WAS JESUS REMEMBERED?

1. Scholars are hard-pressed to locate the source that Matthew seems to have in mind with this reference. It might be the Hebrew word for "root" (*naser*) and thus it could refer to that verse in Isaiah (11:1) which proclaims that the messiah will rise out of the root of Jesse, but there is no unanimity on that issue.

2. The books of 1 and 2 Chronicles, a much later addition to the Jewish sacred scriptures, were to some extent a rewrite of the same material found in the books of 1 and 2 Kings, but written in a much later period of Jewish history. Liturgically, they tended to be ignored or used in place of 1 and 2 Kings.
3. The book of Daniel, now included in our Bibles between Ezekiel and the Book of the Twelve, was a very much later addition to the sacred text of the Jews. A work of the mid-second century BCE, it had not generally established itself in the canon of scripture for liturgical use. It was a popular book filled with dramatic stories and with one crucial image of a figure called the "Son of man," who established the kingdom of God at the last judgment. That image became important in shaping the Jesus story, as I indicated in the chapter on healing miracles. It will also play a part in the section on the earlier images by which Jesus was understood.

CHAPTER 14: JESUS UNDERSTOOD AS THE NEW PASSOVER

1. The dating is not quite as clear in John's gospel, where there are indications that Jesus had been in Judea longer and that the Palm Sunday procession was not his entrance, but another event in the Jerusalem phase of his ministry.

CHAPTER 15: JESUS UNDERSTOOD UNDER THE SYMBOLS OF YOM KIPPUR

1. The phrase is the title from a novel by John Steinbeck. See bibliography for details.
2. There is a second word in Hebrew for "son"—*ben*—which shows up in the Bible in names like Benjamin. In the next chapter we will see that the scriptural phrase *ben adam* is translated literally "Son of man."
3. There may also be a hint of this theme in the story of Abraham. Abraham had two sons, one of whom, Isaac, we are told, was destined to be sacrificed. The other, Ismael, was destined to be banished to the wilderness.

CHAPTER 17: MINORITY IMAGES: THE SERVANT, THE SHEPHERD

1. As evidenced in *The Five Gospels* produced by the Jesus Seminar. See bibliography for details.

CHAPTER 18: JESUS: A MAN FOR ALL JEWISH SEASONS

1. The whole Jewish calendar revolves around the time of Passover, which can come anywhere from March 21 on, depending on the rotation of the moon. Easter, because it is based on Passover, comes on the first Sunday after the first full moon after March 21.
2. The liturgical organization of the synoptic gospels was introduced to me by Michael Donald Goulder, first in his writings and later in person. He was at that time teaching New Testament as a member of the faculty of the University of Birmingham in the United Kingdom. His books were electric to me and were the final piece that I needed to put the Jewish Jesus into a new context. Michael has been one of the three greatest theological and personal influences in my life, John Elbridge Hines and John A. T. Robinson being the other two. I have devoured Michael's scholarship and his writings until I have made them my own. No, I don't agree with Michael on every detail, and he will be the first to tell me that and to disassociate himself from positions I have taken. Still, it would not be appropriate for me not to salute him and to give him credit for developing the broad outlines of the liturgical organization of the synoptic gospels. I commend Michael's books to my readers with the caveat that they were written not for a popular audience, but for an academic one. Furthermore, Michael has backed away from some of the claims he once held. The books to which I particularly refer are: *The Evangelist's Calendar, Midrash and Lection in Matthew* and *Luke: A New Paradigm*. All are listed in the bibliography.

CHAPTER 19: INTRODUCTION: JESUS REALLY LIVED

1. I think of such people as Canadian author Tom Harpur and his book *The Pagan Christ*, and of two Englishmen, Timothy Freke and Peter Gandy, and their book *The Jesus Mysteries: Was the Original Jesus a Pagan God?* Both of these sources lean heavily on the work of Alvin Boyd Kuhn, Gerald Massey and Godfrey Higgins. Harpur, Freke and Gandy appear in the bibliography.
2. After Queen Jezebel was informed by King Ahab that Elijah had beheaded the prophets of Baal following his victorious showdown on Mount Carmel, the queen vowed an oath by God that she would behead Elijah in retribution. Such a vow could not be taken back. The beheading did not happen in Elijah's lifetime, but the oath was enacted by Herod at the request of his queen, Herodias, on Elijah's successor. This was one more way the gospel writers used the Hebrew scriptures to weave their fascinating but nonliteral tale.
3. My daughters inform me that the word "thong" has changed its meaning in recent years, but by this word I am sure the gospel writer meant the leather strap that connected the sandals to the wearer's feet and ankles.
4. This is taken from Harnack's book *The Mission and Expansion of Christianity in the First Three Centuries*. See bibliography for details. The Pauline reference is in volume 1 on the beginning of Christian mission.

CHAPTER 20: WHO IS THE GOD MET IN JESUS?

1. As an exception, one thinks immediately of Gustav Niebuhr, who served as the first religion editor of the *Wall Street Journal* and later wrote for the *New York Times*. The grandson of H. Richard Niebuhr and the grand-nephew of Reinhold Niebuhr, he grew up in the world of academic theology. Another exception is Ariel Goldman, an orthodox Jewish writer who wrote for the *New York Times*. During his tenure at the *Times*, he took a leave and enrolled as a student in the Harvard Divinity School in Cambridge, Massachusetts. Later he wrote a book about his Harvard experience. See bibliography for details.
2. From a story in the *New York Times*, Apr. 6, 2006.

CHAPTER 21: RECOGNIZING THE SOURCES OF RELIGIOUS ANGER

1. Quoted from the book *Why Believe in God?* by Michael Goulder and John Hick. See bibliography for details.
2. The story of John Lewis' role in the civil rights movement is chronicled in a book by David Halberstam entitled *The Children*. See bibliography for details.
3. The *Lynchburg News* in Lynchburg, Virginia, under publisher Carter Glass III was illustrative of this. *Richmond Times-Dispatch* writers James Kilpatrick and Ross MacKenzie were not far behind in their public vitriol.
4. The story of Ray Killen's sentencing was told on CNN and in the *New York Times* among others, June 22, 2006.
5. Polycarp, Jerome and John Chrysostom among others. Their anti-Semitic rhetoric can be read on the Internet by searching for Polycarp and the Jews, Jerome and the Jews, John Chrysostom and the Jews. I chronicled much of this in my book *The Sins of Scripture*, section 6. See bibliography for details.
6. Martin Luther, the father of the Reformation, and to a slightly lesser degree John Calvin both wrote about the Jews in words that literally drip with anger. The Evangelical Lutheran Church of America has actually apologized for the anti-Semitism of its founder. Documentation of this can be found in Frank Eakin's preface to *Dialogue in Search of Jewish-Christian Understanding*, which I wrote with Rabbi Jack Daniel Spiro. Eakin is a professor of the Department of Religion at the University of Richmond. See bibliography for details.

7. This man spoke the words on CNN's *Larry King Live*. His name was Bailey Smith. He also said in this program that he could cure homosexuals if they would just look at his wife in a bathing suit.
8. From the Episcopal Hymnal (1940), hymn 71. The words are by Johann Herrmann (1630).
9. The phrase "original blessing" is the title of a book by Matthew Fox. See bibliography for details.
10. DNA, which stands for deoxyribonucleic acid, contains genetic instructions specifying the biological development of all cellular forms of life. It is thought to date back to 3.5 to 4.6 billion years ago. It can be looked up in any number of scientific journals. Discovered by Francis Crick and James D. Watson in 1953, it helps us to see the relationship between all living things. Human beings are more than 99 percent identical in our genetic makeup to chimpanzees, but we also share significant kinship with cabbages!

CHAPTER 23: JESUS: THE BREAKER OF PREJUDICES AND STEREOTYPES

1. Such stories are powerfully told in books by Alex Haley, particularly *Roots* and *Queen*. See bibliography for details.
2. For a fuller treatment of this parable see my book *A New Christianity for a New World*, p. 134ff.
3. Note the line in the Christian Nicene Creed which says, "I believe in the Holy Spirit, the Lord *and giver of life*."
4. This was the substance of chapter 13 in *Born of a Woman*. See bibliography for details.
5. *Systematic Theology*, vol. 1. Being and God are the correlated ideas in this segment. See bibliography for details.

CHAPTER 24: JESUS: THE BREAKER OF RELIGIOUS BOUNDARIES

1. This quotation is attributed to Karl Marx, though not in this exact form.
2. There is some debate in New Testament circles about the authority and indeed the placement of this story. It appears to dance in various places in some ancient manuscripts. That is not a major concern for me since I doubt the historicity of much that was attributed to Jesus. This story nonetheless reflects a portrait of Jesus that is quite consistent with major parts of the gospel tradition.
3. One thinks of the plagues that were said to have afflicted the whole people of Israel because of the sins of a few or even the sins of the king. In some sense that was the theory behind the destruction of the towns of Sodom and Gomorrah in Genesis 18–19.
4. In Tillich's book *Systematic Theology*, vol. 2: *Christ and Existence*. See bibliography for details.
5. To understand the unlawful quality of this act, see Exodus 14:11.
6. In *Letters and Papers from Prison*, p. 219. See bibliography for details.

CHAPTER 25: THE CROSS: A HUMAN PORTRAIT OF THE LOVE OF GOD

1. I am thinking of such hymns as "Beneath the cross of Jesus, I fain would take my stand" and "In the cross of Christ I glory." They are numbers 341 and 336 in the 1940 Hymnal of the Episcopal Church.
2. The title of one of Paul Tillich's books. See bibliography for details.
3. Elisabeth Kübler-Ross, in her book *On Death and Dying*, outlines this process. See bibliography for details.
4. Borg and Crossan, *The Last Week: A Day-by-Day Account of Jesus's Final Week in Jerusalem*. See bibliography for details.

EPILOGUE: CHRISTPOWER

1. See bibliography for details.

BIBLIOGRAPHY

Altizer, Thomas, and William J. Hamilton. *Radical Theology and the Death of God*. Indianapolis: Bobbs-Merrill, 1966.

Armstrong, Karen. *The Battle for God*. New York: Knopf, 1993.

———. *Beginning the World*. New York: St. Martin's Press, 1983.

———. *A History of God*. New York: Ballantine Books, 1993.

———. *Holy War: The Crusades and Their Impact on Today's World*. New York: Anchor Books, 1988.

———. *One City, Three Faiths*. New York: St. Martin's Press, 1995.

———. *The Spiral Staircase: My Climb Out of Darkness*. New York: Knopf, 2004.

———. *Through the Narrow Gate*. New York: St. Martin's Press, 1980.

Bonhoeffer, Dietrich. *Letters and Papers from Prison*. Edited by Eberhard Bethge. London: SCM Press, 1991; New York: Macmillan, 1997.

Book of Common Prayer. New York: Domestic and Foreign Missionary Society of the Protestant Episcopal Church, 1928, 1979.

Borg, Marcus. *The Heart of Christianity*. San Francisco: HarperCollins, 2004.

———. *Meeting Jesus Again for the First Time*. San Francisco: HarperCollins, 1994.

Borg, Marcus, and John Dominic Crossan. *The Last Week: A Day-by-Day Account of Jesus's Final Week in Jerusalem*. San Francisco: HarperCollins, 2006.

Boswell, John. *Christianity, Social Tradition and Homosexuality*. Chicago: Univ. of Chicago Press, 1980.

Bowker, John. *Problems of Suffering in Religions of the World*. Cambridge: Cambridge Univ. Press, 1975.

Bridge, Anthony. *The Crusades*. New York: Watts, 1982.

Brown, Raymond. *The Birth of the Messiah*. Garden City, NY: Doubleday, 1977.

———. *The Death of the Messiah*. Garden City, NY: Doubleday, 1994.

Buber, Martin. *I and Thou*. Translated by Walter Kaufman. New York: Scribner, 1970.

———. *The Legend of Baal-Shem*. Translated by Maurice Friedman. New York: Harper & Brothers, 1955.

———. *On the Bible: Eighteen Studies*. New York: Schocken Books, 1968.

Buchanan, George Wesley. *To the Hebrews*. Garden City, NY: Doubleday, Anchor Bible Series, 1972.

Bultmann, Rudolf. *The Gospel of John: A Commentary*. Translated by G. R. Beasley-Murray. Oxford: Oxford Univ. Press, 1971.

———. *Jesus and the Word*. Translated by Louise Pettibone Smith. New York: Scribner, 1958.

Caird, George B. *St. Luke: A Commentary*. Baltimore, MD: Penguin Books, 1963.

Campbell, Joseph. *The Hero with a Thousand Faces*. New York: Pantheon Books, 1949.

———. *The Power of Myth* (with Bill Moyers). Garden City, NY: Doubleday, 1988.

Childs, Brevard. *The Book of Exodus: A Critical Theological Commentary*. Philadelphia: Westminster Press, 1974.

Chilton, Bruce. *Judaic Approaches to the Gospels*. Atlanta: Scholars Press, 1994.

———. *Rabbi Jesus*. New York: Doubleday, 2000.

Conzelmann, Hans. *The Theology of Luke*. London: Faber & Faber, 1960.

Cornwall, John. *Hitler's Pope: The Secret History of Pius XII*. New York: Viking Press, 1999.

Crossan, John Dominic. *Jesus: A Revolutionary Biography*. San Francisco: HarperCollins, 1994.

———. *Who Killed Jesus?* San Francisco: HarperCollins, 1995.

Cupitt, Don. *After God: The Future of Religion*. London: Wiedefield & Nicholson, 1997.

———. *Christ and the Hiddenness of God*. London: SCM Press, 1985.

———. *The Great Questions of Life*. Santa Rosa, CA: Polebridge Press, 2006.

———. *Mysticism and Modernity*. Oxford: Blackwell Press, 1998.

———. *Radicals and the Future of the Church*. London: SCM Press, 1989.

———. *The Religion of Being*. London: SCM Press, 1998.

———. *The Sea of Faith: Christianity in Change*. London: BBC Publishing, 1984.

———. *Solar Ethics*. London: Xpress, 1993.

——. *Taking Leave of God.* London: SCM Press, 1980.

Darwin, Charles Robert. *On the Origin of Species by Means of Natural Selection.* London: Penguin, 1989 (originally published in 1859).

Davies, Paul. *God and the New Physics.* London: Dent, 1984; New York: Simon & Schuster, 1992.

——. *The Mind of God.* New York: Simon & Schuster, 1992.

Dawkins, Richard. *The Blind Watchmaker.* London: Hammondsworth, 1991; New York: Norton, 1996.

——. *The God Delusion.* New York: W. W. Norton, 2006.

——. *The Selfish Gene.* London: Granada, 1978; New York: Oxford Univ. Press, 1990.

Dodd, Charles H. *The Epistle of Paul to the Romans.* London: Hodder & Stoughton, 1949.

——. *The Interpretation of the Fourth Gospel.* Cambridge: Cambridge Univ. Press, 1953.

Dollar, James. *The Evolution of the Idea of God and Other Essays.* Greensboro, NC: Outland Press, 2000.

Eakin, Frank E., Jr. *The Religion and Culture of Israel: An Introduction to Old Testament Thought.* Allyn & Bacon, 1971.

Ehrman, Bart. *Lost Christianities/Lost Scriptures.* New York: Oxford Univ. Press, 2003.

——. *Misquoting Jesus: The Story Behind Who Changed the Bible and Why.* New York: HarperCollins, 2005.

Eliade, Mircea. *The Sacred and the Profane.* New York: Harcourt-Brace, 1959.

Evans, Craig A., and Donald A. Hagner, eds. *Anti-Semitism and Early Christianity: Issues of Polemic and Faith.* Minneapolis: Fortress Press, 1993.

Fineberg, Solomon A. *Overcoming Anti-Semitism.* New York and London: Harper & Brothers, 1943.

Fox, Matthew. *The Coming of the Cosmic Christ.* San Francisco: HarperCollins, 1988.

——. *One River, Many Wells: How Deepening Ecumenism Awakens Our Imaginations with Spiritual Visions.* New York: Jeremy Tarcher/Putnam, 2000.

——. *Original Blessing: A Primer in Creation Spirituality.* Santa Fe: Bear Publishing, 1983.

Freke, Timothy, and Peter Gandy. *The Jesus Mysteries: Was the Original Jesus a Pagan God?* New York and London: Random House, 2001.

Freud, Sigmund. *The Future of an Illusion.* Translated by James Strackey. New York: Norton, 1975.

——. *Moses and Monotheism.* Translated by Katherine Jones. New York: Vantage Books, 1967.

——. *Totem and Taboo.* New York: Norton, 1956.

Fromm, Eric. *The Dogma of Christ.* New York: Holt Rinehart & Winston, 1963.

Funk, Robert. *Honest to Jesus: Jesus for the New Millennium.* San Francisco: HarperCollins, 1996.

Funk, Robert, and Roy Hoover, eds. *The Five Gospels: What Did Jesus Really Say?* New York: Macmillan, 1993.

Geering, Lloyd G. *Christianity Without God.* Santa Rosa, CA: Polebridge Press, 2000.

——. *Tomorrow's God.* Wellington, New Zealand: Bridgett Williams Books, 1994.

Goldman, Ari. *The Search for God at Harvard.* New York: Ballantine Books, 1991.

Gomes, Peter. *The Good Book.* New York: William Morrow, 1996.

Goulder, Michael Donald. *The Evangelist's Calendar.* London: SPCK, 1978.

——. *Luke: A New Paradigm.* Sheffield, UK: Sheffield Academic Press, 1989.

——. *Midrash and Lection in Matthew.* London: SPCK Press, 1974.

——. *A Tale of Two Missions.* London: SCM Press, 1994.

Goulder, Michael D., and John Hick. *Why Believe in God?* London: SCM Press, 1983.

Haenchen, Ernst. *The Acts of the Apostles: A Commentary.* Philadelphia: Westminster Press, 1971.

Hahn, Thich Nhat. *Living Buddha, Living Christ.* New York: Riverhead Books, 1995.

Halberstam, David. *The Children.* New York: Random House, 1998.

Haley, Alex. *Queen: The Story of an American Family.* New York: William Morrow, 1993.

——. *Roots: The Saga of an American Family.* Garden City, NY: Doubleday, 1976.

Hall, Douglas John. *The End of Christendom and the Future of Christianity.* Harrisburg, PA: Trinity Press, 1995.

Hamilton, William. *The New Essence of Christianity.* London: Darton, Longman & Todd, 1966.

Hampson, Daphne. *After Christianity.* London: SCM Press, 1996; Harrisburg, PA: Trinity Press, 1997.

Harnack, Adolph. *The Mission and Expansion of Christianity in the First Three Centuries.* Translated by James Moffatt. Freeport, NY: Books for Libraries Press, 1959.

Harris, Sam. *The End of Faith: Religion, Terror, and the Future of Religion.* New York: W. W. Norton, 2005.

———. *Letter to a Christian Nation.* New York: Knopf, 2006.

Harpur, Tom. *The Pagan Christ.* Toronto: Thomas Allen, 2004.

Hartshorne, Charles. *Man's Vision of God and the Logic of Theism.* New York: Harper & Brothers, 1941.

Hick, John. *God and the Universe of Faith.* London: Macmillan, 1993.

———. *The Myth of Christian Uniqueness.* London: SCM Press, 1987.

Holloway, Richard. *Godless Morality.* Edinburgh: Canongate Press, 1999.

Hoskyns, Edwin. *The Fourth Gospel.* London: Faber & Faber, 1939.

James, Fleming. *Personalities of the Old Testament.* New York: Scribner, 1955.

James, William. *The Varieties of Religious Experience.* New York: Random House, 1999.

Josephus. *The New Complete Works of Josephus.* Translated by William Whiston. Grand Rapids, MI: Kregal Press, 1999.

Jung, Carl G. *Aion: Researches into the Phenomenology of the Self.* Princeton, NJ: Princeton Univ. Press, Bollingen Series, 1959.

———. *Answer to Job.* London: Routledge, Kegan & Paul, 1954.

———. *Memoirs, Dreams and Reflections.* New York: Vintage Press, 1965.

———. *On Evil.* Princeton, NJ: Princeton Univ. Press, 1998.

———. *Psychology and Religion, East and West.* New York: Pantheon Books, Bollingen Series, *Collected Works of C. G. Jung,* 1958.

———. *Psychology and Western Religion.* New Haven, CT: Yale Univ. Press, 1960.

Justin. *Dialogue of Justin, Philosopher and Martyr, with Trypho the Jew.* Published in many collections of the early fathers of the church. See especially chapter 84.

Kempis, Thomas à. *The Imitation of Christ.* Garden City, NY: Image Books, 1955.

King, Karen. *The Gospel of Mary.* Santa Rosa, CA: Polebridge Press, 2004.

Kloppenborg, John S. *The Formation of Q: Trajectories in Ancient Wisdom Collections.* Philadelphia: Fortress Press, 1977.

Kübler-Ross, Elisabeth. *On Death and Dying.* New York: Simon & Schuster, 1969.

Küng, Hans. *Does God Exist?* London: Collins, 1980.

———. *On Being a Christian.* New York: Doubleday, 1976.

Latourette, Kenneth Scott. *Christianity in a Revolutionary Age: The 19th Century — The Great Century in the Americas, Australia and Africa, 1800–1914.* New York: Harper & Brothers, 1943.

Laughlin, Paul Alan. *Putting the Historical Jesus in His Place*. Santa Rosa, CA: Polebridge Press, 2006.

Luther, Martin. *Lectures on Romans*. Vol. 25 in *Luther's Works*. Edited by Hilton C. Oswald. St. Louis, MO: Concordia, 1972.

Mack, Burton. *The Lost Gospel: The Book of Q*. San Francisco: Harper-Collins, 1993.

———. *Who Wrote the New Testament? The Making of the Christian Myth*. San Francisco: HarperCollins, 1995.

MacLeish, Archibald. *J. B.: A Play in Verse*. New York and London: Samuel French, 1956.

Mann, Jacob. *The Bible as Read and Preached in the Old Synagogue*. New York: KATV Publishing, 1971.

Meier, John P. *A Marginal Jew: Rethinking the Historical Jesus*. New York: Doubleday, 1991.

Meredith, Lawrence. *Life Before Death: A Spiritual Journey of Mind and Body*. Atlanta: Atlanta Humanics Publishing, 2000.

Milgram, Abraham E. *Jewish Worship*. Philadelphia: Jewish Publication Society of America, 1991.

Mitchell, Stephen. *The God Who Is Everywhere*. London: John Hunt Publishers, 2005.

Moltmann, Jürgen. *God in Creation: A New Theology of Creation and the Spirit of God*. San Francisco: Harper & Row, 1985.

Moule, Charles F. D. *The Origins of Christology*. Cambridge: Cambridge Univ. Press, 1977.

Mountford, Brian. *Why Liberal Christianity Might Be the Faith You've Been Looking For*. Ropley, UK: O Books, 2005.

Nelson, James B. "Reuniting Sexuality and Spirituality." *The Christian Century* 104, no. 8 (Feb. 1987): 187–190.

Ogden, Schubert M. *Christ Without Myth*. New York: Harper & Brothers, 1961.

Pagels, Elaine. *Beyond Belief*. New York: Random House, 2004.

———. *The Gnostic Gospels*. New York: Random House, 1979.

Pannenberg, Wolfhart. *The Apostles' Creed*. London: SCM Press, 1972.

Pelikan, Jaroslav. *The Emergence of the Catholic Tradition (100–600)*. Vols. 1–6. Chicago and London: Univ. of Chicago Press, 1971.

Pike, James A. *If This Be Heresy*. New York: Harper & Row, 1967.

———. *A Time for Christian Candor*. New York: Harper & Row, 1964.

Richardson, Herbert W. T. *Nun, Witch and Playmate: The Americanization of Sex*. New York: Edwin Mellen Press, 1971.

Robinson, John A. T. *Explorations into God*. London: SCM Press, 1962.

——. *Honest to God*. Philadelphia: Westminster Press, 1963.

——. *The Human Face of God*. Philadelphia: Westminster Press, 1973.

Sanders, E. P. *Jesus and Judaism*. Philadelphia: Fortress Press, 1985.

Sandmel, Samuel. *The Genius of Paul*. New York: Farrar, Straus & Cudahy, 1958.

——. *Judaism and Christian Beginnings*. Oxford: Oxford Univ. Press, 1979.

——. *We Jews and Jesus*. New York: Schocken Books, 1970.

Schillebeeckx, Edward. *Christ: The Experience of Jesus*. New York: Seabury Press, 1980.

——. *Jesus: An Experiment in Christology*. New York: Seabury Press, 1979.

Schleiermacher, Friedrich. *The Christian Faith*. London: T. & T. Clark, 1908.

——. *The Experience of Jesus as Lord*. New York: Seabury Press, 1980.

Sheehan, Thomas. *The First Coming: How the Kingdom of God Became Christianity*. New York: Random House, 1986.

Spong, John Shelby. *The Bishop's Voice: Selected Essays*. Compiled and edited by Christine Mary Spong. New York: Crossroad Press, 1999.

——. *Born of a Woman: A Bishop Rethinks the Virgin Birth and the Treatment of Women in a Male-Dominated Church*. San Francisco: HarperCollins, 1992.

——. *Christpower* (arranged by Lucy Newton Boswell Negus). Richmond, VA: Thomas Hale Co., 1975. Reprinted in 2007 by St. Johann's Press, Haworth, New Jersey.

——. *Liberating the Gospels: Reading the Bible with Jewish Eyes*. San Francisco: HarperCollins, 1996.

——. *Living in Sin? A Bishop Rethinks Human Sexuality*. San Francisco: HarperCollins, 1988.

——. *A New Christianity for a New World: Why Traditional Faith Is Dying and How a New Faith Is Being Born*. San Francisco: HarperCollins, 2001.

——. *Rescuing the Bible from Fundamentalism: A Bishop Rethinks the Meaning of Scripture*. San Francisco: HarperCollins, 1991.

——. *Resurrection: Myth or Reality? A Bishop Rethinks the Meaning of Easter*. San Francisco: HarperCollins, 1994.

——. *The Sins of Scripture: Exposing the Bible's Texts of Hate to Reveal the God of Love*. San Francisco: HarperCollins, 2005.

——. *This Hebrew Lord: A Bishop Rethinks the Meaning of Jesus*. San Francisco: HarperCollins, 1973, 1988, and 1993.

——. *Why Christianity Must Change or Die: A Bishop Speaks to Believers in Exile*. San Francisco: HarperCollins, 1998.

Spong, John Shelby, and Jack Daniel Spiro, *Dialogue in Search of Jewish-Christian Understanding*. New York: Seabury Press, 1974.

Steinbeck, John. *East of Eden*. New York: Viking Press, 1952.

Stendahl, Krister. *Paul Among the Jews and Gentiles*. Philadelphia: Fortress Press, 1996.

Strauss, David Friedrich. *Leben Jesu: The Life of Jesus Critically Examined*. 1836. Reprint, London: SCM Press, 1973.

Tacey, David. *The Spirituality Revolution*. Sydney: HarperCollins, 2003.

Taussig, Hal. *A New Spiritual Home*. Santa Rosa, CA: Polebridge Press, 2006.

Taylor, Barbara Brown. *Leaving Church*. San Francisco: HarperCollins, 2006.

Taylor, John V. *The Go-Between God*. Philadelphia: Fortress Press, 1973.

Teilhard de Chardin, Pierre. *Science and Christ*. London: Collins, 1939.

Terrien, Samuel. *The Psalms and Their Meaning for Today*. Indianapolis and New York: Bobbs-Merrill, 1953.

Tillich, Paul. *The Courage to Be*. New Haven, CT: Yale Univ. Press, 1952.

———. *The Eternal Now*. New York: Scribner, 1963.

———. *The New Being*. New York: Scribner, 1935.

———. *The Protestant Era*. Translated by James Luther Adams. Chicago: Univ. of Chicago Press, 1948.

———. *The Shaking of the Foundations*. New York: Scribner, 1948.

———. *Systematic Theology*, vols. 1, 2, and 3. Chicago: Univ. of Chicago Press, 1951–1963.

Toynbee, Arnold J. *Christianity Among the Religions of the World*. New York: Scribner, 1977.

Van Buren, Paul. *The Secular Meaning of the Gospel*. London: SCM Press, 1963.

Vermes, Geza. *The Challenging Faces of Jesus*. New York and London: Penguin Books, 2001.

———. *Jesus, the Jew*. New York: Macmillan, 1973.

Von Rad, Gerhard. *Genesis*. Philadelphia: Westminster Press, 1972.

———. *Old Testament Theology*. San Francisco: Harper & Row, 1965.

Warner, Marina. *Alone of All Her Sex*. New York: Knopf, 1976.

Wemple, Suzanne. *Women in Frankish Society: Marriage and Cloister, 500–900*. Philadelphia: Univ. of Pennsylvania Press, 1982.

INDEX